Lucy Phillimore

Sir Christopher Wren

His Family and His Times

Lucy Phillimore

Sir Christopher Wren
His Family and His Times

ISBN/EAN: 9783337027902

Printed in Europe, USA, Canada, Australia, Japan

Cover: Foto ©ninafisch / pixelio.de

More available books at **www.hansebooks.com**

SIR CHRISTOPHER WREN

HIS FAMILY AND HIS TIMES,

WITH ORIGINAL LETTERS AND A DISCOURSE ON
ARCHITECTURE HITHERTO UNPUBLISHED.

1585—1723.

BY

LUCY PHILLIMORE,

AUTHOR OF 'BISHOP WILBERFORCE, A SKETCH FOR CHILDREN' ETC.

'The modest man built the city, and the modest man's skill was unknown.'—*The Tatler,* No. 52.

WITH TWO ENGRAVINGS.

LONDON:
KEGAN PAUL, TRENCH, & CO., 1 PATERNOSTER SQUARE.
1881.

TO

CATHERINE PIGOTT,

THE LAST DIRECT DESCENDANT OF SIR CHRISTOPHER WREN,

THESE MEMOIRS OF HER ANCESTORS

ARE GRATEFULLY DEDICATED.

PREFACE.

THE materials necessary for writing a life of Sir Christopher Wren are so difficult of access as possibly to explain the unsatisfactory character of such biographies as do exist. Mr. James Elmes, who venerated Wren's genius, published in 1823, a Life which contained a careful if a dry account of Wren's architectural works and of some of his scientific discoveries. He also published a smaller work, 'Sir C. Wren and his Times,' intended perhaps to give a flavour of personal interest to the other volume. Neither book succeeds in doing this, and both have suffered from the circumstance that Mr. Elmes' failing eyesight did not permit him to correct the proofs of either work, and accordingly many serious errors as to names and dates stand unaltered in them. There is a sketch of Wren in the British Family Library, one published by the Society for the Diffusion of Useful Knowledge, and one in the 'Biographica Britannica,' but in them all it is with some of the works of the great architect that we become acquainted, not with himself.

The chief authority to which any biographer of

Wren must perforce turn is, the 'Parentalia, or Memoirs of the Family of the Wrens : viz., of Matthew, Bishop of Ely; Christopher, Dean of Windsor and Registrar of the Garter; but chiefly of Sir Christopher Wren.' This work, a folio, with portraits [1] of the three whose lives it records, was published in London in 1750, dedicated to Mr. Speaker Onslow. It was chiefly written by Christopher, the eldest surviving son of Sir Christopher Wren, finished and finally published by Stephen Wren, M.D., the second and favourite, son of the Mr. C. Wren above mentioned, 'with care of Joseph Ames,' a fellow of the Society of Antiquaries. Several copies were presented to the University of Oxford.

The 'Parentalia,' of which but a small edition was published, is now scarce and little known. It is put together, not quite at hap-hazard, but with no real method or order: digression ensues upon digression until all clue to the original date or subject is lost. Nor is the very imperfect 'index of names' of any real assistance in the labyrinth thus created. Yet, with all its faults, the book is of great interest, and bears amidst all errors and omissions an unmistakably genuine stamp.

'Bishop Wren's Diary,' reference to which will be frequently found in the following pages, was kept by him in the blank leaves of 'Pond's Almanack,' after this fashion :

'August 30.—*Per vim hostilem eripior domo meâ.* 1642.'

---

[1] From which the three vignettes in this volume are taken.

These entries cease with the death of his wife in 1646; even his own release from prison is not mentioned.

The old heirloom copy of the 'Parentalia' intrusted to the writer of these pages contains a large additional number of prints and wood engravings by Virtue, Vandergucht, Loggan, and others, some printed accounts of the City Churches, and several letters, rough drafts of treatises, Garter records, and other MSS. in the handwritings of the Bishop, the Dean, Sir Christopher himself, and of some of their correspondents. Among the curious omissions of the 'Parentalia' are the maiden name of Bishop Wren's wife, the date of the death of Sir Christopher's mother, Mrs. Mary Wren, and the places and the dates at which either of Sir Christopher's two weddings took place. Some of these and other gaps I have, by the aid of 'Notes and Queries,' been able to supply. Wren's son and grandson are both alike silent on all political matters subsequent to the Restoration. The Popish Plot, the Trial of the Seven Bishops, King James's Abdication, the Landing of William of Orange are all passed by in perfect silence. The traditional politics of the Wrens were certainly those of the loyal Cavalier party, and they were in favour at the Court of the Stuarts.

It is curious how all political colouring disappears from the record after the period of the Restoration. Yet Sir Christopher, his cousins, and the very Mr. Wren who writes the book were all in Parliament, and that in more or less critical times. Such accidental hints as there are point, I think, to Sir Christopher as adhering, though very quietly, to the politics of his ancestors; and assuredly neither he nor his descendants had any cause to love the house of Hanover!

Wren was a steady Churchman, bred up in that school of Andrewes, of Laud, and of Matthew Wren, which, if it was anti-Puritan, was equally and emphatically anti-Roman. For this reason, if for no other, after the trial of the Seven Bishops had shaken the confidence of every Churchman in the country, Wren may have acquiesced in a settlement which appeared to promise protection to the Church without finally excluding the Stuart line. The 'Parentalia,' published five years after the last Jacobite rising in 1745, preserves, as has been said, a political silence which may be that of discretion or of disappointment.

One word should be said as to Gresham College, where Wren held his first professorship. It was founded in 1579 by the will of Queen Elizabeth's great merchant Sir Thomas Gresham. The college was no other than his own house in Bishopsgate, forming a quadrangle round a large garden. The seven professors, each of whom gave a lecture a day in term time, had a salary of 50*l.* a year and were lodged in the house. Gresham College escaped the Fire, and gave lodgings at that time to the Lord Mayor and the aldermen, who had been less fortunate. In 1768 it was pulled down by Act of Parliament, to give a site to the new Excise Office, and the original collegiate scheme was destroyed, though the lectures are still given in a lecture hall.

Little is known of Wren in his Masonic capacity. He is said to have been a member and a master of the 'Old Lodge of S. Paul,' now known as the 'Lodge of Antiquity.' All the records of the Lodge belonging to that time have unfortunately been lost, so that they cannot be consulted with reference to this matter.

The question has been raised whether Wren was a Freemason or not. On this point the 'Parentalia' makes no explicit statement, though it appears to imply Wren's connection with the Order.

The Duke of Sussex caused a plate to be engraved in 1827 and affixed to the mallet which Sir Christopher was said to have presented to the Lodge, with this inscription:—'A. L. 5831. A.D. 1827. To commemorate that this, being the same mallet with which His Majesty King Charles II. levelled the foundation stone of S. Paul's Cathedral, A. L. 5677, A.D. 1673. Was presented to the Old Lodge of S. Paul, now the Lodge of Antiquity, acting by immemorial constitution, by Brother Sir Christopher Wren, R.W.D.G.M., Worshipful Master of this Lodge and Architect of that Edifice.'

The statement respecting King Charles's presence is probably an erroneous one. The Lodge possesses also three gilt wooden candlesticks in the form of columns, inscribed 'Ex dono Chr. Wren Eq. A. L. 5680.'

Where quotations have been made directly from the Wren MS., from the 'Parentalia,' or from Evelyn's Diary, the spelling and stopping of the originals have been faithfully reproduced. For the rest, the writer can only hope that these pages may serve as a contribution towards that full and worthy biography of the great architect which may yet, she trusts, be written before London is finally robbed of the Churches with which Wren's genius endowed her.

August 1, 1881.

CONTENTS.

CHAPTER I.
1585-1636.

Ancestry of the Wrens—Matthew Wren—Travels to Spain with the Prince of Wales—Interview at Winchester House—Bishop Andrewes' Prophecy—Wren made Master of Peterhouse—Bishop of Hereford—Consecration of Abbey Dore—Office of Reconciliation—Foreign Congregations and the Norwich Weavers—Result of 'a Lecturer's' Departure. 3

CHAPTER II.
1636-1640.

Dr. C. Wren—Birth of his Son Christopher—East Knoyle—Order of the Garter—How a Murderer was Detected—Christopher at Westminster—A Latin Letter—Diocese of Ely—Impeachment of Lord Strafford—Of Archbishop Laud—Articles against Bishop Wren—Resigns the Deanery of the Chapels Royal. . . . 31

CHAPTER III.
1641-1647.

Bishop Wren accused—Westminster Abbey attacked—Imprisonment of the Bishops—Bishop Wren's Defence—'Utterly Denieth all Popish Affections'—The Garter Jewels—Archbishop Laud Murdered—Christopher at Oxford—Philosophical Meetings. 55

CHAPTER IV.

1647-1658.

Death of Mrs. M. Wren—King Charles Murdered—A monotonous Walk—Inventions—A Dream—All Souls' Fellowship—Beginnings of the Royal Society—Astronomy—An Offer of Release—The Cycloid—Cromwell's Funeral—Letters from London. . 85

CHAPTER V.

1659-1663.

Apostolical Succession—Difficulty of preserving it—Letters from Lord Clarendon—Bishop Wren's Release—The Restoration—Convocation—Savilian Professorship—Royal Society—'Elephant in the Moon'—Pembroke Chapel begun. 109

CHAPTER VI.

1664-1667.

Repair of S. Paul's—Sheldonian Theatre—The Plague—A Letter from Paris—Consecration of Pembroke Chapel—Fire of London—Bishop Wren's Death—His Family. 139

CHAPTER VII.

1668-1672.

Patching S. Paul's—Sancroft's Letters—Wren's Examination of S. Paul's—Salisbury Cathedral—London as it might have been—Letter to Faith Coghill—Wren marries her—Temple Bar—S. Mary-le-Bow—Artillery Company—Gunpowder used to remove Ruins. 165

CHAPTER VIII.

1672-1677.

Birth of his eldest Son—S. Stephen's, Walbrook—S. Bennet Fink—Plans for S. Paul's—The Excavations—Son Christopher born—Death of Faith, Lady Wren—Second Marriage—City Churches—The Monument—Tomb of Charles I.—Remains of the little Princes in the Tower. 191

CHAPTER IX.

1677-1681.

Emmanuel College—Greenwich Observatory—Birth of Jane and William Wren—S. Bartholomew's—Portland Quarries—Dr. and Mrs. Holder—Death of Lady Wren—Popish Plot—Papin's Digester—Sir J. Hoskyns—All Hallow's, Bread Street—Palace at Winchester. 215

CHAPTER X.

1681-1686.

Chelsea College—S. James's, Westminster—A hard Winter—Chichester Spire—An Astronomical Problem—A Seat in Parliament—More City Churches—A curious Carving. 239

CHAPTER XI.

1687-1696.

Parliament dissolved—Church building—Acquittal of the Seven Bishops—James the Second's Flight—William and Mary—College of Physicians—Hampton Court—Greenwich Hospital—Richard Whittington—S. Paul's Organ. 259

CHAPTER XII.

1697-1699.

Opening of S. Paul's Choir—A moveable Pulpit—Letter to his Son at Paris—Order against Swearing—Peter the Great—S. Dunstan's Spire—Morning Prayer Chapel opened—Westminster Abbey. . 279

CHAPTER XIII.

1700-1708.

Member for Weymouth—Rising of the Sap in Trees—Prince George's Statue—Jane Wren's Death—Thanksgiving at S. Paul's—Letter to his Son—Son marries Mary Musard—Death of Mr. Evelyn—Queen Anne's Act for Building fifty Churches—Letter on Church Building. 297

CHAPTER XIV.

1709–1723.

Private Houses built—Queen Anne's Gifts—Last Stone of S. Paul's—Wren deprived of his Salary—His Petition—'Frauds and Abuses'—Interior work of S. Paul's—Wren Superseded—Purchase of Wroxhall Abbey—Wren's Thoughts on the Longitude—His Death—Burial in S. Paul's—The End. 317

APPENDIX.

I. Reverendo Patri Domino Christophoro Wren S.T.D. et D. W. Christophorus Filius Hoc Suum Panorganum Astronomicum D.D. xiii. Calend. Novem. Anno 1645. 337

II. Churches, Halls, Colleges, Palaces, other Public Buildings, and Private Houses built and repaired by Sir Christopher Wren. 338

III. A Discourse on Architecture, from Original MS. . . 340

INDEX 351

THE PRINCIPAL WORKS OF SIR CHRISTOPHER WREN
FROM A DRAWING BY C. R. COCKERELL, R.A.

CHAPTER I.
1585–1636.

ANCESTRY OF THE WRENS—MATTHEW WREN—TRAVELS TO SPAIN WITH THE PRINCE OF WALES—INTERVIEW AT WINCHESTER HOUSE—BISHOP ANDREWES' PROPHECY—WREN MADE MASTER OF PETERHOUSE—BISHOP OF HEREFORD—CONSECRATION OF ABBEY DORE—OFFICE OF RECONCILIATION—FOREIGN CONGREGATIONS AND THE NORWICH WEAVERS—RESULT OF 'A LECTURER'S' DEPARTURE.

Time, like an ever-rolling stream
Bears all its sons away.

CHAPTER I.

THE name of Christopher Wren is no doubt familiar to the great majority of English people, and to Londoners especially; but it is to many of them little more than a name with which is connected S. Paul's Cathedral and a now, alas! diminished number of City churches. Yet the great architect's ninety-one years of life were passed among some of the most stirring times of our history, in which his family played no inconsiderable part, and he himself was not only the best architect of his day, but was also the foremost in many other sciences. A singularly patient and far-seeing intellect aiding a strong religious faith enabled him 'to keep the even tenour of his way' through a life of incessant labour and considerable temptation. It has been truly said,

> 'It seems almost like a defect in such a biography as that of Wren, that it presents nothing of that picturesque struggle, in the rise from a lower to a higher condition, which has so commonly attended the conquest of genius over difficulty.'[1]

Far otherwise, the Wren family was an old one, tracing its descent from the Danes; one of the house

[1] *Warwickshire Worthies*, p. 845. Article by C. Wren Hoskyns, Esq., M.P.

fought in Palestine under Richard I., and his fame long survived, as in Charles I.'s time it was quoted against one of the knight's descendants.

In 1455, during the reign of Henry VI., in the Black Book (or register) of the Order of the Garter, mention is made of a Wren who probably belonged to this family:—

> 'The Lord of Winchester, Prelate of the order, performed the Divine Service proper for S. George the Martyr, but the Abbots Towyrhill and Medmenham being absent, were not excused, in whose stead Sir William Stephyns read the gospel and Sir W. Marshal the epistle, both of them singing men of the king's choir. The dean of the same choir presented the gospel to the sovereigne to be kissed, and the next day celebrated Mass for the deceased, Sir J. Andevere and John Wrenne assisting in the reading of the epistle and gospel. The reader of the gospel, after censing the reader of the epistle, reverently tendered the heart of S. George to the sovereigne and knights in order to be kissed.'

The heart of S. George was presented by Sigismund, Emperor of Germany, on his admission to the Order of the Garter.

The spelling of 'Wrenne' was a very common form of the family name, and it seems very likely that John Wrenne belonged to this family, who were much connected with S. George's, Windsor.

William Wren was in Henry VIII.'s time the head of the family; his younger brother Geoffrey, who was a priest, was of Henry VII.'s privy council, and was confessor both to him and to Henry VIII. He held the living of S. Margaret's, Fish Street, in the City of London, from 1512 till his death.[1] Geoffrey Wren was also a canon of S. George's at Windsor, where he founded the seventh stall. There he died in 1527, and was buried in the north aisle of the chapel under a brass bearing his effigy in the Garter mantle, with this inscription at his feet:

> 'Sub saxo ponor, et vermibus ultimis donor,
> Et sicut ponor, ponitur omnis honor.'[2]

This tomb and brass have disappeared, as has the 'South Lodge' with its window displaying his coat of arms and emblem; the latter, a wren holding a trefoil in its claw, and his motto—'Turbinibus superest coelo duce praescius.' Dean Wren explains this emblem as chosen because, 'the trefoil or clover shrinking before a storm foretold a change of weather,' and the wren was supposed to have the same prescience. Both motto and emblem were changed by the descendants of the family.

William Wren's grandson, Francis, was born 1552, two years before the close of Queen Mary's reign, at Monk's Kirby in Warwickshire, where the family had property. He was a mercer and citizen of London,

---

[1] S. Margaret's, standing close to Pudding Lane, where the Fire of London began in 1666, was the first church consumed. Its site is now occupied by the Monument, and the parish incorporated with that of S. Magnus the Martyr, London Bridge.

[2]   Laid under the stone,
        For the worms alone,
        All mortal pride
        Is laid aside. (G. A. D.)

and was steward to Mary Queen of Scots during her captivity in England. He married Susan, daughter of William Wiffinson; they lived in the parish of S. Peter's Cheap, and had three children: a daughter Anna, and two sons; Matthew, born 1585, and Christopher, born 1589. Both were educated at the Merchant Taylors' School, and there Matthew especially attracted the notice of Lancelot Andrewes, then Dean of Westminster, who frequently came to the school where he had been bred, and examined the boys in various subjects, particularly in the Hebrew Psalter. He was struck by the proficiency of the eldest of the Wrens, and obtained for the boy a scholarship at Pembroke Hall, Cambridge, of which he was himself master. From that time Dr. Andrewes appears never to have lost sight of Wren, but to have guided his studies and fostered 'the most passionate affection for the ministry of the Church' which the young man showed. Nor was Wren's university life undistinguished, for he became Greek scholar of his college, and when King James visited Cambridge, Matthew Wren, then in priest's orders, 'kept the Philosophy Act' before him with great applause. The subject given was, 'Whether dogs were capable of syllogisms.' Old Fuller says of this extraordinary 'Act,' 'he kept it with no less praise to himself than pleasure to the king; where if men should forget even dogs should remember his seasonable distinction what the king's hounds could perform above others by virtue of their prerogative.'[1] Pro-

[1] Bishop Andrewes was so well pleased that he 'sent the moderator

bably this speech and its ready wit remained on the mind of the King, who dearly loved a compliment to the royal prerogative, and determined him to favour Matthew Wren.

Lancelot Andrewes, who had been Bishop of Chichester, was in 1609 translated to Ely, and so enabled to watch over the University and 'to search out,' as he entreated his friends to do also, 'hopeful and towardly young wits,' and train them up for Holy Orders.[1] He made Matthew Wren his chaplain, gave him the living of Feversham in Cambridgeshire, and some years later made him a canon of Winchester. But very different duties from the ordinary ones of a parish priest devolved upon Wren. King James planned for the Prince of Wales the famous 'Spanish match,' and gave a most reluctant consent to the Duke of Buckingham's scheme, that the Prince should himself go to Spain to fetch home his bride. Two of his chaplains were to attend the Prince, and by the advice of Bishop Andrewes and of Laud, then Bishop of S. David's, Dr. Leonard Maw, afterwards Bishop of Bath and Wells, and Dr. Matthew Wren were chosen. The Prince and Buckingham departed hastily, leaving the chaplains and suite to follow as they could. King James had no sooner allowed the expedition than he repented of it, and being unable to recall his permission, was tormented by a thousand fears for the Prince's safety. The nation was in a state of ferment,

(Dr. Meade), the answerer (Mr. M. Wren), the varier, and one of the repliers that were all of his house (i.e. Pembroke), twenty angels apiece.'
Life of Bishop Andrewes, Lib. Anglo-Catholic Theology, p. xxi.

[1] *Life of Bishop Andrewes*, Lib. Anglo-Catholic Theology, p. xvii.

persuaded that the Prince's faith would be tampered with as well as his person endangered. Thus the two chaplains had by no means an enviable post. They went down to Newmarket, took their leave of the King and received his last instructions :—

'So as all their behaviour and service should prove decent and agreeable to the purity of the Primitive Church, and yet so near the Roman form as can lawfully be done ; "for," said he, " it hath ever been my way to go with the Church of Rome *usque ad aras*."' [1]

'The two bishops gave them also written and detailed instructions that there might appear a face of the Church of England in all forms of worship ; that in the sermons there may be no polemical preachings to inveigh against the Romanists or to confute, but only to confirm the doctrine and tenets of the Church of England by all positive arguments either in fundamental or moral points.'

A full list followed of vestments for the clergy, ornaments and hangings for the altar, and altar lights, Latin service books, directions for a room to be adorned chapel-wise, and for frequent services, all to be read in Latin so that the Spaniards might comprehend them. All this careful provision seems to have been defeated by the fact of the Prince and his suite being lodged in the palace at Madrid, so that there was no public service, only bed-chamber prayers. Contemporary letters show that the chaplains' position was not an easy one, though the Prince remained steadfast, and in the congenial

[1] *Cypr. Ang.*, p. 100. Heylin.

atmosphere of the dignified Spanish court became every day more gracious. 'Dr. Wren forbears,' says one of these letters, 'to write any particulars, but intimates all is not as it should be.' It was no doubt a necessary precaution on the chaplain's part to preserve this discreet silence, but it is tantalising to have only a hint concerning the transactions in Spain. How the negotiations were delayed, how the King recalled the Prince and the marriage was broken off, are historical facts too well known to need repetition here. One result seems to have been a strong bond of affection between the Prince and those who went with him on this singular expedition.

That his departure was attended with some sea-peril appears from one of Edmund Waller's[1] early poems on 'the Danger which His Majesty, being Prince, escaped in the Road at S. Andero':—

> 'Now had his Highness bid farewell to Spain,
> And reached the sphere of his own pow'r, the main;
> With British bounty in his ship he feasts
> The Hesperian princes his amazed guests,
> To find that wat'ry wilderness exceed
> The entertainment of their great Madrid.'

A description follows of the Prince being rowed in a barge to his own ship, a sudden storm arises in which there is a great difficulty in making the ship; at length the Fates allow the rope to be successfully thrown, knowing it to be for England:—

---

[1] Edmund Waller, born March 3, 1605. He was connected by his marriage with Cromwell, and wrote one of his best poems as a panegyric on the Protector, but was supposed to be a Cavalier at heart and rejoiced at the Restoration; died 1687.

> 'Whose prince must be (as their own books devise)
> Lord of the scene where now his danger lies.'

On October 8, 1623, Dr. Wren's diary records 'we landed at Portsmouth,' and his first and only journey out of Great Britain was over.

The sea-voyage, probably a stormy one, made an impression on his mind and he preached before the Universities on the text 'One deep calleth to another.' This is said to have been a remarkable sermon, and old Fuller declares that he became an excellent preacher. The one sermon of his now extant, preached at a later date, on the text 'Fear God, honour the King,' shows that he modelled his style greatly on that of Bishop Andrewes, though without attaining to the same excellence. The sermon is a bold and outspoken one, and has its striking passages. King James, in testimony of his approval of Dr. Wren's conduct as his son's chaplain, bestowed on him the valuable living of Bingham, in Nottinghamshire, to which he was inducted during the next year, resigning his fellowship of Pembroke and the living of Feversham.

Previous to this event, and soon after the Prince's return, a singular incident occurred. Wren, who had been down to Cambridge, came up, as he says, 'suddenly' to London, and as it was late, lodged with his sister in Friday Street, instead of going to Winchester House, where the Bishop kept 'three rooms near the garden' fitted and reserved for him, and where he had lodged twice or thrice. He had, however, seen the Bishop twice, also the Bishops of Durham and S. David's, had taken leave of them on a Saturday, and was prepared to return to Cambridge on the Monday morning following. His journey was, however, delayed by an event which shall be given in his own words:—[1]

'On Monday morne by break of the day there was a great knocking at the door where I lay. And at last the apprentice (who lay in the shop) came up to my bedside, and told me there was a messenger from Winchester House to speak with me. The business was to let me know, that my Lord, when he came from Court last night, had given his steward charge to order it so that I might be spoken with, and be required as from him without fail to dine with him on Monday; but to be at Winchester House by ten of the clock, which I wondered the more at, his lordship not using to come from his study till near twelve. My businesse would hardly permit this, yet because of his lordship's importunity, I got up presently, and into Holborn I went, and there used such despatch, that soon after ten of the clock, I took a boat and went to Winchester House, where I found the steward at the water gate waiting to let me in the nearest way; who told me that my lord had called twice to know if I were come. I asked where his lordship was? He answered, in his great gallery (a place where I knew his lordship scarce

---

[1] 'A transcript of a certain narrative written by the late Bishop of Ely (Dr. Matthew Wren) with his own hand, of that remarkable conference, which after his return from Spain with Prince Charles, 1636, he had with Dr. Neile, then Bishop of Durham, Dr. Andrewes, Bishop of Winchester, and Dr. Laud, Bishop of S. David's, touching the said Prince, whereat something propheticall was then said by that Reverend Bishop of Winchester.' Printed from a MS. in the Ashmolean Museum. *Life of Bishop Andrewes*, Lib. Anglo-Catholic Theology, p. lvii.

came once in a year), and thither I going, the door was locked, but upon my lifting a latch, my lord of St. David's opened the door, and, letting me in, locked it again.

'There I found but those three Lords, who causing me to sit down by them, my Lord of Durham began to me : " Doctor, your Lord here will have it so, I that am the unfittest person must be the speaker. But thus it is. After you left us yesterday at Whitehall, we entering into further discourses of those things which we foresee and conceive will ere long come to pass, resolve to again to speak to you before you went hence.

'" We must know of you, what your thoughts are concerning your master the Prince. You have now been his servant above two years, and you were with him in Spain. We know he respects you well ; and we know you are no fool, but can observe how things are like to go." " What things, my Lord ? " (quoth I). " In brief," said he, " how the Prince's heart stands to the Church of England, that when God brings him to the Crown we may know what to hope for."

'My reply was to this effect, that however I was most unfit of any opinion herein, attending but two months in the year and then at a great distance, only in the closet and at meals ; yet, seeing they so pressed me, I would speak my mind freely ; so I said, " I know my master's learning is not equal to his father's, yet I know his judgement to be very right ; and as for his affection in these particulars which your Lordships have pointed at, for upholding the doctrine and discipline and right estate of the Church, I have more confidence of him than of his father, in whom they say (better than I can) is so much inconstancy in some particular cases."

'Hereupon my Lords of Durham and St. David's began to argue it with me, and required me to let them know upon what ground I came to think thus of the Prince. I gave them my reasons at large; and after many replyings, (above an hour together,) then my Lord of Winchester (who had said nothing all the while) bespake me these words :—

'"Well, Doctor, God send you may be a good prophet concerning your master's inclinations in these particulars, which we are glad to hear from you. I am sure I shall be a true prophet : I shall be in my grave, and so shall you, my Lord of Durham; but my Lord of St. David's and you, Doctor, will live to see that day that your master will be put to it, upon his head and his crown, without he will forsake the support of the Church."

'Of these predictions made by that holy father,' adds the writer, 'I have now no witness but mine own conscience and the Eternal God who knows I lie not; nobody else being present when this was spoken but these three Lords.'

After this the four friends separated and Wren returned to Cambridge.

In two years from the time of that conference King James died, in the following year the saintly

Bishop Andrewes, the kind and unfailing friend of both the Wrens, died also. It is to the great discredit of James I., and probably was the inconstancy to which Dr. Wren alluded, that, as has happened in our own day, the greatest Prelate, the 'incomparable preacher,' the truest and wisest champion of the Church, was passed over when the archbishopric was vacant, an inferior man put above him, and at last the see of Winchester offered to him in tardy amends. At Archbishop Bancroft's death in 1610, everyone's eyes had turned to Bishop Andrewes as his natural successor: but, in the words of a contemporary letter from Lord Baltimore (then Mr. Calvert) to Sir T. Edmonds,

'The Bishop of London (Abbot) by a strong north wind blowing out of Scotland is blown over the Thames to Lambeth; the king having professed to the Bishop himself as also to all the Lords of this council that it is neither the respect of his learning, his wisdom nor his sincerity (although he is well persuaded there is not any one of them wanting in him), that hath made him to prefer him above the rest of his fellows, but merely the recommendation of his faithful servant Dunbar that is dead, whose suit on behalf of this Bishop he cannot forget, nor will suffer to lose his intention.'[1]

The consequences of such an ecclesiastical appointment made for so insufficient a reason were disastrous indeed. Had Andrewes succeeded Bancroft, and had Laud succeeded Andrewes, 'the Church had been

[1] *Life of Bishop Andrewes*, Lib. Anglo-Catholic Theology, p. x.

settled on so sure a foundation that it had not easily been shaken.'[1]

There was general lamentation when Andrewes died, and few can have mourned him more sincerely than Matthew Wren, whom he had loved as a son. Wren attended the funeral, received the gold ring which was the Bishop's bequest to him, and composed the Latin epitaph for his tomb in S. Saviour's, Southwark, which is no unworthy tribute to the holy Bishop.

During this year Dr. Wren was elected, by the unanimous wish of the fellows, Master of Peterhouse, Cambridge, where he 'exercised such prudence and moderation in his government that he reduced all the fellows to one sacred bond of unity and concord.' Besides this he rebuilt the college in great part from the ground, and perceiving that the absence of a chapel was a great obstacle in the way of reverent and frequent services, he did not rest until he had raised subscriptions enough to build a handsome chapel, and to ornament it richly.[2] The wood-panelled hexagonal roof, the marble steps on which the altar stands, flanked by two tall candlesticks, give a character to the interior enhanced by the east window, which is in part a copy of that famous picture of the Crucifixion, then just finished, by Rubens, at Antwerp. This window was carefully taken down in the Rebellion before the college was

---

[1] *Cypr. Ang.*, p. 59. Heylin.

[2] Evelyn, who visited Cambridge in 1655, says of Peterhouse, 'a pretty neate college having a delicate chappell.'

The chapel, especially the west front, of S. Peter's College, is one of the best specimens of the Renaissance Art at Cambridge.—*Hist. of Modern Architecture*, p. 275. Fergusson.

visited, and hidden away in boxes. A wise precaution, for the commissioners destroyed all the other ornaments, pulling down 'two mighty angels with wings, divers other angels, the four evangelists, and Peter with his keys on the chapel door, together with about a hundred cherubim and many superstitious letters in gold. Moreover,' they say, 'we found six angels on the windows which we defaced.' After the Restoration the hidden glass was brought forth again and put back in its place over the altar.[1] While Dr. Wren was thus adorning his college chapel King Charles did not show himself forgetful of Bishop Andrewes' well-loved pupil and chaplain, but in 1628 appointed him Dean of Windsor and registrar of the Order of the Garter. The year after this appointment the peace between England and France was solemnly ratified in the chapel at Windsor and Dean Wren administered the oath to the French ambassador, the Marquis de Châteauneuf.

About this time, as his diary says, he was 'joined together in happy matrimony.' His wife was Eliza Brownrigg, the widowed daughter of Thomas Cull, Esquire, of Ipswich; she had one daughter by her first marriage, and seems to have been possessed of some property in Suffolk. The marriage was in truth as happy as the cruel times in which their lot was cast would allow, though chequered with many sorrows; for of the twelve children whose birth Wren records in his diary, six died while very young. When King Charles journeyed to Scotland for his coronation he summoned

---

[1] *Beauties of England and Wales* (Cambridgeshire).

Wren to attend him. No shadow of the coming trouble showed itself then. The young King was everywhere received with enthusiasm. Whether Dr. Wren, mindful of Andrewes' words, suspected what lay under this fair show, there is no record left to tell us. In after years Sir Thomas Widdrington's venomous attack on himself must have strangely recalled his tones when on this occasion he addressed the King in terms of fulsome adulation at Berwick. On his return from Scotland the King passed the holy week at York, where on Maunday Thursday Dr. Wren washed the feet of thirty-nine poor old men in warm water, drying them with a linen cloth, and Dr. Curle, Bishop of Winchester, washed them over again in white wine and then kissed them.

Shortly after this, Dr. Lindsell, the Bishop of Hereford, died, and Matthew Wren was appointed (1634) to the vacant see. He thereupon resigned the Mastership of Peterhouse, probably with much regret, for all his life he retained a strong affection for his University. His successor was one whose name is well known in church history, Dr. John Cosin, afterwards Dean of Durham and Bishop of Peterborough, a great authority on the ritual and ornaments of the Church. The King would not then suffer Wren to resign the Deanery of Windsor. When Dr. Juxon, who was Clerk of the Closet, was made Bishop of London, the King showed how highly he valued and esteemed Bishop Wren by giving him the post which Juxon resigned, and Dr. Wren then gave up his Deanery. His new post was one of great nearness to the King; to fill it well required great tact and a discreet deafness to the whispers of court intriguers. King Charles was well aware of this, and as soon as Wren had settled himself in his new post said to him:[1]

'Now you are at my elbow there will be many devices to set you and the Archbishop (Laud) at odds. But I warn you of it that you suffer no such trick to be put on you, and therefore I require you both, by that faith which I am sure you will both perform to me, to bind yourselves mutually neither of you to believe any report against the other; and if you meet with any such thing, believe it not, yet presently impart it to each other.'

The wisdom of the King's counsel was quickly shown, for when Dr. Hackett came in his turn of office as the next month's chaplain, he told Wren how they had expected him to be made Bishop of London, and but for the Archbishop preferring Juxon, as a man of whom he had experience and on whom he could rely, it would have been done. Wren paid no regard to these suggestions, suspecting them to be the device of some discontented courtier in order to make him the Archbishop's enemy. To keep his faith with the King and the Archbishop, he presently told them what had passed. The King praised his conduct and told him, ' there was no truth in the report, but only a plot to kindle coals between them two.'

Bishop Wren began vigorous work in Hereford,

---

[1] *Life of Archbishop Juxon*, p. 27. Rev. W. H. Marah.

holding a visitation, collecting and setting in order the statutes of the cathedral, which were in a state of great confusion. Another congenial piece of work came also into his hands. John, Viscount Scudamore, a friend of Laud's, had inherited, with other property, the old Cistercian abbey of Dore, near Monmouth; the building had been greatly damaged in the reign of Henry VIII., but the transepts, chancel, and lady chapel still stood, as they do now, and Lord Scudamore was minded to restore the building to its true use. He accordingly repaired it, setting up again the old stone altar on its four pillars, and providing the church with everything needful for service. Bishop Wren was unable to consecrate the building himself, being in constant attendance on the King, but he busied himself in drawing up an office for the occasion, like, but not identical with, that used by Bishop Andrewes, and commissioned Bishop Field of S. David's to act for him. Bishop Wren was, as Lord Clarendon testifies, 'much versed in the old liturgies, particularly those of the Eastern Church.' He employed himself, at Laud's request, in preparing a service for the reconciliation of those who had apostatised when in slavery with the Moors, and when released wished to return to the faith. The merchants and seamen who were taken by 'Barbary pirates,' and when released came sadly back to England with their story of cruel sufferings undergone and faith reluctantly forsworn, were numerous enough to require a special provision to be made for them.

Knolles' quaint 'Historie of the Turks' shows that

they even made descents on the western coasts of England and carried off men, women, and children into slavery. In 1636, with some of the much-grudged 'ship-money,' a very successful expedition was made under Lord Rainsborough against Sallee, which resulted in the release of large numbers of captives and a promise from the Moorish king to suppress Christian slavery. It is significant that the real leader of the expedition was John Dunton, a reformed renegade taken *off the Isle of Wight* in command of a Sallee ship. He was tried and condemned, but saved his life by offering to show the assailable points of the Barbary ports, and sailed as master on Lord Rainsborough's ship.[1]

The 'Form of Penance and Reconciliation of a Renegado or Apostate from the Christian Religion to Turcism,'[2] which Wren and Laud prepared together, is a very striking one. First came the solemn excommunication, then for two Sundays the penitent came to the door of his parish church in a white sheet carrying a white wand, craving the prayers of all 'good Christians for a poor wretched renegado;' on the second Sunday he was allowed to enter and kneel by the font and pray to be 'restored to the rights and benefits of the blessed sacrament which I have so wickedly abjured,' and then return to the church porch as before. On the third Sunday, when the Apostles' creed had been said, after being publicly put in mind

---

[1] *Annals of England*, p. 407.
[2] *Eccles. Hist.*, vol. ix. p. 388, ed. 1841, Collier, where the office may be found entire.

of his sin, and advised 'that a slight and ordinary sorrow is not enough for so grievous an offence,' the penitent, kneeling eastward, and bowing to the very pavement, was to confess his sin and declare his sorrow and repentance, and to ask the prayers of the congregation. Also to 'thank God for His mercies, especially for the divine ordinance of His Holy Sacraments, and of His heavenly power committed to His Holy Priests, in His Church for the reconciliation of sinners unto Himself and the absolving them from all their iniquity.'

'Then,' says the rubric, 'let the Priest come forth to him, and stand over him, and laying his hand on his head, say, as is prescribed in the Book of Common Prayer, thus :—

Our Lord Jesus Christ, who has left power to his Church to absolve all sinners which truly repent and believe in Him, of His great mercy forgive thee thine offences; and, by His authority committed unto me, I absolve thee from this thy heinous crime of renunciation, and from all thy other sins, in the name of the Father, and of the Son, and of the Holy Ghost. Amen.'

After this follows, with slight alteration, a collect, also from the Visitation of the Sick, and then the priest was to take the penitent by the hand, take away from him the white sheet and the wand, and address to him, once again as dear brother, an affectionate exhortation to walk worthy 'of so great a mercy,' and promise him re-admission to the Holy Communion on the next opportunity. How often this service was employed does not appear. The whole form is so beautiful that it is matter for regret it should be so much forgotten.

Wren had been Bishop of Hereford but one year, when the Bishop of Norwich, Dr. R. Corbet, was translated to Oxford, and Bishop Wren translated in turn to the vacant see. It is easy to see Laud's hand in this. Norwich was a large wide diocese, much shaken by schism and faction and abounding with lecturers who were the torment of the Church at that time and were not unaptly compared 'to bats or reremice, being neither birds nor beasts, and yet both together,'[1] i.e. neither clerk nor layman.

They were not unfrequently men who had been ordained without cure of souls and served as chaplains in gentlemen's houses, or men whose orders were doubtful, or mere laymen who had failed in other callings. They were all strong Calvinists, seldom read the services, but called a fast, quite irrespective of those of the Church, and gave a lecture. This speedily became a 'running lecture,' i.e. was not confined to one place but ran from parish to parish. Every possible check was put by the Archbishop upon these lectures, which were fatal to the proper order of the parishes and all church discipline. Private gentlemen were forbidden to have chaplains, all who preached were compelled to wear a surplice and first to read the Church Service, and in the afternoon to teach the Church Catechism. Wren, Mainwaring, Corbet, Montague, and other like-minded bishops set themselves vigorously to enforce the Archbishop's plans,

[1] *Cypr. Ang.*, introduction, p. 9. Heylin.

esteeming the discipline and doctrine of the Church more valuable than the popularity which their firmness forfeited. Norwich presented an especial difficulty to the Bishop in the great number of weavers and other workmen who had taken refuge there from the Low Countries in times of persecution, and who still kept up their schismatic services.

As his treatment of the Norwich weavers has always been the principal ground of attack against Wren, from Lord Clarendon down to writers of the present time, it is needful to enter somewhat into the question, and to see where the truth lies.

These foreign workmen had settled in England at various times, escaping from persecutions in the Low Countries and in France, and, though they had never had any distinct permission to use their own services, their doing so had been winked at by Queen Elizabeth and King James. Now they had reached a third generation and continued to profit by an exemption which was enjoyed by no other body of the kingdom. It will be borne in mind that as the laws then ran and were understood, every English subject was required to be also a member of the Church of England. The first generation of refugees were an exception, but when they reached a second and third generation, had their own ministers and pretended to the power of Ordination, they became an anomaly, and as Laud, when Bishop of London, said, 'The example is of ill-consequence in Church affairs to the subjects of England, many being confirmed by it in their stubborn ways and inconformities.' The matter was not likely to be mended by Archbishop Abbot; but when Laud succeeded him he addressed himself, in 1634, vigorously to the business, and set out this dilemma: 'If they were not of the same religion' (as the Church of England), 'why should they, being strangers, born in other countries, or descending from them, expect more liberty of conscience than the Papists had, being all natives, and descending from English parents? If of the same, why should they not submit to the government and forms of worship, being the outward acts and exercises of the religion here by law established?'

Every art that could be used was employed by the congregations to avoid returning an answer to the Archbishop's inquiries, whether the English-born members would conform and use the Liturgy in their own language. The two congregations in Norwich resisted vehemently and remonstrated with Bishop Corbet, who was then bishop of the diocese; but Archbishop Laud himself visited the diocese and caused the injunction to be published in the congregations. It had been modified until it only ordered that, while strangers, as long as they were strangers, might use their own discipline, yet that the English Liturgy should be translated into French and Dutch for the better fitting of their children to the English Government. In Canterbury, he kept them 'on a harder diet,' and allowed only the translated Liturgy. All this took place before Bishop Wren came to Norwich, so it is manifestly unjust to accuse him of having set the measure, moderate as it was, on foot. The congregations remained a focus of Calvinism and discontent, secretly encouraged by all the leading Puritans, and envied by the lecturers who wished themselves in the like case.

Another trouble in Norwich, was the failure of business amongst the cloth weavers, whose trade was the chief industry of the town; the failure appears to have been, in a great measure, caused by the plague, which raged in London in 1636,[1] and put a stop for a considerable time to the weekly traffic between it and Norwich. Many of the workmen in consequence betook themselves to Holland, to obtain the means of livelihood. The same thing had happened in Bishop Corbet's time, but as in this instance it coincided with Wren's first visitation, there were not wanting those who said that his severity in enforcing conformity was the main reason of their departure. This accusation seems never to have been made at the time, but only later on, when every conceivable charge was being raked up against the Bishop. He truly says, that, often as at the council board the failure of the weaving trade and the emigration of the skilled workmen to Holland was lamented, it was never suggested that his severity was in any way the cause of it. In his defence, prepared for the House of Commons, the

[1] 'On August 29, 1636 (the plague then raging in London), King Charles, the Queen, and the Court arrived at Oxford. The Chancellor (Archbishop Laud), the Vice-Chancellor, and numerous doctors and masters went out to meet the royal retinue. The Chancellor, accompanied by the Lord Treasurer (Bishop Juxon), the Bishop of Winchester (Dr. Curle), the Bishop of Norwich (Dr. M. Wren), and the Bishop of Oxford (Dr. Bancroft), rode in a coach.' The Court was entertained with very brilliant festivities, and a series of masks and interludes arranged by Inigo Jones.—*Oxfordshire Annals*, p. 25, by J. M. Davenport.

Bishop, besides accounting for much of the emigration by the failure of trade, consequent on the plague, reduces the number, by comparing it with the records kept at the various ports, from the alleged 3,000 to about 300, and drily says: 'The defendant humbly conceiveth that the chiefest cause of their departure was the small wages given to the workmen, whereby the workmasters grew rich, and the workmen were kept very poor.'

The charge has been often revived, the more so as though the accusation is well known enough, the defence, only to be found in the 'Parentalia,' is hardly known except to the few who have threaded the labyrinth of that scarce volume. That Wren was a great upholder of discipline and authority, a man of a fiery energetic temper, decided opinions, and an unyielding, perhaps a severe, disposition, is certainly true; but it is also true that he practised, as Laud and Strafford did, an even-handed justice, laying his hand on rich and poor alike, and would not turn aside for any suggestion of policy or expediency. It should, however, in fairness be added, that though he made his authority felt and obeyed, he did not press matters to extremity against any clergyman without grave cause, and was very ready to receive those who showed any readiness to submit. Of the 1,300 clergy in the diocese, not including those attached to the Cathedral or the schoolmasters, in spite of 'many disorders,' there were in 1636 but thirty excommunicated or suspended, some for contumacy, some for obstinately refusing to publish the King's declaration, some 'for contemning all the Orders and Rites of the Church and intruding themselves, without licence from the Ordinary, for many years together.' His returns to the Archbishop show how very thoroughly and diligently he, to use a modern phrase, 'worked his diocese,' visiting parish after parish, causing the fabrics to be repaired,[1] the clergy to reside, to hold the appointed services and to catechise the children. Here and there a lecturer who promised conformity was allowed to remain, but generally they were checked and discouraged. Great Yarmouth must have gladdened the Bishop's heart, as, two years before Bishop Wren came to the Diocese, the lecturer had gone to New England, 'since which time,' the Bishop says, 'there hath been no lecture and very much peace in the town and all ecclesiastical orders well observed.' It was in truth a great undertaking to bring the Diocese of Norwich into order; but Wren did not shrink from the task, and had all the support which the King and the Archbishop could give, a support afterwards imputed as a crime both to those who gave and to him who received it.

[1] The state of the diocese is vividly shown in Bishop Corbet's charge of 1634 (for the repairs of old S. Paul's Cathedral). 'Some petitions,' he says, 'I have had since my coming to this diocese, for the pulling downe of such an isle [aisle] or for changing lead to thatch, soe far from reparations that our sute is to demolish. . . . Since Christmas I was sued to and I have it yett under their hands, the hand of the minister and the hand of the whole parish, that I would give way to their adorning their church within and out, to build a stone wall round the churchyard which now had but a hedg. *I took it for a flout at first*, but it proved a very sute; they durst not without leave mend a fault forty yeares ould.' The spire of Norwich Cathedral where Bishop Corbet was preaching had fallen in, and during three years but two yards had been rebuilt. See *Documents relating to S. Paul's* by Dr. Sparrow Simpson, p. 137. Camden Society.

CHAPTER II.

1630–1640.

DR. C. WREN—BIRTH OF HIS SON CHRISTOPHER—EAST KNOYLE—ORDER OF THE GARTER—HOW A MURDERER WAS DETECTED—CHRISTOPHER AT WESTMINSTER—A LATIN LETTER—DIOCESE OF ELY—IMPEACHMENT OF LORD STRAFFORD—OF ARCHBISHOP LAUD—ARTICLES AGAINST BISHOP WREN—RESIGNS THE DEANERY OF THE CHAPELS ROYAL.

Instead of kitchen-stuff, some cry
A gospel-preaching ministry,
And some for old suits, coats, or cloak,
No surplices nor service-book.
A strange harmonious inclination
Of all degrees to Reformation.
                    Hudibras, pt. i. canto 2.

CHAPTER II.

LESS is known of the early years of Christopher Wren than of his brother's more eventful life. Christopher went to Oxford, to S. John's College, was admitted to Holy Orders, and, like his brother, became chaplain to Bishop Andrewes, from whom in 1620 he received the living of Fonthill Bishops in Wiltshire.

It may be said in passing, that to receive preferment from Lancelot Andrewes was in itself a proof of merit, for it was his especial care, in the three dioceses which he successively governed, only to promote able and good men to 'such livings and preferments as fell within his gift, and to give Church preferment to *none that asked for it.*' To this rule he rigidly adhered, and his disciple, Matthew Wren, followed the same plan when he became a Prelate of the Church.

Christopher did not hold this living more than three years, and then received, also from Bishop Andrewes, the neighbouring living of East (or Bishop's) Knoyle, very near Fonthill Abbey, afterwards a place famous for its beauty and its curiosities, then the property of a Mr. Robert Cox. This gentleman had an only child, Mary, who inherited his property; she became the wife of Christopher Wren, probably a few years after his appointment to East Knoyle, where their seven children were born—five girls, of only one of whom there is any subsequent record, and two sons. A Christopher, baptized in the November of 1630, who probably died very young, as in the register the record stands, 'Christopher, first sonne of Doctor Wren,' 'first' is added above in another hand. The next baptism is, 'Christopher, 2nd (*sic*) sonne of Christopher Wren, Dr. in Divinitie and Rector now.' This is in the entries for 1631 (O.S.), followed by those for March, and is dated only '10th.'

This 'second Christopher' is the one who was to make the name afterwards so famous; but the date is very perplexing. Dr. Wren and his son both reckoned the latter's age from his birthday, October 20, 1632, as appears again and again in the 'Parentalia,' notably in Dr. Wren's own MS. note to a letter from his son.[1] The East Knoyle Register would, if the baptism is rightly put among the entries for *March* 1631. (O.S.), make the birthday October 20, 1631; but it seems more likely that this is an error, and 1632 the correct date.

At East Knoyle Dr. Wren appears to have passed most of his time, leaving it occasionally, as he had done his previous living, to attend on Bishop Andrewes. He was a good scholar, if less deeply learned than his brother; a mathematician, a good musician, and had besides some knowledge of drawing and architecture. He employed himself in decorating East Knoyle chancel, and to him, in all probability, are

[1] *Vide infra*, p. 43.

owing the [1] 'flower borders, figures, and texts of Scripture in raised plasterwork' which, though much defaced, still cover the chancel. The subjects are— 'Jacob's Dream,' 'The Ladder with the Angels,' 'Jacob anointing the Pillar.' Over the chancel arch 'The Ascension of our Lord.' Round the capitals of the columns are quaint inscriptions :

$$\text{Sic}_{\text{ut}}\text{pr}_{\text{o}}^{\text{ae}} \quad \text{sis.} \quad \text{Am}_{\text{or}}^{\text{a}}\text{.} \quad \text{A Deo}_{\text{o}}^{\text{a}} \text{ pta.}$$ [2]

'Unum necessarium.' The texts of holy Scripture, which are very well chosen, are all quoted from that earlier translation known as the 'Bishops' Bible,' to which the Psalms, Offertory sentences, and 'Comfortable Words' of the Prayer Book belong.

Besides this, Wren contrived a new roof for the church, as the old one was falling into decay. In the hall of the rectory he put up the following inscription :

> 'In quamcunque domum introeritis primum dicite :
> paX sIt hVIC DoMVI
> Tam solenni præcepto, tempestivo voto
> Subscripsi introiens
> C. W. Rector,
> Julii 28. Anno dicto.' [3]

[1] I am indebted to the kindness of the Rev. R. N. Milford, rector of East Knoyle, for this account. See Sir R. C. Hoare's History of Wiltshire. The inscriptions on the columns have been destroyed.

[2] So guide and govern as to profit souls. Love, Pray. One thing needful. Ask fit things from God.

[3] Into whatsoever house ye enter, first say
Peace be to this house.
To so solemn a precept, by a seasonable vow,
I, entering, have set my name.
C. W. Rector.
July 28. In the said year, i.e. MDCXVVIII.

The inscription is not a little characteristic of the gentle, peace-loving nature of Christopher Wren, and the quaint conceits in which the wits of the time delighted. This form of chronogram was one which he frequently used. His second daughter, Susan, was born in 1627, and as she and the 'second Christopher' clung closely together in after life, and the others are never mentioned, it seems likely that they two were the only survivors of the seven children. Christopher was a very delicate, weakly boy, who early gave promise of brilliant abilities. No records say when Mrs. Wren died, but various things seem to show that she died when her children were still very young.

Dr. Wren had been one of the King's chaplains in ordinary since 1628, and so well did he acquit himself that when his brother the Bishop resigned the deanery of Windsor and the registrarship of the Garter, the King appointed Christopher to the vacant post. It was an appointment which suited him well; he took up with equal energy his brother's work, of arranging the documents and records, and continuing the history of the Order. Two autograph letters relating to this are preserved in the 'Parentalia,' one from the chancellor of the Garter, Sir Thomas Rowe :—

> 'Reverend Sir,—I had wayted on you before this tyme, but that I have been punished with Lamenes, both for my owne advantage to learne of y^u and to acquaint y^u with some orders I have received from his ma^{tie} and to give y^u ye summe of ye last chapter as I conceived it.'

Sundry particulars follow, and he promises a record

of the members of the Garter from its foundation. The King, he says, is anxious that every 'chapter of the Order' should be fully recorded. Sir Thomas asks for 'the papers of Sir John Fynnet' in order to send them to King Charles, 'who is very curious of them.' 'On all occasions,' the letter concludes, 'I shall be glad to give y^u ye testimonye of my desire to be esteemed and to be y^r affectionate friend to serve y^u,

'THO. ROWE.

'Cranford, 9 Jan. 1636 (O.S.)'

The Dean's answer comes promptly :—

'Jan. 10, 1636 (O.S.)

'Honorable Sir,—How much you obliged me I shall endeavour to demonstrate to you upon better opportunities. For ye present I returne y^r books and promise you ye sight of another some^{wt} of them (?) wch phaps you will not dislike, though I begin to think your exact diligence hath lefte none of those monuments lye undiscryed, where they might be gained. I send back likewise Sir John Finet's Paps; whereof I reserve ye copyes. And now that I begin to finde a little respiration, I will draw y^m up into acte. Till I had y^m I could not well begin, and now that you are pleased to send me ye last, drawne up into forme, I shall ye better accomplish ye whole business of my little time. Whereof I will send you ye whole contextures, Deo dante, ere longe. I should however give you a formall thanks that you imploy yourselfe soe largely, soe nobly for me in present, and in promise more. Knowing your reality in all worth, I abstain from other compliments then those wherein Affection must pforce speake yf she speake at all. Once for all, that branch of our comon oath is never out of my minde: Sustentabis Honores hujus Ordinis atq. omni^m qui in eo sunt. Of wch omni^m you are Pars Magna and shall ever be to your affectionate ob: servant friend,

'CHR. WREN.

'To the Honble Sr. Tho. Row Chancelor of ye most Honble Order of ye Garter.'

The Garter history appears to have been carefully continued, and Dean Wren describes, in a long picturesque account, the admission on May 19, 1638, of the Prince of Wales, then but eight years old, as a 'companion of the Garter.' The little Prince, Dean Wren says, acquitted himself admirably during the three days of intricate ceremonial, doing his part with accuracy and spirit, a sweet dignity, and an unwearied patience until all was completed.

He must have been a very hopeful, engaging, boy, and it is sad to think how little his after life fulfilled its early promise: had he remained in his father's care a very different record might have been left of him in English history. The Service of Admission is a curious one, and the prayers on the putting on the Garter, the ribbon, the collar, and the mantle have considerable beauty. On this occasion the festival was celebrated with great splendour. King Charles presented two large silver flagons, cunningly carved and very richly gilt, offering them on his knees with these words: 'Tibi, et perpetuo Tuo servitio, partem bonitatis Tuae offero Domine Deus Omnipotens.'[1]

These were added to the treasury of the Garter, which contained many articles of great value. There was a set of triple gilt silver plate wrought by Van Vianen[2] of Nuremberg, estimated at over 3,000*l.*, several other pieces of plate, Edward IV.'s steel armour, gilt, and covered with crimson velvet embroidered with pearls, rubies and gold, fifteen rich copes embroidered in gold, altar-cloths and hangings worked with the same costly material.

There was also the blue velvet mantle, the George and Garter of Gustavus Adolphus, each letter of the motto made in diamonds. These had been sent to the King of Sweden by Charles I. at the close of the campaign in 1627 as a mark of friendship and respect for his valour, and were the richest ever sent even to a sovereign.

After the heroic king's death on the field at Lutzen, in 1634, a solemn embassy brought the mantle and the jewels back to England, when they were consigned to the Dean and Chapter of Windsor, with a charge from King Charles to lay them up in the treasury 'for a perpetual memorial of that renowned King, who died in the field of battle wearing some of those jewels, to the great honour of the Order, as a true martial prince and companion thereof.'

---

[1] 'To Thee, and to Thy service for ever, I offer a portion of Thy bounty, O Lord God Almighty.'

[2] Christian Van Vianen was an embosser and chaser of plate, much esteemed by Charles I. The gilt plate above mentioned was wrought at the rate of 12*s.* per oz.—*Anecdotes of Painting*, Walpole, vol. ii. p. 323.

A few years later King Charles presented Dean Wren to the rectory of Great Haseley [1] near Oxford, with a fine old church containing two crusaders' tombs.

In the parish of Haseley is the manor of Ryecote (or Ricot), which by marriage had become the property of Sir Henry Norris, Queen Elizabeth's ambassador to France, whom she created Baron Norris (or Norreys) of Ryecot, and whose descendants, now the Earls of Abingdon, possess the manor to this day. During Dr. Wren's incumbency, a strange event took place. Among the retainers of Lord Norris was an old man who had charge of the fish ponds; he had one nephew, who was the heir of all his uncle's possessions and savings. The nephew enticed the old man out one night, waited till he fell asleep under an oak tree, murdered him by a blow on the head, dragged the body to one of the ponds, tied a great stone to the neck and threw the corpse in. There it lay *five weeks*, during which time Lord Norris and all the neighbours wondered what had become of the old man. At length the body was found by the men who were about to clean the pond, and were attracted to the spot by the swarms of flies; they raised the corpse with great difficulty and recognised it.

The stone tied to the neck was evidence of foul play, though no one could guess at the murderer.

---

[1] William Lenthall (born at Henley-on-Thames 1591), Speaker of the House of Commons 1640–1653 and 1660, lived chiefly at Lachford Manor in Great Haseley parish, which had been in his family since the reign of Edward IV. The property was sold by his eldest son. It may have been owing to the influence of the Speaker that Dean Wren escaped imprisonment during the Rebellion.

Lord Norris, in order to detect the criminal, after the usual manner, commanded that the corpse, preserved by the water from the last extremity of decay, should on the next Sunday be exposed in the churchyard, close to the church door, so that everyone entering the church should see—and touch it. The wicked nephew shrank from the ordeal, feigning to be so overwhelmed with grief as to be unable to bear the sight of his dearest uncle. Lord Norris, suspecting that the old man had been murdered by the one person whom his death would profit, compelled him to come, and to touch with his finger, as so many had willingly done, the hand of the dead. At his touch, however, 'as if opened by the finger of God, the eyes of the corpse were seen by all to move, and blood to flow from his nostrils.' At this awful witness the murderer fell on the ground and avowed the crime, which he had secretly committed and the most just judgment of God had brought to light. He was delivered to the judge, sentenced, and hanged.

The event must have made a deep impression on Dean Wren, who recorded it at length in Latin and signed the record to attest its truth.

He also mentions that in the east window of the church was the

> 'Coat of France azure fretté and semé of Flower de Lyces or, put there together with his own coat by Lord Barentine, knight of Rhodes and a great benefactor to that church. A man of great valour and possessions in France as well as in England, his tomb at the north-east side of the chancel shows he was of a

gigantic stature; and his statue of one entire stone, which I digged out of a heap of rubbish there, makes it appear he was (not two inches lower than) seven foot high.'

Dr. Wren seems to have divided his residence between Haseley and Windsor, probably spending most of his time at the Deanery, where many of the learned men and philosophers' of the day sought his society. Among these was the Prince Palatine Charles, who was a frequent guest at the Deanery, enjoying its learned quiet, and interested in his host's young son, whose great gifts were early remarkable. Many a little note did Dean Wren make of curious things that came under his observation, particularly of an oak that grew in the New Forest and sent out young fresh leaves on Christmas Eve. So much discussion was raised about it at court and King James would so little believe it, that good Bishop Andrewes sent a chaplain on Christmas Eve to the forest, who gathered about a hundred fresh shoots, stuck them into wet clay, and sent them straight to the court, where Dr. Wren witnessed the opening of the boxes. The tree was then cut down by some spiteful fellow, 'who,' says the Dean, 'made his last stroke on his own leg, whereof he died, together with the old wondrous tree.'

King Charles engaged Dr. Wren to make an estimate for a building at Windsor for the use of the Queen; it was to be of considerable size, containing a chapel, a banqueting room, galleries and rooms for the Lord Chamberlain and court officials. The estimate exists in business-like detail, the total amounting to 13,305*l*.; but it was probably not even begun.

To his other employments the Dean added the tender care of his young son. Christopher's case was one of those rare ones in which a precocious child not only lives to grow up, but also amply fulfils his early promise. His delicate health was the cause of much anxiety to his father and to his sister Susan, and it may be that the skill in nursing and medicine for which she was afterwards famous, had their beginning in her watchful care of her little brother.

His frail health seems to have been rather a spur than a hindrance to his studies, and when very young he had a tutor, the Rev. W. Shepheard, who prepared him for Westminster, where he was sent in his ninth or tenth year. Westminster was then under the rule of its famous headmaster Dr. Busby, to whose especial care young Christopher was committed.

The school with its stir of life, the grand abbey, the Houses of Parliament then empty and silent, Lambeth, from which his uncle's friend, Archbishop Laud, might be seen frequently coming across the river in his barge; the whole surroundings must have been wonderful to the country-bred boy who was one day to connect his name indissolubly with that of London. Did he, one cannot but wonder, ever on a holiday take boat down the river, shooting the dangerous arches of London Bridge, and look at S. Paul's with its long line of roof, its tall tower and shattered spire; little S. Gregory's nestling by its side, and all the workmen busied on the repairs which had been begun after King James's solemn thanksgiving in 1620? Laud, while Bishop of London, had carried on the works with a vigour that had given them a fresh impetus, and was one great cause of his unpopularity. Inigo Jones had superintended them and finished the interior, and at the west end, the stately portico of Portland stone, which, though incongruous, was in itself beautiful, was being erected by King Charles's orders. How little could the boy have guessed at the ruin which was approaching those pious builders, or the desecration and destruction that awaited the fine old building itself!

At school no pains were spared with so promising a pupil as young Wren soon showed himself to be. His sister Susan married, in 1643, Mr. William Holder, subdean of the Chapel Royal, of a Nottinghamshire family, a good mathematician, and one 'who had good skill in the practic and theoretic parts of music.'[1] Susan Wren was sixteen when she married, and though childless the marriage was a very happy one.

Mr. Holder early discerned his young brother-in-law's talent for mathematics and gave him private lessons. Mr. Holder was subsequently appointed to the living of Bletchingdon in Oxfordshire, which he held until 1663.

Among the few autograph letters of Christopher Wren's which remain in the family, is one written to his father from Westminster in a boy's unformed hand, the faintly ruled lines still showing.

[2]'Venerande Pater,—Sententia apud antiquos vulgata

---

[1] Wood, *Fasti Oxon.*, p. 139.

[2] 'Revered Father,—There is a common saying among the ancients which I remember to have had from your mouth; there is no equivalent that can be given back to parents. For their cares and perpetual labours

est, quam ex ore tuo me habuisse memini, Parentibus nihil posse reddi æquivalens. Frequentes enim curae et perpetui labores circa pueros sunt immensi quidem amoris indicium. At praecepta illa mihi toties repetita, quae animum ad bonas Artes, & Virtutem impellunt, omnes alios amores superant. Quod meum est, efficiam, quantum potero ne ingrato fiant hac munera. Deus Optimus Maximus conatibus meis adsit et Tibi, pro visceribus illis Paternae Pietatis, quae maximè velis praestet.

'Id orat Filius tuus, Tibi omni obsequio devotissimus,

'CHRISTOPHORUS WREN.

> 'Has tibi primitias Anni, Pater, atq. laborum
> Praesto (per exiguas qualibet esse sciam)
> Quas spero in messem posse olim crescere, vultu
> Si placido acceptes tu, foveasque sinu.'

> 'To you, Deare Sir, your Son presenteth heere
> The first-fruits of his pains and of the yeare ;
> Wich may (though small) in time an harvest grow,
> If you to cherish these, your favour shew.

'E. Musaeo Meo.
'Calendis Januarii 1641 (1642 N.S.)'

---

concerning their children are indeed the evidence of immeasurable love. Now these precepts so often repeated, which have impelled my soul towards all that is highest in man, and to virtue, have superseded in me all other affections. What in me lies I will perform, as much as I am able, lest these gifts should have been bestowed on an ungrateful soul. May the good God Almighty be with me in my undertakings and make good to thee all thou most desirest in the tenderness of thy fatherly love. Thus prays thy son, most devoted to thee in all obedience,

'CHRISTOPHER WREN.'

'Script. hoc, A° Ætatis suae, Decimo. Ab Octobris 20° elapso' is the note in different hand of Dean Wren, who may very probably have felt that in the fast-rising storm all this fair promise might be swept away.

While young Christopher was thus delighting his father with his 'first-fruits,' his uncle the Bishop was encountering many adversities. While he was busied in Norwich, and in the midst of his work, Dr. White, Bishop of Ely, died; he had resided mostly in London, as was then too commonly the habit of the bishops, and it is to be supposed that there was plenty of work to be done in the diocese. Laud reckoned it as a very important one on account of its university, and could think of no one so well suited to the post as Bishop Wren, who was a distinguished Cambridge scholar. To Ely accordingly the Bishop was trans-. lated, May 5, 1638, and rejoiced in renewing his connection with the university where his early years had been spent. The expenses attending so many removals must have fallen heavily upon him; all the more, as in Norwich the palace was out of repair and he lived for some time in a house of his own at Ipswich, which was probably a part of Mrs. Wren's property, finding that much attention was required by that part of his diocese. Prynne was born at Ipswich, and though shut up in the Tower of London,[1] retained friends in his native town; thus the Bishop knew he was entering a hornet's nest. Prynne speedily produced his 'Quench-Coal,' which professed to answer a tract called 'A Coal from the Altar,' wherein were explained the reasons for placing the Holy Table altarwise, and railing it in. Next came 'The News from Ipswich,' which reviled all bishops under the names of 'Luciferian Lord Bishops, execrable Tray-

---

[1] Heylin, *Cypr. Ang.*, p. 309.

tors, Devouring Wolves,' and the like; especially attacking Wren, and declaring, that, 'in all Queen Marie's time, no such havoc was made in so short a time of the faithful ministers in any part, nay in the whole Land, than had been made in his Diocese.' There was one great riot at Ipswich, which the Bishop was able to quell. Prynne was fined, branded, and imprisoned in Carnarvon Castle, and the town was for the time tranquil, but Prynne was destined to be a deadly and utterly unscrupulous enemy.

For nearly two years after his translation to Ely, Dr. Wren was able to govern his new diocese in comparative peace. Little opposition seems to have been made, for the factious spirit which was rampant in Norfolk and Suffolk was less violent here. In his beloved university there were many points which needed amendment. When he was master of Peterhouse and built the chapel, he gave it that which many colleges then lacked, and were lacking still when he returned, to visit Cambridge.

The churchyards of the parish churches had been in many instances encroached upon and profaned, and in most of the chancels were 'common seats over high and unfitting that place.' 'In all these businesses,' says Archbishop Laud in his yearly report to the King, 'the Bishop hath been very tender, both out of his respect to his mother the University of Cambridge, and because divers of the benefices are impropriations belonging to some of the Colleges there.' Nor was Wren's care alone for the fabrics of the Church; he was careful to secure resident and diligent clergy in all the parishes as far as he could and to see that they did their duty. His advice and help were readily given. A clergyman, Mr. John Bois, applied to him for advice in the case of a woman of twenty-nine, of whom no one knew whether or no she was baptized. Mr. Bois had applied by letter and word of mouth to the previous Bishops of Ely (Bishops Buckeridge and White), and could get no answer. Bishop Wren replied to him promptly, directing him to baptize her forthwith, which was accordingly done.[1] Upon these peaceful labours the long-pending storm broke and called Wren to harder duties.

In 1640 the discontent of the times declared itself openly in Scotland, where the Puritan party took up arms against the King, and began to league themselves with the party in England whose opinions or prejudices coincided with their own. King Charles had summoned a parliament, and again dismissed it, having obtained no assistance against the Scotch. 'The minds of men had taken such a turn,' says Hume, 'as to ascribe every honour to the refractory opposers of the King and the ministers. These were the only patriots, the only lovers of their country, the only heroes, and perhaps, too, the only true Christians.' The mob of sectaries in London, encouraged by the successes obtained by the Scotch, burst into S. Paul's,

---

[1] *Desiderata Curiosa*, p. 336. Peck. It will be borne in mind that the Office for the Baptism of such as are of Riper Years was only added to the Prayer Book at the last revision in 1662. Mr. John Bois was made a Prebendary of Ely by Bishop Andrewes, and was one of the translators of the Bible (1604–1611); he was on the Cambridge Committee, and assisted in the translation of the Apocrypha.—*Key to the Holy Bible*, p. 28. Rev. J. H. Blunt.

where the High Commission then sat, and tore down the benches, with cries of 'No Bishops—no commission!' Before this they had attacked Lambeth Palace, threatening to tear the Archbishop in pieces, and would probably have done so had he not been prepared for them. From that time he knew his life to be in constant peril. An unknown friend had written to warn him that the Scotch Puritans justified assassination, and openly hoped the Primate might meet the same fate as his early friend and patron, the Duke of Buckingham. His integrity and singleness of mind, to which Clarendon gives high testimony, had made him bitter enemies. A hasty temper and sharp mode of speech alienated many who could not but respect him. The difficulties of his task had been doubled by the lax, un-Catholic rule of his predecessor at Lambeth. Both Puritans and Romanists alike reckoned him as their greatest opponent. He was nearly seventy years old, and sadly felt that 'there wanted not many presages of his ruin and death.' The King's return, on October 30, brought a gleam of sunshine.

Evelyn[1] says :—

'I saw His Majesty (coming from his Northern expedition) ride in pomp and a kind of ovation with all the markes of a happy peace, restored to the affections of his people, being conducted through London with a most splendid cavalcade; and on 3 November following (a day never to be mentioned without a curse), to that long, ungrateful, foolish, and fatal Parliament, the beginning of all our sorrow for

[1] *Diary*, October 30, 1640.

twenty years after, and the period of the most happy monarchy in the world.' In truth its opening augured ill for the country and for the Church.

Lord Strafford was impeached and sent to the Tower, and the Archbishop next attacked. Sir Harbottle Grimston, in a virulent speech, vented his hatred against Archbishop Laud ; 'and those prelates he hath advanced—to name but some of them : Bishop Manwaring, the Bishop of Bath and Wells, the Bishop of Oxford, and Bishop Wren—the last of all those birds, but one of the most unclean ones.' The debate which followed ended—as in the temper of the House it was certain to do—in a vote that the Archbishop was a traitor. Allowed the afternoon at Lambeth to collect papers for his defence, he attended the evening prayers for the last time in the chapel that he had repaired and adorned with loving care. The service, which he had restored to its full beauty, soothed that bitter hour. 'The Psalms of the day (December 18) and chapter l. of Isaiah gave me great comfort. God make me worthy to receive it,' he wrote in his diary. The poor thronged round Lambeth Palace, and bitterly lamented the departure of their best friend, showering blessings on his head as he was carried away. He remained in the custody of Maxwell, the Usher of the Black Rod, ten weeks, compelled to pay 436*l.* for his charges, besides a fine of 500*l.* He was then transferred to the Tower.

The Archbishop being secured, the Bishops were next attacked. Hampden came to the Lords with a message to acquaint their lordships that the Commons had received matters of a high kind against the Bishop of Ely, for the 'setting up of idolatry and superstition in divers places, and acting the same in his own person;' adding that he was intending to escape from England, and that they therefore desired he might be put in security, to be forthcoming and abide the judgment of Parliament. Bishop Wren was in his place in the House when this summons came, and was ordered to find bail for 10,000*l*.; helped by three of the bishops, he managed to do so. When the Primate was in custody, and Wren under censure, at the beginning of the next year Lord Strafford was attacked. Dr. Williams, Bishop of Lincoln, not long released from the Tower, anxious to please the Commons, declared that the canon law forbade the Bishops to sit as judges in a case of blood. He spoke in the name of the other Bishops; and the decision was too welcome to Strafford's enemies not to be agreed to instantly; but it was a concession afterwards very dangerous to those who made it. The issue of that iniquitous trial, perhaps as great a perversion of justice as England had ever then known, needs no repetition here.

The King's best advisers were in prison or under restraint, except good Bishop Juxon, who bravely told him he ought not, upon any considerations in the world, to do anything against his conscience; and Bishop Williams, who hated Strafford and Laud alike, sent by the Commons to induce the King to sign the deathwarrant, had a fatal success.

Bishop Wren came to Windsor after this to marry Princess Mary, the King's eldest daughter, to William, eldest son of Henry Frederick, Prince of Orange, whom he succeeded in six years. The alliance was one which gratified the Parliament, being so Protestant a connection. Little, however, could they have guessed how deadly an enemy Princess Mary's son would prove to the house of Stuart. Ten days after this wedding came May 12, when 'the wisest head in England was severed from the shoulders of Lord Strafford.' So writes John Evelyn. To the Archbishop, his friend's death must have been a terrible blow. He was just able to bestow a parting blessing through his prison window, and to hear Lord Strafford say, 'Farewell, my lord. God protect your innocency.' The Princess's marriage was the last occasion on which Bishop Wren was to officiate as Dean of the Chapels Royal.

The Commons had been industriously at work against him since the first attack in December, and as Archbishop Laud said of Prynne, 'by this time their malice had hammered out somewhat.' The committee sent in a report, charging the Bishop with 'excommunicating fifty painful ministers, practising superstition in his own person, placing "the table" altarwise, elevation of the elements, the "eastward position," as it is now called, at the Eucharist, bowing to the Altar, causing all seats to be placed so that the people faced east, employing his authority to restrain "powerful preaching," and ordering catechising in the words of the Church Catechism only, permitting no prayer before the sermon but the bidding prayer (canon 5), publishing a book of articles, to which the churchwardens were sworn, containing 187 questions.'

Upon this report a debate ensued, ending in a vote that it was the opinion of the House that Matthew Wren was unworthy and unfit to hold or exercise any office or dignity in the Church, and voting that a message be sent to the House of Lords to desire them to join the Commons in petitioning his Majesty to remove Bishop Wren from his person and service. Evelyn's expression, 'to such an exorbitancy had the times grown,' aptly describes the state of matters when, for details such as these of the government of a diocese, and for practices which, if they had been proved, were both legal and reasonable, an assembly of laymen presumed to pronounce a bishop unfit for his office in the Church. Whether the petition ever came before the King does not appear, but Wren thought it best to take the initiative; for he writes in his diary five days after the debate: 'I hardly obtained leave from the King to resign the deanery of the Chapels Royal.'

CHAPTER III.
1641–1647.

BISHOP WREN ACCUSED—WESTMINSTER ABBEY ATTACKED — IMPRISONMENT OF THE BISHOPS — BISHOP WREN'S DEFENCE — 'UTTERLY DENIETH ALL POPISH AFFECTIONS'— THE GARTER JEWELS—ARCHBISHOP LAUD MURDERED—CHRISTOPHER AT OXFORD —PHILOSOPHICAL MEETINGS.

For though outnumber'd, overthrown,
And by the fate of war run down,
Their duty never was defeated, ·
Nor from their oaths and faith retreated ;
For loyalty is still the same,
Whether it win or lose the game ;
True as the dial to the sun,
Although it be not shined upon.
     Hudibras, pt. iii. canto 2.

CHAPTER III.

The concession Bishop Wren had thus made did not satisfy the Commons, and on July 20 they drew out the report into twenty articles of accusation, containing all the former charges and several additional ones, among which were the setting up of altar-rails, ordering the Holy Communion to be received kneeling, ordering the reading of the 'Book of Sports,' and preaching in a surplice; causing by prosecutions 3,000 of the King's poor subjects to go beyond the sea.

For these offences they prayed that Bishop Wren might answer, and suffer such punishment as law and justice required. The articles were transmitted to the House of Lords at a conference, and were read by Sir T. Widdrington, Recorder of York,[1] who prefaced them by a venomous speech against the Bishop of Ely, whom he compared to 'a wolf devouring the flock; an extinguisher of light; a Noah, who sent out doves from the ark, and refused to receive them back unless they returned as ravens, to feed upon the carrion of his new inventions, he himself standing with a flaming sword to keep such out of his diocese.' He accused the Bishop of raising fines for his own profit; called him a great robber, a malefactor, 'a compleat mirror of

[1] *Vide supra*, p. 17.

innovation, superstition, and oppression: an oppugner of the life and liberty of religion, and a devouring serpent in the diocese of Norwich.'

These are but a few phrases from Sir Thomas's speech; he used no argument, adduced no proof, but contented himself simply with clamour and reviling, and these were amply sufficient. In the Long Parliament it was enough to accuse anyone, especially a bishop, of Popery, superstition and 'innovation'—which was a term invented by Bishop Williams, then as now commonly applied to the oldest dogmas and practices of the Church—to insure his imprisonment, or at the least a heavy fine. In Wren's Diary opposite the day of the month is merely, ' Let God arise, and let his enemies be scattered.' Dr. Pierce, Bishop of Bath and Wells, was attacked at the same time; but at first no active steps were taken against them, perhaps because the Commons found matters not yet ripe for a wholesale imprisonment of the Bishops. Dr. Wren well knew that matters would not stop here, and while awaiting the next attack began to prepare his Defence against the Articles of Accusation.

The mob in the meanwhile were encouraged by caricatures, libels, and invectives to rail against the Bishops and impute every misfortune and every trade failure to them, by which means the Puritan leaders contrived to stir up a yelling mob of men and women.

All petitions against the Church were received and the petitioners encouraged and praised. The populace insulted the Bishops whenever they appeared, and threatened their lives. Westminster Abbey was attacked, when the Bishops were there, by a violent mob, led by Wiseman, a knight of Kent. The officers and choirmen of the Abbey with the boys of the School, among whom must have been Christopher Wren, defended it gallantly, and the fray ended when Wiseman was killed by a tile thrown from the battlements by one of the defenders. After this the Bishops who were in London met in the Deanery at Westminster, the lodging of Williams, Archbishop of York, who had just been translated from Lincoln to York, in succession to the late Archbishop Neile,[1] to consult what should be done. At the Archbishop's suggestion, they drew up a paper, remonstrating against the abuse offered them, and the manner in which they had been hindered from coming to the House of Lords, their coaches overset, their barges attacked and prevented landing, and they themselves beset and threatened. They claimed their right to sit in the House of Lords and vote, and protested against all that had been done since the 27th of that month (December, 1641), and all that should hereafter pass in time of this their forced and violent absence. This paper was signed by the Archbishop and eleven Bishops, of whom Bishop Wren was one, and presented to the King, who delivered it to Littleton, the Lord Keeper, to be communicated next day to the Peers. The Lord Keeper, who had already deserted his benefactor, Lord Strafford, contrary to the King's orders showed

[1] R. Neile, successively Bishop of Rochester, Lichfield, Lincoln, Durham and Winchester, and Archbishop of York, died 1640. Godwin speaks strongly of his loyalty to Church and King, and the hatred borne to him by the Puritans.—*Praesul. Ang.*

the paper first to 'some of the preaching party in both Houses,' and then to the Peers. Upon the reading a conference was desired between the Houses, and the Lord Keeper declared that the Bishops' paper contained ' matters of high and dangerous consequence, extending to the deep intrenching upon the fundamental privileges and being of Parliament.' The Commons, whose part, like that of the Lord Keeper,[1] was pre-arranged, impeached the Bishops of high treason ; the usher of the Black Rod was despatched to find and bring them before the House. They, lodging in different parts of London, were not all collected until eight o'clock on the winter's night, and then, their offence being signified, were committed to the Tower.[2] The Bishops of Durham and Lichfield, both aged and infirm, obtained leave to be in the custody of the Black Rod. The other bishops were carried to the

[1] 'The Commons not being able to come at their intended alterations in the Church while the Bench of Bishops remained entire in the House of Peers, formed several schemes to divide them.'—*Hist. of the Puritans*, vol. ii. p. 388. Neale.

[2] 'We, poor souls,' says Joseph Hall, Bishop of Norwich, in his *Hard Measure*, 'who little thought we had done anything that might deserve a chiding, are now called to our knees at the bar, and charged severally with high treason, being not a little astonished at the suddenness of this crimination compared with the perfect innocency of our own intentions, which were only to bring us to our due places in Parliament with safety and speed, without the least purpose of any man's offence ; but now traitors we are in all the haste, and must be dealt with accordingly. For on December 30, in all the extremity of frost at eight o'clock on the dark evening, are we voted to the Tower; only two of our number had the favour of the Black Rod, by reason of their age, which though desired by a noble lord on my behalf would not be granted ; wherein I acknowledge and bless the gracious Providence of my God, for had I been gratified I had been undone both in body and purse ; the rooms being strait, and the expense beyond the reach of my estate.'—*Annals of England*, p. 420.

Tower on the following morning. A libellous pamphlet was published at this time, entitled 'Wren's Anatomy, discovering his notorious Pranks &c., printed in the year when Wren ceased to domineer,' has in the title-page a print of Bishop Wren sitting at a table; out of his mouth proceed two labels: on one, 'Canonical Prayers;' on the other, 'No Afternoon Sermon.' On one side stand several clergy, over whose heads is written 'Altar-cringing Priests.' On the other, two men in lay habits, above whom is this inscription, 'Churchwardens for Articles.' It serves to show what were considered as really the Bishop's crimes, and that he had a fair proportion of faithful clergy.[1] The Archbishop of York had served the Commons' turn in procuring the King's assent to Lord Strafford's death-warrant, and had enjoyed for a short time a remarkable though transient popularity both on that account and as Laud's bitter opponent. The Commons were, however, soon weary of him, and gladly availed themselves of the pretext afforded by the protest to throw him aside. A pamphlet was published, which had a great success, entitled the 'Decoy Duck,' in allusion to the fens of his former diocese of Lincoln, in which he was represented as only released from the Tower in order to decoy the other bishops there. It was thought prudent that the bishops should make no attempt either to see each other, or Archbishop Laud, who had preceded them to that dreary lodging, so that only loving messages passed between the prisoners. So many bishops being in custody, and five sees vacant,

[1] *Biographical History of England*, vol. ii. p. 157. Grainger.

the Commons took their opportunity, and brought in a Bill depriving the Bishops of their seats in Parliament, and of the power of sitting as judges or privy councillors. It was feebly opposed by the Churchmen, who had been alienated by the prelates' desertion of Lord Strafford, and was finally carried. The remark made a little later by Lord Falkland on Sir E. Deering's 'Bill for the Extirpation of Episcopacy,' when the Churchmen, weary of their attendance, left the House at dinner-time, and did not return—'Those who hated the bishops, hated them worse than the devil, and those who loved them did not love them so well as their dinner,'—appears to have been applicable to this occasion also. Not very long after the first-named Bill had passed, some of the bishops were set at liberty, but Bishop Wren was not released until May 6, 1642.

It was a brief respite. He went down to his diocese, to a house at Downham, near Ely, where his wife and children were living, and there, August 17, he kept the last wedding-day that he and his wife were ever to celebrate together. On August 25 King Charles set up his standard at Nottingham and the Civil War began. On the 30th of the month Bishop Wren's house was entered by soldiers and he was taken prisoner, without, it will be observed, the shadow of a legal charge against him. On September 1st he was again thrown into the Tower, leaving Mrs. Wren with a daughter only eight days old and mourning for their son Francis, who had died in the previous month. Matthew, the eldest son, was then only thirteen years old. Bishop Wren's was a singularly steadfast, hopeful nature, and it may be that he expected to be speedily released by the victorious Royalist armies. Could he have foreseen the duration of his imprisonment and the miseries which were to befall the Church and the country, even his dauntless spirit might have been crushed. He did not seek an interview with Archbishop Laud, lest they should be accused of plotting, and so each injure the other. Otherwise it would not have been difficult, as the Archbishop was at first carelessly watched, in the hope that he would, by escaping, rid the Commons of a difficulty. The Archbishop 'would not, at seventy years, go about to prolong a miserable life by the trouble and shame of flying,' though Grotius sent him an intreaty to copy the example of his own marvellous escape from Loevenstein Castle twenty-one years previously.[1] The services in the Tower Chapel, where they probably met at first, could have given them little comfort, marred and mangled as the services were by the intruders, who came often with no better object than to preach insulting sermons against the prelates.

Dr. Wren busied himself in the completion of the 'Defence,' to which allusion has been made in the first chapter.[2] It is too long to allow of being set out in full, but a few points may be touched upon. Of the 'fifty painful ministers' whom he was said to have excommunicated, for some of the sentences there was, as has been said, very sufficient reason. As the Bishop says, 'Excommunication doth by law fall upon those

[1] *Vide Life of Barnevelde*, vol. i. p. 408. Motley.   [2] P. 26.

that are absent, either from visitation, or synods; and suspension is a censure which in the practice of those courts is incurred in one hour and taken off in another, and is of little or no grievance at all except it be wilfully persisted in.' He complains of so vague a charge, not stating who the clergy were, and proceeds as well as he can recollect to mention those who had fallen under his censure. For those whose licence to preach had been withdrawn, the greater number ought never to have received it at all; one had been a broken tradesman in Ipswich, one a country apothecary, another a weaver, another 'no graduate, not long translated from common stage-playing to two cures and a publick lecture.' Yet still when all were reckoned who had ever been censured or admonished, the Bishop thinks that the fifty will hardly be made up.[1]

It is a curious instance of the temper of the times that one head of so serious an indictment should be that ' To manifest his Popish Affections, he in 1636, caused a crucifix to be engraven upon his Episcopal seal.' Bishop Wren carefully addresses himself to the defence of this point, and to that of bowing at the name of our Lord, and to the Altar.

'He began so to do by the example of that learned and holy Prelate Bishop Andrewes, now with God,

[1] 'Certainly,' says Nalson, 'notwithstanding this black accusation (he is speaking of the ' fifty painful ministers '), there cannot be a greater demonstration of the innocence of this worthy prelate than the very articles; and that this accusation wanted proof to carry it further than a bare accusation, and a commitment to the Tower, where, with the courage and patience of a primitive Christian, he continued prisoner till the year 1660.'—*History of the Puritans*, vol. ii. p. 223. Grey, Examination of Neale's.

under whom this defendant was brought up from his youth, and had depended upon him more than forty years since, and constantly and religiously practised the same upon all occasions . . . . as his own years and studies increased he found first, the bowing at the name of the Lord Jesus, had not only been practised by the clergy but had also been enjoined to all the people, ever since the first reformation, as appeareth by the Injunctions, 1° Eliz. Cap. 52, thereby to testify our due acknowledgment that the Lord Jesus Christ, the true and Eternal Son of God, is the only Saviour of the world, in whom alone the mercies, graces and promises of God to mankind for this life and the life to come are fully and wholly comprised, 1° Jac. Can. 18.' For bowing to the Altar, while setting out how old a practice of the Church it was, designedly continued at the Reformation, how a like reverence was paid always to the King, or to his chair of estate if he was not in the Presence Chamber,

' No Christian would ever deny that bowing or doing adoration, was to be used as a part of God's worship, the affirmative act being necessarily included in the negative precept, " Non adorabis ea, ergo adorabis Me."' 'No more as he humbly conceiveth is it any superstition, but a sign of devotion, and of an awful apprehension of God's divine Presence, to do Him reverence at the approach into the House of God, or unto the Lord's Table. . . .

For the crucifix—' He utterly denieth all popish affections, and saith that the figure of Christ upon the Cross may be had without any popish affection, and that the said figure upon his seal did itself declare what affection it was to manifest. For there was this posy engraven with it, "'Εν ᾧ κόσμος ἐμοὶ κἀγὼ τῷ κόσμῳ," being taken out of S. Paul, Gal. vi. 14. . . . . . In an holy imitation whereof this defendant beareth divers coats of arms (as the use is) upon the said seal, to wit, the arms of the See of Norwich, and the arms of the See of Hereford, and of the Deanery of Windsor, and of the Mastership of Peterhouse, together with his own paternal coat of an ancient descent; he, considering with himself, that these were emblems all, and badges but of worldly and temporal glories, and desiring that the world should have a right apprehension of him, and to testify that he did no way glory in any thing of this transitory world, but humbly endeavoured to wean himself from all temporal and vain rejoycing, he therefore caused such a small figure of Christ on the Cross to be set over all the said coats.'

He adds that he principally used it in signing 'presentments of Popish recusants.' . . . not to say that although the said seal lay all the year long locked up in a chest, but at the time of sealing, and that when any sealing there was no worship done by any; yet nevertheless, as soon as he understood that any had taken scruple at it, he presently, to avoid all pretence of scandal, caused the said seal to be altered and the figure of Christ to be wholly omitted.'[1]

[1] It is curious that nearly as violent an attack was made a hundred

The part of the Defence, which has been most challenged, is that for the use of the 'Eastward position.' It is, however, important to remember that the Bishop had to defend himself against the charge, that once, while celebrating in the Tower Church at Ipswich, he had 'used idolatrous actions' in administering the Holy Communion, Consecrating the Elements with his face eastward, elevating the Paten and Chalice 'above his shoulders and bowing low either to or before them when set down on the Table.'

The charge of 'idolatry' divides itself into three heads. The last two Wren met by a full denial, the first he confesses, while explaining his reason for his position in *that special instance*, when, as he says, the Elements being on the middle of the Holy Table, 'were farther from the end thereof than he, being but low of stature, could reach over his book unto them and yet still proceed in reading the words without stop or interruption and without danger of spilling the Bread and Wine . . . and he humbly conceiveth that although the Rubric[1] says that the Minister shall stand at the north side of the Table, yet it is not so to be meant as that upon no occasion during all Com-

---

years later upon Bishop Butler (the author of the *Analogy*), because, when Bishop of Bristol, he put up a plain, inlaid, black marble cross in the Chapel of the Palace there. He died 1752.

[1] The Rubric before the Prayer of Consecration in the Prayer Book of 1559–1604, was simply :—
 'Then the Priest, standing up, shall say as followeth.'
The first rubric of position at the beginning of the service had placed him 'at the north side of the Table.' For a full and very interesting defence of Bishop Wren, see *Worship in the Church of England*, Right Honourable A. B. B. Hope, and, Dean Howson '*Before the Table*,' by the same author, in the *Church Quarterly Review*, January, 1876.

F

munion time he shall step from it.' For the rest, the whole tone of the Defence is brave and dignified; and despite the knowledge that his life was at stake, despite of the 'humbly conceiveth' which runs through it, it is evident that the Bishop considered his position to be in reality unassailable, and that he was more or less condescending in making these explanations. There is an irony in the studied simplicity with which the scholar and theologian explains elementary truths and ordinary rules of church discipline to a House of Commons who certainly stood in need of instruction in such matters.

The Bishop, when his part was done, and he had received notice to prepare for trial on a day appointed, put his manuscript, with an injunction of secresy, into the hands of a lawyer who was supposed to be friendly, that he might give his advice on the technical and legal parts.

' The person,' says the 'Parentalia,' 'thus intrusted discovering (on the perusal) matters of such moment, as he conceived might be very expedient for the Prosecutors to be forewarned of, betrayed his trust, and to ingratiate himself treacherously delivered up the Bishop's papers to the chief persons in power of the governing faction. The consequence thereupon was—that the resolution which had been taken to bring him to trial for life was suddenly countermanded and an order by the House of Commons made to continue him in prison during their pleasure.'

So began the long years of Bishop Wren's captivity. Few trials could have been harder for a man of vigorous active nature to bear than this one which rendered him powerless, when all he held dear was at stake, loaded him with calumnies and prevented his uttering a word in his defence. The diary gives no hint of what his feelings were. In silence he resigned himself, resolved to afford no triumph to his enemies. Dean Wren was somewhat better off, though he had his share of misfortunes. The valuable plate and treasures belonging to the Order of the Garter were a serious responsibility, and, though the treasure-house was strong, he could not feel that it offered a sufficient security. The plate and armour were not easily hidden, but the Diamond George and Garter of Gustavus Adolphus he determined, if possible, to save. Accordingly, with the help of one trustworthy person and every precaution for secresy, he dug a hole in the treasury floor and there deposited them, concealing the place with the utmost care, and leaving a note in the hand of one worthy person intimating where the jewels might be found in the event of his death. He had good cause to rejoice in this precaution, for a few months later, in October 1642, down came

'one Captain Fogg pretending a warrant from the King and demanding the keys of the Treasury, threatening if they were denied him by the Dean and Prebendaries, to pull the Chapel about their ears.'

As his threats had no effect, he forced the stone jambs of the doorway with crowbars, and carried off all the treasures except those which the Dean had buried. These, however, did not long remain secure, for in 1645 they were discovered and placed in the keeping of Colonel Ven, then governor of Windsor Castle, and finally, through several hands, reached the trustees of the Long Parliament, who sold the jewels to Thomas Beauchamp, their clerk. The Deanery was not spared during the first pillage of the chapel, though the Dean possessed a formal protection from the Committee of Public Safety, but was ransacked by the soldiers, and the Registry of the Garter, sealed by order of the House of Lords, broken open, and the records stolen. Dean Wren lost many things of value—books and manuscripts dear to the careful scholar, and also plate, including two large silver tankards, the gifts of the Elector Palatine. Of his own effects the Dean was only able, after an interval of six years, to recover one harpsichord valued at ten pounds; but he succeeded, after much expense and frequent attendances at Somerset House, by the favour of the trustees' chairman, Major Wither, in regaining the registers of the Order of the Garter, known from the colours of the velvet in which they were bound as 'the Black, the Blue, and the Red,' though not until a considerable space of time had passed; they contained all the principal records of the Order, and were therefore very valuable. The diamonds however, he was never able to regain, or the Altar Plate. After the first plunder of the Chapel and the Deanery Dr. Wren appears to have left Windsor and to have followed the Court for a time.

Christopher, meanwhile, was at Westminster advancing steadily in learning, while the loyal principles of his family must have been confirmed by the whole tone of the school which was ardently royalist. South, in a sermon for January 30, says,[1] speaking of Westminster : 'Upon that very Day, that black and eternally infamous Day of the King's murder, I myself heard, and am now a witness, that the King was publickly prayed for in this School but an hour or two (at most) before his sacred head was struck off.'

Whether at this period Christopher ever saw his uncle in the Tower does not appear. The Bishop's position was sad enough. During 1643 and 1644 his diary records the death of five of his children ; in the monotony of his prison life these sorrows must have pressed on him with double force. Nor was there any consolation to be derived from public matters. The royal cause, prosperous at first, grew less and less so, as the King's lack of money became an ever-increasing difficulty. Another grief, keenly felt by all Churchmen, was the order of the Parliament for the abolition of the Prayer Book and the alteration of the Thirty-nine Articles in a sense pleasing to the Puritans. Then came the long-deferred trial of the Archbishop of Canterbury. He was treated with a cruel disregard of his high position and of his age, every kind of insult and indignity being offered him. He however rose superior to it all, and defended himself with an eloquence, vigour, and courage which dismayed and enraged his enemies, though it could not change their purpose. The Bishop of Ely's name was frequently mentioned, and his promotion objected to as one of the

[1] South's *Sermons*, vol. v. p. 45, ed. 1727.

Archbishop's crimes; but no further steps were taken against him then, as he was safe in custody, and the Commons had enough on their hands.

In his defence, the Archbishop thought it prudent to say nothing respecting the Bishops whose advancement was objected against him, deeming it for their interest to entangle them as little as possible in his misfortunes. They were able to speak for themselves he said, but the memory of the dead Archbishop Neile he warmly defended. The trial was long protracted in order to give a specious colouring of justice to the predetermined sentence.

For this Prynne 'kept a school of instruction' for the witnesses, and tampered with the Archbishop's papers, of which he had forcibly possessed himself. The spirit that guided the whole trial was shown in his reply to one who said the Archbishop was a good man. 'Yea, but we must make him ill.' The Peers raised a feeble opposition. The King, whose consent the Parliament had not attempted to procure, sent to the Archbishop by a sure hand, from Oxford, a full pardon under the Great Seal, but neither received the least attention.

On January 10, on Tower Hill, the unjust sentence was fulfilled. Few things are more touching than the account given by his chaplain and biographer, Heylin, of the way in which the Archbishop met that cruel fate. It is some comfort to remember that, though the Church Services were then forbidden, yet his enemies did not interfere, but suffered the Burial Service to be read in All Hallows, Barking, where he was first interred. After the Restoration, the coffin was removed to S. John's College, Oxford, and buried under the altar in the chapel. He left Bishop Wren and Dr. Duppa, Bishop of Salisbury, executors of his will. It contained a great number of bequests for charitable foundations, especially for his native town of Reading; but as his whole estate had been taken from him, these were unfulfilled. His murder was an immense triumph to all the Sectarians in England and Scotland, who probably considered it as a death-blow to the Church.

The Bishop of Ely in his cell must have listened in grief and horror to the tolling of the Tower bell which proclaimed the bloody death of the friend with whom he had laboured for many years, latterly his patient fellow-prisoner. The entry in the diary is brief: 'Parce, O Deus Requisitor sanguinis.' The same fate seemed very near to himself, and he was ready to follow the Archbishop; but he had eighteen years of close imprisonment to endure, and a different work to do.

Early in 1644, George Monk, then a colonel in the King's service, was taken prisoner by Fairfax in his attack upon the army besieging Nantwich, in Cheshire. He was imprisoned first at Hull, and then, as he was thought too important to be exchanged except for some considerable prisoner, he was sent to the Tower, and there remained two years. The Tower charges were high, and a long confinement in its walls was a strain upon the resources of a prisoner, which reduced those, whose fortune, like that of Monk, was scanty, to extreme poverty. The King, who knew Monk's condition, contrived to send him a hundred guineas, and upon this he existed for some time, and resisted the offers of Cromwell, then rapidly rising in power and authority.

Somehow or other, Monk contrived to obtain several interviews with Bishop Wren, who did his best to confirm the soldier in his loyalty. He perceived that Monk, whose popularity with the army was very great, and whose military talents were thought to be of a high order, might one day be a valuable ally, and a useful counterpoise to Cromwell. At length, when the King's cause appeared for the time lost, and Monk himself was reduced to extreme poverty, he yielded to Cromwell's request, and accepted a commission in the Irish army, under his kinsman Lord Lisle. Before his release, Monk had a final interview with the Bishop of Ely, and, as he knelt to ask the Bishop's blessing, bound himself with a solemn engagement never to be an enemy to his king, and said he was going to do his majesty the best service he could against 'the rebels in Ireland, and hoped he should one day do him further service in England.'

Bishop Wren held firmly to his trust in Monk's loyalty, though many things might well have shaken his confidence. In the curious life of Dr. John Barwick, one of the King's most faithful agents, from whom Sir Walter Scott may have taken many of the features of his indefatigable plotter 'Dr. Rochecliffe,' it is said that [1] 'he' (Dr. Barwick) 'often heard the

[1] *Life of Dr. Barwick*, p. 267, ed. 1724.

Right Reverend Bishop of Ely promise himself all he could wish from the General's fidelity.' As Monk gave no other hint of his intentions, refusing even to receive Charles II.'s letters, this assurance was precious to the Royalists.

In 1646, Christopher Wren left Westminster, and at the age of fourteen went up to Oxford, and was entered as a Gentleman Commoner at Wadham College. He had, young as he was, distinguished himself at Westminster, inventing an astronomical instrument, of which no description remains, and dedicating it to his father in a short Latin poem,[1] which has been often praised for the flow and smoothness of its lines ; a set of Latin verses in which the signs of the Zodiac are transformed into Christian emblems, is, in spite of its ingenuity, much less successful; a short poem on the Nativity also in Latin, belongs probably to the same date, and is of the same order of poetry.

Far more graceful are the playful lines cut on the rind of an immense pomegranate sent to 'that best man, my dearest friend E. F., by Christopher Regulus,' in which on the ' Pomo Punico,' as he calls it, Christopher rings the changes on ' Punic gifts ' and ' Punic faith,' and declares his pomegranate is connected neither with the one nor the other.

One English poem, an attempt to paraphrase the first chapter of S. John's Gospel, fails of necessity from the impossibility of such an attempt, and Wren handles the English verse far more stiffly and uneasily than he did the Latin. What however is striking is the pen-

[1] See *Appendix I.*

manship of the 'Parentalia' autograph; the writing, the capital letters, and the little flourishes are executed with a delicate finish really remarkable.

There is no date to this autograph, but the handwriting appears firmer and more regular than that of the dedication to his father, and it was probably an Oxford composition.

Christopher came up to Oxford a slight, delicate boy, with an understanding at once singularly quick and patient, readily seconded by very dexterous fingers, and keen powers of observation. He brought with him a reputation for, in the phrase of the day, 'uncommon parts,' and speedily showed that besides a classical education, he had acquired a strong bent for the experimental philosophy of the 'New learning.'

Oxford, when Wren came there, was not only the seat of learning, it was a Court and a Camp as well, to which all the Royalist hearts in England turned. In the midst of these curiously differing influences, Christopher pursued his studies under the care of the 'most obliging and universally curious Dr. Wilkins,'[1] as Evelyn calls him, a man as devoted to experiments as Christopher himself. Dean Wren had been in Bristol with his daughter and son-in-law, accompany-

---

[1] Dr. Wilkins published a book (*A Discovery of a New World*), concerning the art of flying, in which he said he did not question but in the next age it will be as usual to hear a man call for his wings when he is going a journey, as it is now to call for his boots. The Duchess of Newcastle objecting to Dr. Wilkins the want of baiting places on the way to his New World, he expressed his surprise that the objection should be made by a lady who had all her life been employed in building castles in the air. (*The Guardian*, No. 112. Addison.) This scheme does not seem to have reached the length of an experiment!

ing Prince Rupert, and on the Prince's unexpected surrender of the town to Fairfax (1645), seems to have returned with Prince Rupert and Mr. and Mrs. Holder, either to his own living of Great Haseley, or to Mr. Holder's at Bletchingdon.

In those times no place could long be a tranquil habitation. The King's affairs went from bad to worse, and at length the near approach of Fairfax with his victorious army made it evident that Oxford could no longer be a safe refuge for the Court. King Charles accordingly left Oxford in disguise, and, attended only by Mr. Ashburnham and Dr. Michael Hudson,[1] who was well acquainted with the lanes and byeways of the country, proceeded by Henley-on-Thames and St. Albans, to Southwell in Nottinghamshire, throwing himself on the loyalty of the Scots, then encamped at Newark. How unworthy of his confidence they proved to be, and how they finally sold him to the Parliament, are matters of history too notorious for repetition here.

Oxford, thus saved from the ruin of a siege, capitulated to Fairfax June 24, 1646, on the express condition that the University should be free from 'sequestrations, fines, taxes and all other molestations whatsoever.' But the Parliament was not famous for keeping its engagements, and at once proceeded to break through those made with Oxford and reduce it to the same condition as Cambridge, which they had devas-

---

[1] A most zealous Royalist; King Charles called him 'my plain-dealing chaplain,' because Dr. Hudson told him the truth when others would not. He was murdered at Woodcroft House, Northamptonshire, 1648. *Desiderata Curiosa*, p. 378. Peck.

tated in 1642. A passage from 'Querela Cantabrigiensis,' which is supposed to be written by Dr. Barwick, gives some idea of what this condition was:

'And therefore,' he says, 'if posterity shall ask "Who thrust out one of the eyes of this kingdom, who made Eloquence dumb, Philosophy sottish, widowed the Arts, and drove the Muses from their ancient habitation? Who plucked the reverend and orthodox professors out of their chairs, and silenced them in prison or their graves? Who turned Religion into Rebellion, and changed the apostolical chair into a desk for blasphemy, and tore the garland from the head of Learning to place it on the dull brows of disloyal ignorance?" If they shall ask "Who made those ancient and beautiful chapels, the sweet remembrances and monuments of our forefathers' charity and the kind fomenters of their children's devotion, to become ruinous heaps of dust and stones?" . . . 'Tis quickly answered—"Those they were, who endeavouring to share three Crowns and put them in their own pockets, have transformed this free kingdom into a large gaol, *to keep the liberty of the subject*: they who maintain 100,000 robbers and murderers by sea and land, *to protect our lives and the propriety of our goods*. . . . they who have possessed themselves of his majesty's towns, navy, and magazines, *to make him a glorious king*; who have multiplied oaths, protestations, vows, leagues and covenants, *for ease of tender consciences*; filling all pulpits with jugglers for the Cause, canting sedition, atheism, and rebellion, *to root out popery and Babylon and settle the kingdom of Christ: . . . The very same have stopped the mouth of all learning (following herein the example of their elder brother the Turk), lest any should be wiser than themselves, or posterity know what a world of wickedness they have committed.* "'[1]

Wadham College probably suffered less than many, as its head, Dr. Wilkins, who had married Cromwell's sister, was very submissive to the then Government. As matters settled down somewhat at Oxford towards 1648, Dr. Wilkins, Dr. Jonathan Goddard, Dr. Wallis, Mr. Theodore Hank, who came from the desolated Palatinate, and Mr. S. Foster, the Gresham Professor of Astronomy, met together weekly, 'to discourse and consider,' writes Dr. Wallis, ' (precluding theology and state affairs), of philosophical enquiries, and such as related thereunto: as physick, anatomy, geometry, astronomy, navigation, staticks, magneticks, chymicks, mechanicks, and natural experiments with the state of those studies as then calculated at home and abroad.'

The meetings, at which Christopher Wren, young as he was, appears to have been a constant attendant, were frequently held at the house of Dr. Goddard for the convenience of his having there a workman skilled in the nice work of grinding glasses for microscopes and telescopes. Dr. Goddard became body physician to Cromwell, was by him made Warden of Merton College, Oxford, and subsequently represented the university in Parliament. Dr. Wallis, a famous Oxford

[1] *Annals of England*, p. 432.

mathematician, was employed by the Parliament to decipher the King's cabinet of letters taken at Naseby, and also was proved by Matthew Wren, the son of the Bishop, to have deciphered several very important letters sent by Charles II. to England, and intercepted at Dunkirk.

As by degrees these meetings were more largely attended, and men came who held very different opinions from those of Dr. Goddard and Dr. Wallis, the exclusion of theology and politics from the discussions was a needful precaution. Many inventions of Christopher's date from this time, a design for a reflecting dial for the ceiling of a room, ornamented with quaint figures and devices, some Latin lines ending in a chronogram of his age, and the date of the invention, suggested probably by the one in the rectory at East Knoyle, which he had known from a child; an instrument to write in the dark; and an instrument of use in gnomonics.[1] At the same time he had attracted the notice of Sir Charles Scarborough, a friend of Dean Wren's, then just rising to fame as a surgeon. Christopher, whose health, as has been said, was delicate, fell dangerously ill and considered that he owed his life to the skilful care of his new friend. Dr. Scarborough, who could recite in order all the propositions of Euclid and Archimedes, and could apply them, found in his patient a kindred spirit, and induced Wren, young as he was, to undertake the translation into Latin of the 'Clavis Aurea,' by the Rev. W. Oughtred, a mathematical treatise of great reputation.

[1] i.e. the art of dial-making.

That Christopher was able to satisfy the old man is evident from the preface, even while making allowance for the complimentary style of the time. Mr. Oughtred speaks of—

'Mr. Christopher Wren, Gentleman Commoner of Wadham College, a youth generally admired for his talents, who, when not yet sixteen years old, enriched astronomy, gnomonics, statics and mechanics, by brilliant inventions, and from that time has continued to enrich them, and in truth is one from whom I can, not vainly, look for great things.' [1]

Mr. Oughtred was a Canon of Chichester, and after the siege of the city and the wanton sack of the cathedral by Sir E. Waller in 1642, deprived and heart-broken, wandered to Oxford, refusing the offers of home and emolument which came to him from France, Italy, and Holland. He gladly availed himself of young Wren's services in the work of translation, which he had not energy to undertake himself, and waited, hoping for better times. When at length they drew near, and he heard of the vote passed at Westminster (May 1, 1660), for the Restoration of the Royal Family, the relief was too great, and Mr. Oughtred 'expired in a sudden ecstasy of joy.' [2]

Dean Wren, in the meanwhile, though deprived of his living, does not seem to have been in any personal danger, having a protection from Parliament, possibly obtained by his friend the Elector Palatine, or Speaker Lenthall, by favour of which he boldly attended the

---

[1] *Lives of the Gresham Professors.* Ward, p. 96.
[2] *Memorials of the See of Chichester*, p. 290.

Committee Meetings at Somerset House. He made an attempt to gather together the Knights of the Garter, and addressed the following petition, an autograph copy of which is contained in the 'Parentalia':

'*To ye Right Honble ye Knights of ye Most Noble Order of ye Garter.*

'Dr. C. Wren Register and Secretarye of ye sd Most Noble Order of ye Garter in discharge of his sworne service.

'Prayeth, that according to ye commission directed to all ye Honble Peers of ye said Most Noble Order or to any Three of them [to muster and consult in ye absence of ye Sovraine upon all such emergent occasions as may concerne ye advancement or indemnity of ye said Most Noble Order]

'It may therefore please your Honors to give yr. consent for some sett Time and Place of meeting with such convenient speed as may best stand with ye great Affairs. That yr. humble Servant ye Register may Represent to yr. Honors some few Things, wch hee humbly conceaves may much concerne ye Honor & Interest of ys. Most Honble Order to bee provided for.'

'I delivered this Petition in ye Parliament Howse before they sate, Jan. 23d. 1647.' (O. S.)

A copy of this Petition he sent to the Deputy Chancellor. It would seem to have startled the Knights, and Dr. Wren evidently wishes the way smoothed. His letter, also an autograph, is headed

'Copye of my letter sent to the Deputie Chancelor for removal of some scruples wch arose among ye Knights of ye Order before ye Time of their meeting in Council.'

'Honble Chancelor.—I have no pticular aime in this my humble suite to ye Lords of ye Order to propose any private or Personal Interest of my owne, or any other man's, much lesse to engage their Honors in anything that may seeme to contest wth or dissent from ye Highe Court of Parliament wherein they now sit & from whence I am not ignorant ye Most Honble Society of ye Most Noble Order receaved as at first Life and Being soe now holds its establishment. My humble & earnest desires, are to represent such Things only as I humbly conceave may nearly concerne ye Honor & Interests of their Most Noble Order. To w^{ch} (next as yr. Selfe Honored Sir) I am by oath obliged: (to preserve ye Honor thereof, & of all in itt to my utmost Power) For zeale of this duty wch upon ye intimation of what I here profess, I presume they will not reject, I beseech you to give y^m this assurance as yf itt were from ye tender of my owne mouthe, who am at this period God's Prisoner, & under Him,

'Yr servant, C. W.'

Whether the Dean succeeded in gathering the Knights together, and what the 'Things nearly concerning their Honor' may have been if they were *not*, as the letter implies they were not, the King's deliverance, the 'Parentalia' does not say, neither does it give any hint of the illness to which the end of the Dean's letter appears to point.

CHAPTER IV.
1646–1658.

DEATH OF MRS. M. WREN—KING CHARLES MURDERED—A MONOTONOUS WALK—INVENTIONS—A DREAM—ALL SOULS' FELLOWSHIP—BEGINNINGS OF ROYAL SOCIETY—ASTRONOMY—AN OFFER OF RELEASE—THE CYCLOID—CROMWELL'S FUNERAL—LETTERS FROM LONDON.

La Royauté seule, depuis vingt ans, n'avait pas été mise à l'épreuve ; seule elle avait encore à faire des promesses auxquelles on n'eut pas été trompé. . . . On y revenait enfin, après tant d'agitations comme au toit paternel qu'a fait quitter l'espérance et où ramène la fatigue.—*Monk*, par M. Guizot, p. 69.

CHAPTER IV.

A HEAVY sorrow fell upon the imprisoned Bishop of Ely at the close of 1646. His wife was worn out by grief for the loss of her children and anxiety for her husband, for whom Laud's fate seemed but too probable, and the Bishop's diary records that on 'December 8, 1646, Ad Christum evolavit pia anima conjugis E. mediâ post 5^{vum} matutinam.'[1] The diary contains no remark, no murmur, though this loss left Bishop Wren very desolate and full of anxiety for his seven surviving children, of whom the eldest, Matthew, was but seventeen. Upon such troubles as these prison life must have pressed heavily, and if Bishop Wren's captivity was half as strict as was that of Dr. John Barwick, who was consigned to the Tower in 1650,[2] it was a sufficient hardship. Every rumour which reached his ears from the tumultuous world outside must have added to his grief. The King's affairs grew more desperate, and the shadow of Cromwell loomed larger and larger. Probably the Bishop did not expect a long captivity. It must have come to his ears that in the proposed treaty of Newport (1648), 'the persons only who were to expect no pardon

---

[1] 'December 8, 1646. The pious soul of my wife Eliza flew up to Christ at half-past five in the morning.'

[2] *Life of Dr. Barwick*, ed. 1724, p. 122.

were the Princes Rupert and Maurice; James, Earl of Derby; John, Earl of Bristol; William, Earl of Newcastle; Francis, Lord Cottington; George, Lord Digby; Matthew Wren, Bishop of Ely,' and some fifty others.[1]

Condemned thus without a trial, without a chance of his vindication being known, the Bishop betook himself to prayer, and to writing a commentary on the Holy Scriptures, a task for which, as a fine Hebrew, Greek and Latin scholar, he was well qualified. In this work he found solace and support, and quietly waited until the tyranny should be overpast.

There is no need to recall in detail the thickcoming sorrows of that time; it is but too easy to guess how doubly galling imprisonment must have been to Bishop Wren when the royalists who were at liberty were straining every nerve, exhausting every device to save if possible their beloved King from his fate. In vain— at length came the fatal January 30 (1649), and King Charles, attended by Bishop Juxon, walked to the scaffold and uttered his final words, 'I have a good cause and a gracious God on my side; I go from a corruptible to an incorruptible Crown where no disturbance can be, no disturbance in the world.' There was one of the King's loyal subjects who, we may well believe, envied Bishop Juxon his privilege of attendance on his master to the last—Bishop Wren, who had been with him in bright early days, had attended him when Prince of Wales, on his romantic journey to Spain, and, when the weight of the corruptible crown first came

---

[1] Grey's Examination of Neale's *History of the Puritans*, vol. iii. p. 333.

upon the prince's head, had accompanied him on the journey to Scotland for his coronation at Scone, who ever since then had been so trusted by him.

No word of his own grief, of his unavailing longing to see his King once more, and once more kiss his hand, is expressed in the brief record in his diary. It is simply 'A sanguinibus, O Deus!'

Horror at the crime, at the stain of innocent blood which now defiled his country, seems to have swallowed up all expression of personal feeling. By degrees the rigour of his imprisonment appears to have been a little relaxed, and by the connivance of his gaoler he obtained the opportunity, rarely granted to prisoners, of walking upon the leads of one of the towers. Thither he daily went for his exercise, and, says the writer of the 'Parentalia,'

'by a just computation, he walked round the world. The earth being affirmed to be 216,000 miles in compass (at a calculation of sixty miles to a degree) ;[1] if it were possible to make a path round the earth, an able footman going constantly twenty-four miles a day, would compass it in 900 days, and so on in proportion of time and miles.'

It would seem that the Bishop, finding his life was for the time spared, and having a steady conviction that the evil days would pass, had determined to keep himself ready in body, as in soul, for what work the future might bring. A prison life leaves little to be recorded ; the days wore away in the Tower, divided between devotion, study, and that unchanging monoto-

[1] It is really 24,899 miles.

nous walk which at least gave the prisoner a distant glimpse of the world from which he was excluded.

He was allowed the Bible and paper and ink, but no other books. It is the testimony of one who has studied Bishop Wren's manuscript—

' He wrote in an exquisite hand, in very fair Latin, a commentary on much of Holy Scripture enough to fill an oak box of no mean dimensions. This box he committed to the care of Dr. Beaumont, master of S. Peter's College.[1] Had the Puritans read the MS. they would have found some antidote to their poison.'

Two sermons and some treatises were also written during his captivity. Probably suspicion attached to anything that he did, for it is said to have been all written by stealth.

His nephew's life differed as widely from his own as did their characters. Christopher was at Oxford, deep in the experiments of the 'New learning,' and in the inventions which it suggested to his ready brain and dexterous fingers.

One invention which he was at the time proud of was that of a—

' diplographic instrument for writing with two pens,' whose uses he thus describes ; ' by the help of this instrument, every ordinary penman may at all times be suddenly fitted to write two several copies of any deeds and evidences, from the shortest to the longest

---

[1] The box is, I believe, in Peterhouse Library to this day, but a portion of the Commentary was published as a treatise against the Socinians by the Bishop's son Matthew, under the title of *Increpatio Bar Jesu, sive polemicae adsectiones locorum aliquot S. Scripturae ab imposturis perversis in Catechesis Racoviana collectae.*

length of lines, in the very same compass of time, and with as much ease and beauty, without any dividing or ruling ; as, without the help of the instrument, he could have despatched but one.'

So successful was this instrument, that he obtained a patent for it for seventeen years. In the same year an exact duplicate of this invention was brought from France, and another patent taken out for the same number of years, by Mr. William Petty,[1] who claimed to be the inventor.

Wren was indignant at the notion that he had copied another person's idea, and gives good reasons for his belief that his own instrument had been described to Petty by a friend of his. Three years later Wren wrote of it as 'an obvious Thing, a cast-off Toy ;' ending, 'Indeed though I care not for having a Successor in Invention, yet it behoves me to vindicate myself from the Aspersion of having a Predecessor.'

Another invention Wren describes as a 'weather clock.' It consisted of a clock affixed to a weather cock that moved a rundle covered with paper, upon

[1] Petty's history is a curious one. The son of a clothier of Rumsey ; he educated himself; was some years in the navy; became Gresham professor of music ; then a physician of some fame ; was also Henry Cromwell's secretary; was a commissioner for Ireland, and married Sir Hardress Waller's daughter. Soon after the Restoration he was knighted by Charles II. Petty invented a ' double-bottomed ship to sail against wind and tide ; it was flat-bottomed, had two distinct keels cramped together with huge timbers, so as a violent stream run between : it bore a monstrous broad sail.' It excited much interest at the time, made one very successful voyage, and was afterwards wrecked in a frightful storm. Its model is still preserved at the Royal Society, of which he became a member. He died in 1687. *Lives of the Gresham Professors*, p. 217. Ward. See also Evelyn's *Diary* of March 22, 1675, for an interesting ccount of Petty's career.

which the clock moved a black-lead pencil, so that the observer, by the traces of the pencil on the paper, might certainly conclude what winds had blown in his absence for twelve hours' space. The 'Parentalia' contains a careful drawing in pen and sepia of this invention elaborately worked out and remarkable for the truth and finish of the drawing. Some of these designs, and an instrument for sowing corn, nearly identical with a modern 'drill,' he dedicated in a quaintly formal letter to his father's friend, the Prince Palatine. He appeared before the Prince in another character, due probably to his Westminster training. A play was performed (about 1652) at Oxford before the Prince, Dr. Seth Ward,[1] and several others, entitled 'Hey for Honesty, down with Knavery,' translated by Thomas Randolph from the Plutus of Aristophanes, in which Christopher sustained the part of Neanias.[2] It is provoking to have this bare record merely, and no clue as to the success or failure of any part of the

[1] Seth Ward, born 1617. Was Savilian Professor of Astronomy at Oxford and an active member of the Royal Society. Afterwards Bishop of Exeter and then of Salisbury; died 1689.

[2] *Life of Sir C. Wren*, by J. Elmes, p. 12. The full title of the play was 'Πλουτοφθαλμία Πλουτογαμία,' a pleasant comedy intituled *Hey for Honesty*, &c., augmented and published by F. J. A copy, published in 1651, and containing a MS. note saying that Wren took the part of 'Neanias Adolescens,' was in the possession of Isaac Reed, a commentator on Shakespeare and a great book collector, who died in 1807. His epitaph (given in *Notes and Queries*, series v., xiii. p. 304) was as follows:—

> 'Reader of these few lines take heed,
> And mend your ways for my sake;
> For you must die like Isaac Reed,
> Tho' you read till your eyes ache.'

T. Randolph was a friend and pupil of Ben Jonson's; he published *The Muses' Looking Glass*, which satirised the Puritans; died 1634.

performance, especially where the young actor was concerned.

To about the same date belongs a Latin letter written by Christopher to his father, signed 'Christophorus Regulus,' describing in glowing terms a visit paid in the spring to a friend's house. Some pretty touches give 'the lofty woods with their clamorous republic of rooks, the great fountains, the placid pools—without, you might say a terrestrial paradise, but within, heaven itself.' It may have been, though there is nothing in its favour but conjecture, that this was Bletchingdon House, and that among 'the virgins singing holy psalms,' whom he mentions, was his future bride Faith, (or as she spelt it, 'ffaith') Coghill. The letter says much, as does all that passed between them, for the warm affection existing between father and son, and the sincerely religious tone of Christopher's mind.

The desperate efforts of the Royalists shortly after this period to overthrow Cromwell's tyranny and to put Charles II. on the throne, received a cruel check in the disastrous battle of Worcester (1651), Cromwell's 'crowning mercy.' This crushed the hopes of the Royalists and obliged them to turn their every effort and thought to effecting the escape of their prince. He must have passed very near Knoyle Hill, when he crossed Salisbury Plain and met at Stonehenge the friends who at last succeeded in conveying him to the coast. Knoyle Hill had its own fugitive to shelter.

Aubrey, the Wiltshire Antiquary, gives the account of a vivid dream which Christopher Wren had, when staying, in the autumn of 1651, with Dean Wren at Knoyle. He

'dreamed he saw a fight in a great market-place, which he knew not, where some were flying and others pursuing; and among those who fled, he saw a kinsman of his, who went into Scotland with the King's army. They heard in the country that the King was come into England, but whereabouts he was they could not tell. The next night came his kinsman to Knoyle Hill, and brought with him the disastrous news of Charles II.'s defeat at Worcester.'[1]

It seems likely that this 'kinsman' was Bishop Wren's son Matthew, who afterwards went to the Hague. There also, when his escape had been with great difficulty contrived, went King Charles, as his brother-in-law, the Prince of Orange, was his steady friend. In the hope of utterly putting down the Cavaliers, the greatest severity was shown at this time to all who had helped the King, and even to those who merely boasted of their good will towards him. Among those who suffered was Inigo Jones, who had been architect to James I. and to Charles I., had been steadily loyal to the Stuarts, and was therefore an object of suspicion. He lived to see what was thought the utter downfall of the monarchy, and following upon this the desecration and ruin of the finest churches in England. S. Paul's, on which he had spent much labour and skill, was, as being connected with Archbishop Laud, an object of special hatred to the Puritans. It suffered

[1] Miscellanies, ed. 1696.

every possible injury. The fine portico designed by Inigo Jones was filled with stalls, blocked up by booths, and used as a market-place. The year after the battle of Worcester, Inigo Jones died, poor and lonely, in a lodging close to the defaced cathedral. He and Christopher Wren must probably have met. Wren had a sincere admiration for his predecessor's skill, and spoke of the S. Paul's portico as 'an exquisite piece in itself.'

In the autumn of 1653, Wren, then just twenty-one, was elected to a fellowship at All Souls, and happy in the comparative tranquillity of Oxford, pursued the various studies which he loved. All this time he was 'making himself,' as was said of Sir Walter Scott in his childhood on the Scotch hills, though perhaps at the time no one could have guessed the particular manner in which he would distinguish himself.

In the following summer he made acquaintance with John Evelyn, who had come up to Oxford to hear the 'Philosophy Act.' Evelyn mentioned that after a dinner at All Souls he 'visited that miracle of a youth Mr. Christopher Wren, nephew to the Bishop of Ely.'[1]

'A day or two later Evelyn dined with 'that most obliging and universally curious Dr. Wilkins at Wadham College, who showed him his " transparent apiaries, built like castles, and so ordered one upon another as one might take the honey without hurting the bees," his " hollow statue, which gave a voice

[1] *Diary*, July 13, 1654.

and uttered words, by a long, concealed pipe that went to its mouth, whilst one speaks through it at good distance;" and his gallery filled with mathematical and other curiosities; a "thermometer," still a curiosity, though fifty-two years had elapsed since Galileo invented the first; a "way-wiser," which, when placed in a coach, exactly measured the miles it travelled, and showed them by an index; "a monstrous magnet," and many other inventions, most of them of his owne and that prodigious young scholar, Mr. Christopher Wren, who presented me with a piece of white marble which he had stained with a lively red very deepe, as beautiful as if it had been natural.'

The acquaintance thus made with Christopher Wren ripened into a friendship lasting until Evelyn's death in 1706.

Dr. Wilkins was also of Evelyn's friends, though he was very submissive to Cromwell.[1] It is curious to contrast two accounts which occur in the same page of Evelyn's diary.

'*December* 25, 1655. There was no more notice taken of Christmas Day in churches. I went to London, where Dr. Wild preached the funeral sermon of Preaching, this being the last day, after which Cromwell's proclamation was to take place, that none of the Church of England should dare either to preach or administer Sacraments, teach schoole etc. on paine of imprisonment or exile. So this was the mournfullest day that in my life I had seene, or

[1] *Præsul. Ang.*, p. 779. Godwin.

the Church of England herselfe since the Reformation; to the greate rejoicing of both Papist and Presbyter. So pathetic was his discourse (on 2 Cor. xiii. 9) that it drew many teares from the auditory. Myself, wife, and some of our family received the Communion; God make me thankfull that hath hitherto provided for us the food of our soules as well as bodies! The Lord Jesus pity our distressed Church, and bring back the captivity of Sion!

'*February* 10, 1656. I heard Dr. Wilkins preach before the Lord Mayor in S. Paul's, shewing how obedience was preferable to sacrifice. He was a most obliging person, who had married the Protector's sister, and tooke greate paines to preserve the Universities from the ignorant sacrilegious commanders and souldiers, who would faine have demolished all places and persons that pretended to learning.'

Dr. Wilkins appears, like too many of that time, to have regarded the Church as utterly overthrown, and probably believed honestly in his peculiar interpretation of the text upon which he preached. Much credit is however due to him for the idea of the Oxford meetings, and for the hospitality which he showed. These meetings were the germ of the Royal Society, and to them Dr. Thomas Sprat (afterwards Bishop of Rochester), a great friend of Christopher Wren's, bears testimony:—

'Wadham College,'[1] he says, 'was then the place of resort for virtuous and learned men. Their first

---
[1] *Hist. of Royal Society.* Bishop Sprat, ed. 1722, p. 53.

purpose was no more than only the satisfaction of breathing a freer air, and of conversing in quiet, one with another, without being engaged in the passions and madness of that dismal age. And from the institution of that assembly it had been enough if no other advantage had come but this; that by these means there was a race of young men provided against the next age, whose minds receiving from them their first impressions of sober and generous knowledge, were invincibly armed against all the enchantments of enthusiasm. . . . It was in good measure by the influence which these gentlemen had over the rest, that the university itself, or at least any part of its discipline and order, was saved from ruin. . . . Nor indeed could it be otherwise, for such spiritual frenzies, which did then bear rule, can never stand long before a clear and deep skill in nature. It is almost impossible, that they who converse much with the subtilty of things, should be deluded by such thick deceits. There is but one better charm in the world than real philosophy, to allay the impulses of the false spirit, and that is the blessed Presence and assistance of the True.'

In 1656, on the 29th of May, Dean Wren died. Sorrow and anxiety, the desolation of the Church, the apparent ruin of the monarchy, had worn out his gentle spirit; and probably little thinking how great a change was approaching to free the country, he passed away, aged 69, at the house of his son-in-law, Mr. Holder, and was buried in the chancel of Bletchingdon Church.[1]

[1] 'Dr. Christopher Wren, Deane of Windsor, was buried June 3,

When we look back to the years of the Rebellion, their darkness is lightened for us by the knowledge that the Restoration came at last, and it is difficult to realise fully how the times appeared to those who actually lived in them, to whom the years brought only fresh losses and sorrows, and the sickness of hope deferred.

Knowing how, on the 29th of May, but four years later, all England was welcoming back the King to 'enjoy his own again,' one can hardly forbear wishing that Dean Wren might have been spared to see that day; yet those who loved him best cannot have grudged him the fulness of that peace which all his life he had desired, and which he had invoked upon his first home. Christopher was very warmly attached to his father, as all his letters show, and must have grieved greatly for his death.

Soon after this he was summoned to London. The Gresham professor of astronomy, Mr. Laurence Rooke, retired in 1657, and the chair was offered to Wren. He was but twenty-four and doubted whether he should accept such a post while so young, and he clung to Oxford and his studies there.

The friends whom he consulted advised him differently; accordingly he came up to London and delivered his opening address to a considerable audience. It was in Latin, and after a brief apology for his youth passed into a sketch of the history of astronomy. He dwells on the great riches of the science, how it is the handmaid of theology, the queen

1656,' is the entry in the register; there does not appear to be any monument or brass to his memory. The *Parentalia* and Elmes's Life give 1658, but the dates are frequently inaccurate in both books.

of sciences, speaks of the vast discoveries made by its means, touches upon Copernicus, whose mind first grasped the idea that the earth moved round the sun, then upon Kepler and upon Galileo, and the storms that had arisen, when in 1632 he had demonstrated that truth at which Copernicus had guessed; he praises highly Galileo's invention of the telescope, pays a tribute to the great men who had lectured at Gresham on these subjects, and especially to his own predecessor, Rooke, and winds up with an eloquent description of London as a Pandora of cities to whom each of the choir of planets gave a peculiar blessing, on whom the sun shines benignly, who possesses more inhabitants than any city in the world, a healthy air, a fertile soil stretching far around her, beautiful buildings springing as of themselves from the earth, and, lastly, is blessed by the moon, 'the governess of floods,' who alluring the seas thus far inland by means of the beloved Thames, makes her the city which nourishes the best seamen of the world. The rough draft of this address, written by Christopher in a bold hand with a few changes and corrections, is preserved in the 'Parentalia.'

This professorship obliged him to come up to London and give a course of lectures every Wednesday in term time at Gresham College. None of these lectures have been preserved, and it seems from a hint in one of Dr. Sprat's letters, that Wren was in the habit of lecturing from rough notes merely, and used no pains to keep any record of them.

At this time he made acquaintance with Richard

Claypole, who was married to Elizabeth, Cromwell's favourite daughter; both she and her sister, Lady Falconbridge, were faithful members of the persecuted Church of England. Dr. Hewet still read the Prayer Book services in S. Gregory's Church, which adjoined S. Paul's, and there the two sisters resorted, there Dr. Hewet secretly married Mary Cromwell to Lord Falconbridge, as neither would be satisfied with the ceremony performed by an independent preacher. Cromwell's daughters used all their influence with their father on the side of mercy, but when the excellent Dr. Hewet fell under his displeasure they pleaded in vain for his life.[1] Mr. Claypole professed a fondness for mathematical science and frequently invited Christopher Wren to his house. On one of these occasions when Wren was dining there, Cromwell himself entered, and, as was his custom in his own family, sat down to table without speech or ceremony. After a while he fixed his eyes on Christopher and said, 'Your uncle has been long confined in the Tower.' 'He has so, sir,' said Wren; 'but he bears his afflictions with great patience and resignation.' 'He may come out an he will,' was Cromwell's unexpected reply. 'Will your Highness permit me to take him this from your own mouth?' said Wren, hardly able to believe his ears. 'Yes, you may,' said

[1] Evelyn's *Diary*, March 31, 1658. 'That holy martyr Dr. Hewer condemned to die, without law, jury or justice by a mock council of State as they called it. A dangerous, treacherous time. June 8, *ib*. That excellent preacher and holy man Dr. Hewer was martyred for having intelligence of his Majesty, through the Lord Marquess of Ormond. He was beheaded on Tower Hill. The name was spelt Hewer, Hewet, and Hewett.

Cromwell briefly. At the earliest possible moment Christopher hurried to the Tower to communicate to his uncle the tidings that the long years of his imprisonment were over. When he had poured out his news the Bishop replied warmly that it was not the first time he had received the like intimation from that miscreant, but he disdained the terms proposed for his enlargement, which were a mean acknowledgment of his favour and an abject submission to his detestable tyranny; that he was determined to tarry the Lord's leisure, and owe his deliverance, which was not far off, to Him only. Such an answer must have been startling enough to Christopher, and may have opened his eyes to the causes of Cromwell's seeming leniency. He left the brave old man to await the deliverance which the keen sight of faith showed him as drawing near, and returned to his own work.

The death of Mrs. Claypole in the following summer must have checked an intimacy upon which Bishop Wren looked with little favour. She died of a terrible illness, and in the paroxysms of her pain bitterly reproached Cromwell for the innocent blood that he had shed, and particularly for that of Dr. Hewet.

At about this period some experiments were made by Wren's philosophical friends wherein he took a principal part, and to which the barometer, now in common use, is mainly due. The first instrument of the kind was invented by Torricelli, the pupil of Galileo, who used it in order to ascertain the pressure of the air on fluids, the supposed cause of which pressure was the passing by of the body of the moon. Pascal, in those earlier days when his great genius employed itself on natural philosophy, made several experiments at Rouen, in 1646, with a friend, M. Petit, using 'Torricelli's tube,' as it was called. Similar trials were afterwards made by M. Perier, his brother-in-law, among the mountains of Auvergne. They then discovered that the rising and falling of the mercury was due not to the moon, but to the differences in the specific gravity of the atmosphere. Wren's experiments led him to the same conclusion, and at a later period he and Robert Boyle continued them until they produced the barometer, though it was not used commonly as a weather-glass until a much later date. Pascal did not pursue his discovery, but was satisfied with having proved the point for which he was contending.

Though Wren and Pascal never met, some communication passed between them. Pascal, who was Wren's senior by eleven years, propounded a problem, under the name of Jean de Monfert, to the mathematicians of England, adding a challenge to them to solve it by a given day. Christopher sent a solution, and in his turn propounded a problem which seems never to have been answered. Pascal is said to have considered Wren's solution very carefully, but the promised prize of twenty pistoles was withheld by some trickery. Besides this, Wren wrote four mathematical tracts on the cycloid, and sent them to Dr. J. Wallis, who was publishing a book on mathematics. He corresponded with Pascal,[1] who was writing on the

---

[1] Pascal is said to have written his treatise on the cycloid from a

cycloid by the name of *la Roulette*, the problem being 'to determine the curve made in the air by the nail of a coach wheel from the moment it rises from the ground, till the moment when the continual rolling of the wheel brings it back to the ground, after a complete turn, supposing the wheel a perfect circle and the ground perfectly level.'

Wren was engaged also in a series of observations on the planet Saturn. These pursuits were, however, interrupted by an event that convulsed all England. On September 3, 1658, during a fearful storm which swept over London, Oliver Cromwell died. Hume [1] gives a terrible account of the state of constant suspicion and fear of assassination in which Cromwell passed the last year of his life; the secret armour which he wore, his constant guard of soldiers wherever he moved, his fears on a journey, his habit of never returning the way he had come, nor by the direct road, seldom sleeping above three nights together in the same chamber, or in any he did not choose himself, or without sentinels. His body lay in state for a considerable time. The funeral, on October 22, Evelyn calls 'superb.' He says :—

'I saw the Protector carried from Somerset House on a velvet bed of state drawn by six black horses,

religious motive. It was a common opinion in France that the study of natural sciences, especially of mathematics, led to infidelity. Accordingly Pascal, writing for geometricians and mathematicians, wished to show, by the solution, vainly sought before, of this problem, that the same man who wrote the *Lettres à un Provincial* could also instruct them in abstract science, and he published his treatise in the intervals of writing the *Pensées*. See *Vie de Pascal, par sa sœur Mad. Perier, Pensées de Pascal*, p. 13, ed. 1839.

[1] *Hist. of England*, vol. vii. ch. lxi. p. 292.

houss'd with the same; the pall held up by his new lords; Oliver lying in effigie in royal robes, crown'd with a crown, sceptre, and globe like a king . . . a knight of honour armed *cap-à-pie*, and, after all, his guard, soldiers, and innumerable mourners. In this equipage they proceeded to Westminster; but it was the joyfullest funeral I ever saw, for there were none that cried but dogs, which the soldiers hooted away with a barbarous noise, drinking and taking tobacco in the streets as they went.'

Under the feeble rule of Richard Cromwell at first and then under the multiform tyranny of the re-assembled 'Long Parliament,' every kind of disorder and oppression had free course. Monk grievously disappointed the Royalist hopes by proclaiming Richard Cromwell. The day of deliverance appeared more than ever distant.

The Gresham Professors were all driven out of the college except Dr. Goddard, Cromwell's physician, and the place was garrisoned by soldiers, who did it great damage. Matthew Wren made an attempt two days after Cromwell's funeral to enter the college, and sent a curious account to Christopher, who had returned to All Souls at Oxford. He writes:

'Dear Cousin,—Yesterday being the first of the term, I resolved to see whether Dr. Horton [1] entertained the new auditory at Gresham with any lecture, for I took it for granted that if his divinity could be spared your mathematics would not be expected.

[1] Gresham Professor of Divinity, confirmed in his post by Cromwell.

But at the gate I was stopped by a man with a gun, who told me there was no admission upon that account, as the college was reformed into a garrison. Then changing my pretension, I scarce got permission to go in to Dr. Goddard, who gave me assurance enough that none of your colleagues intend to appear this term unless the soldiers be removed, of which there is no probability. Upon these premises it is the opinion of all your friends that you may save that journey hither, unless some other occasion calls you; and for these I expect you will make me your agent, if they be such as I am capable of despatching.

' But it will not perhaps be amiss to take from hence the occasion of a short and civil letter to the Committee, signifying that you hope you have not deceived their expectations in choosing you, and that you are ready to attend your duty but for this public interruption and exclusion from your chamber; or what else you will that looks towards this.

' I know no more domestic news than what everybody talks of. Yesterday I was in Westminster Hall, and saw only Keudigate and Windham in the two courts, and Wild and Parker in the Exchequer. In the Chancery none at all; Bradshaw keeps the seal as if it were to be carried before him in the other world, whither he is going. Glyn and Fountain pleaded at the bar. They talk much of the mediation of the two Crowns, and proceed so far as to name Marshall Clerambault for the Embassador who is to come hither from France. My service to all friends. Dear Cousin, your most humble servant,

'M. W.

'London, October 25, 1658.'

Dr. Sprat[1] writes also to Christopher at about the same time:

'Dear Sir,—This day I went to visit Gresham College, but found the place in such a nasty condition, so defiled, and the smells so infernal that if you should now come to make use of your tube, it would be like Dives looking out of hell into heaven. Dr. Goddard, of all your colleagues, keeps possession, which he could never be able to do had he not before prepared his nose for camp perfumes by his voyage into Scotland, and had he not such excellent restoratives in his cellars.'

[1] Thomas Sprat, D.D., Dean of Westminster, and afterwards Bishop of Rochester; was an active member of the Royal Society, and was educated at Wadham College with Sir C. Wren, whose intimate friend he was: born 1636; died 1713.

CHAPTER V.
1659-1663.

APOSTOLICAL SUCCESSION—DIFFICULTY OF PRESERVING IT—LETTERS FROM LORD CLARENDON—BISHOP WREN'S RELEASE—THE RESTORATION—CONVOCATION—SAVILIAN PROFESSORSHIP—ROYAL SOCIETY—'ELEPHANT IN THE MOON'—PEMBROKE CHAPEL BEGUN.

Yet bethink thee that the spirit whence those princely bounties flowed
To the ties of private feeling all its force and being owed ;
Severed from the bonds of kindred, taught his lonely heart to school,
By his Father's chastening kindness or his Church's sterner rule ;
Oft to spots by memory cherished, where his earliest love began,
In his age's desolation, fondly turned the childless man.
Phrontisterion, by Dean Mansel.

CHAPTER V.

ALL was confusion, doubt and anxiety in the country; the Royalist plots failed; the Parliament was powerless; no one knew whether Monk intended, as was still hoped by a few, to bring back the King, or to support the Parliament, or to make himself dictator; those were keen eyes which could discern through the darkness any ray of approaching light.

Nowhere perhaps did matters seem more desperate than in the Church. Her discipline and order, barely revived by the murdered Archbishop, had been for eighteen years trampled upon and neglected; 'by the licentiousness of the times,' many were growing up unbaptised and ignorant of Christianity. The number of bishops living was but small, many sees being already vacant when the Civil War broke out, and imprisonments and hardships had so reduced the Prelates that, in 1659, but ten survived, one of whom, Dr. Brownrigg, Bishop of Exeter, very soon died. Of the nine others, many were very old; the Bishop of London (Juxon) was very ill, and the Bishop of Ely was in prison. How was the succession to be preserved if the troubles of the times continued? The Scotch Church had been reduced by persecution; the Irish Bishops were in as evil a plight as their English brethren, and the difficulty of communication was great. There was then no daughter Church in America or in the Colonies to render back in time of need the grace they had themselves received. It was hardly possible for the English Bishops to meet for consultation; but the indefatigable Dr. Barwick was authorised [1]—

> 'not only to ride about among them all, and by proposing and explaining to each what was thought for the Church's Service; to collect the opinions and resolutions of every one of them upon all difficult affairs; but also to procure the communication of all that was needful between their lordships and His Majesty, which he frequently did by letters written in characters' (*i.e.* cypher).

Great difficulties lay in the way of the first step—a canonical election—and in the face of the watchful enmity of the Church of Rome, no doubtful step could be taken; and even were this difficulty surmounted and three Bishops got together, the risk of imprisonment and death to both consecrators and consecrated needed no one to point it out. The two with whom Dr. Barwick principally consulted were the Bishops of Ely and Salisbury. Many letters passed between Dr. Barwick and Mr. Hyde,[2] at Brussels, in one of which, written on July 8, 1659,[3] the latter speaks of—

> 'much preferring the Bishop of Ely's judgment and advice in that point (the method of election) before any man's. I pray remember my service with all

---

[1] *Life of Dr. Barwick*, p. 201.   [2] Afterwards Lord Clarendon.
[3] *Life of Dr. Barwick*. p. 424.

imaginable reverence to my Lord of Ely and assure him, that the King will always return that candour, benignity and equality to both the Universities, which he wishes; and I hope all who shall be entrusted by him in that great affair will be as just and dispassioned in all their interpositions and look upon them as equal lights to learning and piety and equally worthy of all encouragement and protection. And if at present my Lord of Ely will recommend any person to his Majesty for the Bishoprick of Carlisle, he shall be approved. And if my Lord will transmit a list of persons to be specially recommended to the King for any dignities of the Church, I dare promise the persons shall find that they could not have been better recommended. I know not what more to add but my hearty service to your sick friend,[1] whose health I pray for as a publick concernment. To yourself I shall say no more but that I shall think myself very faulty if I do not serve you very heartily, and if you do not with the first receive some evidence of the sense the King hath of your service.

'I am very heartily, Sir, your most affectionate servant, 'HYDE.'

These letters, thirty-six in number, were transmitted in cypher, and with the utmost precaution and considerable delay in awaiting a safe opportunity; the one quoted from is endorsed 'Received not till Aug. 29.' Nor was the cypher, however carefully contrived,

[1] Probably Bishop Juxon, more than once alluded to under this name in these letters.

always a security when the letters fell into the wrong hands. Dr. Wallis, the mathematician, was a most skilful decypherer, and was the person who decyphered the King's papers taken in his cabinet at Naseby, though the Royalists considered this a vain boast until Matthew Wren, the Bishop's eldest son, obtained the proof of it from Dr. Wallis himself. One important letter from Dr. Barwick to Mr. Hyde fell into Dr. Wallis' hands; Mr. Allestry his coadjutor coming from Brussels was seized and imprisoned as soon as he landed. Bishop Morton of Durham, the last surviving Prelate of the province of York, had died, as his epitaph says, 'deprived of all his goods except a good name and a good conscience.' The rising in Cheshire had been unsuccessful. Monk refused to give even his brother any hint of his intentions, and made no reply to the letter which King Charles sent to him from Breda. In short, matters were as adverse as it was possible for them to be, but yet Dr. Barwick was undiscouraged; with fresh precautions the correspondence with Mr. Hyde was resumed, and in truth the matter pressed; 'for,' says Dr. Barwick, writing in Sept. 1659, after mentioning his circuit among some of the surviving Bishops,[1] 'I fear this winter will go hard with some of them that may worst be spared in the due performance of such a work.' It is evident that Dr. Barwick was able to see and consult the imprisoned Bishop of Ely whenever it was needful. These hurried meetings, full of anxiety and peril as they were, must have been a great refreshment to the

[1] *Life of Dr. Barwick*, p. 437.

Bishop, who thus still took part in the work of the Church. He declined to send any list of names to the King, though he pressed Dr. Barwick to accept the Bishoprick of Man. Mr. Hyde[1] wrote a letter in September, which was not received till November 10, where he says :—

'The King hath done all that is in his power to do ; and if my Lords the Bishops will not do the rest, what is to become of the Church ? The conspiracies to destroy it are very evident; and if there be no combination to preserve it, it must expire. I do assure you the names of all the Bishops who are alive, and their several ages, are as well known at Rome as in England, and both the Papist and the Presbyterian value themselves very much upon computing in how few years the Church of England must expire.' . . . And again : 'His Majesty is most confident that the Bishop of Ely will give all the assistance and advice which his restraint will permit him to do. . . . I do beseech you,' says the next letter, 'present my humble service to my Lord of Ely, whose benediction, I do hope to live to receive at his own feet. I pray send me word our sick friend is in perfect health.'

But little progress appears to have been made, since Mr. Hyde writes, Nov. 28 :—

'I can say no more with reference to the Church, but that if there be nothing hinders it but the winter it be quickly over, whilst preparations are making ;

[1] *Life of Dr. Barwick*, p. 449.

and yet, God knows, it will be almost a miracle, if the winter doth not take away half the Bishops that are left alive ; and I must still lament that some way is not found that the Bishop of Ely may be at liberty; which would carry on this work more than any expedient that I can think of.'

An entry in Evelyn's diary shows the general state of affairs at this time :—

'*October* 11. The armie now turned out the Parliament. We had now no government in the nation ; all in confusion ; no magistrate either own'd or pretended but the souldiers, and they not agreed. God Almighty have mercy on and settle us !'

Evelyn was not slack in doing what in him lay towards this much-desired settlement :—

'*November* 7. Was published my bold "Apologie" for the King in this time of danger when it was capital to speake or write in favour of him. It was printed twice, so universally it took.'

A fast was kept in secret, apparently about once a fortnight, by the Churchmen in London to pray 'for God's mercy to our calamitous Church.'

On *February* 3, 1660, Evelyn writes :—

'General Monk came to London from Scotland, but no man knew what he would do or declare. Yet he was met on all his way by the gentlemen of all the counties which he passed, with petitions that he would recall the old, long-interrupted Parliament, and settle the nation in some order, being at this time in most prodigious confusion and under no government, everybody expecting what would be next and what he would do.'

Later in the same month Mr. Hyde wrote almost in despair to Dr. Barwick :[1] ' It would be very good news if I could hear of my Lord of Ely being in full liberty, to whom I pray present my humble service. The truth is I have but little hope of the business of the Church but by his being at liberty, and therefore I hope he will make no scruple of accepting it if it be offered, or if it can be reasonably obtained.'

The suspense which Evelyn describes had not long to be endured. On February 11, the very day after Monk had dismayed the city by breaking down its gates and allowing the soldiers to march about it in triumph, he turned out the Parliament then sitting at Westminster, and called together the former one, to the great joy of the people. From this moment all hearts and wishes turned to the exiled royal family as the one hope left of tranquillity and order ; thus suddenly, when the royalist hopes were lowest, their hearts' desire was given to them.

Monk, now in supreme power, did not forget the Bishop of Ely, whose fellow-captive he had been and who must have rejoiced to see Monk at last justify his confidence. On March 15 the lieutenant of the Tower received the order ' That Dr. Wren, Bishop of Ely, be discharged from his imprisonment.' Thus the eighteen years of captivity came to an end, and the

[1] *Life of Dr. Barwick* p. 496.

Bishop came forth from the Tower, an old man of seventy-five, broken by many sorrows.

It cannot have been with unmixed joy that he once more trod another path than that wonted one on the leads of the Tower. True, the King was coming home in peace to a people longing to receive him. This return was a promise of deliverance for the Church, and an end to that difficulty of preserving the Apostolical Succession which had so nearly proved a fatal one. And yet, the flood, which in those eighteen years had passed over the land, had swept away many whom the Bishop loved well. The King might return in triumph, but he was not the sovereign whom, from his youth, Bishop Wren had loved and served. The primate with whom he had worked, had been cruelly murdered; and none could restore the wife and children who had pined and died during the long years of his imprisonment. The Church, however, remained, and for her Bishop Wren would work while life lasted. Part of his employment in the Tower had been the writing of treatises and sermons, one of which on the Scotch Covenant, from the text 'Neither behave thyself frowardly in the covenant,' he dispersed over the dioceses of Norwich and Ely, lodging the while where he could in London, as he was not yet allowed to go back either to Downham in Suffolk or to Ely House in Holborn. It appeared, as was truly said, as if he had not been 'so much released as thrust out of prison.'

Homeless and penniless as he then seemed, Bishop Wren's spirit was in no respect daunted; when he left in safety the Tower where he had once thought to lay his head on the block, he planned the thank-offering which he would make to God. His children, from whom he had been so long separated, who were scattered everywhere and had been reduced to the greatest straits, he with much difficulty gathered together again, and they awaited the event of Monk's decision.

At length came that 29th of May so often described in history and fiction. Evelyn's [1] account of it is interesting, as that of an eyewitness :—

'This day his majestie Charles II. came to London, after a sad and long exile and calamitous suffering both of the king and church, being seventeen yeares. This was also his birthday; and with a triumph of above 20,000 horse and foote, brandishing their swords and shouting with inexpressible joy; the wayes strewed with flowers, the bells ringing, the streetes hung with tapestry, fountaines running with wine; the maior, aldermen, and all the companies in their liveries, chaines of gold, and banners; lords and nobles clad in cloth of silver, gold, and velvet; the windowes and balconies well set with ladies: trumpets, music, and myriads of people flocking even so far as from Rochester, so as they were seven houres in passing the citty, even from two in afternoone till nine at night. I stood in the Strand and beheld it, and blessed God. All this was don without one drop of bloudshed, and by that very army which rebelled against him.'

By degrees matters settled down to a more ordinary level. The Church Service was restored at

[1] *Diary*, May 29, 1660.

Whitehall, and on June 28 Pepys mentions [1] 'poor Bishop Wren going to chapel, it being a thanksgiving day for the King's returne.'

The vacant sees were now filled up as speedily as possible. Bishop Juxon was translated to Canterbury, Sheldon succeeding him as Bishop of London; the northern province, then wholly without bishops, had its losses supplied.

The Prayer Book was not by any means commonly used again for some time. Pepys characteristically says—[2]

'*July* 1.—This morning come home my fine camlett cloak, with gold buttons, and a silk suit which cost me much money, and I pray God make me able to pay for it. In the afternoon to the Abbey, where a good sermon by a stranger, but no Common Prayer yet.'

In the following November, to quote the same writer, 'men did begin to nibble at the Common Prayer.' Matters were really progressing, the cathedrals and the court chapels as well as those in the Bishop's palaces setting the example. In February (1661) Evelyn heard 'Dr. Baldero preach at Ely House on St. Matthew vi. 33; after the sermon the Bishop of Ely gave us the blessing very pontifically.' [3]

Ely House was an ancient possession of the see,[4] the gift of William de Ludd, who in the reign of Edward I. gave the house and endowed it with his manor of Ouldbourne, a name which soon grew into Holbourn. The garden and its strawberries are immor-

---

[1] *Diary*, vol. i. p. 112, ed. 1828.   [2] Ib., p. 114.
[3] *Diary*.   [4] *Repertorium*, vol. ii. p. 273. Newcourt.

talised by Shakespeare. It was leased to Sir Christopher Hatton by Bishop Cox in Queen Elizabeth's reign, and a struggle between the Hatton family and the Bishops of Ely then began which lasted until 1772.[1] In Wren's time, the Bishops had recovered some of the buildings, and he had lived here before the rebellion. During that time the house had been used as a prison for 'malignant priests,' especially those of the city of London, and he must have found the whole building sorely defaced and injured.

The chapel, dedicated to S. Etheldreda, is a beautiful piece of Gothic architecture; and there, when it had been cleansed and restored to some order, many of the new bishops were consecrated, and Bishop Wren assisted at that preservation of the Apostolical Succession which but two years before had seemed well-nigh hopeless.

Much was done at Ely House. In the May of 1661 the Convocation of Canterbury met in S. Paul's, its marred, plundered condition not inaptly showing the adversities through which the Church of England had passed. The Convocation had much work before it, the most pressing being to prepare a service for the baptism of those of riper years and for May 29. In order to this a committee of both Houses of Convocation was formed, which met at Ely House, and of which Bishop Wren appears to have been the ruling

---

[1] In that year the last Lord Hatton died; the bishops resigned Ely House to the Crown, and received No. 37 Dover Street in exchange. The chapel, after years of neglect, has also been suffered to pass out of the hands of the Church into those of the Romanists. See *Walks in London* by A. C. Hare, vol. ii. pp. 196-201.

spirit. Many were still half afraid of their true position and afraid of the Puritan party; eighteen years of confusion and persecution had slackened all discipline, and many things seemed natural to the new generation which neither Bishop Andrewes nor Archbishop Laud would have tolerated for a day. It is implied in Dr. Barwick's Life that many of those who should have upheld the Church discipline were willing, from a mistaken notion of conciliation and peace, to let it go. Bishop Wren set his face resolutely against this doctrine.

In November the Convocation met again. Dr. John Barwick had been appointed to the deanery of S. Paul's, and in spite of very failing health, had resumed the weekly Communions, daily prayers, and musical services of the cathedral, and had succeeded in making the choir, where the Puritans had stabled their horses, once more fit for Divine service. At this session of Convocation the Prayer Book was finally revised, after the Bishops had heard at the Savoy Conference all that the Puritans could urge against it. Bishop Wren had been actively engaged in this work, and suggested a considerable number of alterations and additions, many of which were adopted. A large number of grammatical errors had crept in to the old book: for example, 'which' instead of 'who' was in almost all the collects and the Apostles' creed. It still, by some oversight, survives in the Lord's Prayer.[1] 'The altering whereof,' says Bishop Wren, 'if it may seem strange

---

[1] *Fragmentary Illustrations of the History of the Book of Common Prayer*, edited by the Bishop of Chester, p. 47, *et seq.*

at first to unskilful ears, yet will it not be a nine days' wonder, but for ever after a right expression in all our addresses unto God.'

Page after page he corrected with the utmost care, from the very title-page and calendar to the end. July has the characteristic note, 'Out with Dog-days from amongst the Saints.'—A considerable number of his suggestions are part of the Prayer Book to this day. The final clause of the prayer for the Church Militant beginning 'We also bless, etc.,' though not Bishop Wren's composition, as he intended to have replaced the Commemoration of the Saints and the Thanksgiving as it stood in the first Prayer Book of Edward VI., is yet due to his suggestion. The whole series of notes and emendations is very interesting, though they are more than can be given here. Two things plainly appear: that he wished to return as nearly as possible to the first Prayer Book of Edward VI., as the one most closely resembling the offices of the Early Church; that he was very desirous to have the book made as full, as plain, and as clear as the English language could make it. He was anxious that no needless stumbling-blocks should remain in the path either of Churchmen or of Nonconformists, but at the same time he had no intention of bartering any portion of Church truth or discipline for the doubtful advantages of 'comprehension.'

It is a proof that he was not, with all his highminded firmness, the persecuting prelate of Puritan pamphleteers, or the sour and severe man which, in early days, Lord Clarendon thought him, that both in

Norwich, his former diocese, and in the one he then ruled, most of the clergy renounced the Covenant.¹

S. Bartholomew's day, 1662, was the time fixed for those who refused to conform to the Church to resign their livings. It has been easy to represent this as a piece of cruel tyranny, as the turning out of a body of pious men who were labouring in the work which others neglected. In truth, as even Milton says, they were 'time-servers, covetous, illiterate persecutors, not lovers of the truth, like in most things whereof they had accused their predecessors.' To this grave indictment must be added that they were, in the strictest sense, intruders, thrust into charges by Cromwell's authority, while the true priests were imprisoned, fined, forbidden to minister, or even to teach as schoolmasters, and literally left to starve.

'The majority of these were dead and none had been ordained to fill up the gaps, during all the long years since the Church's overthrow. . . Of the eight thousand intruding Nonconformists, a bare two thousand

---

¹ Bishop Kennet says, 'One particular will appear' (from Bishop Wren's *Register*), 'that there were but few of the parochial clergy deprived in this diocese (Ely) in 1662, for not submitting to the Act of Uniformity, though more of the old legal incumbents had been sequestered about 1644 than in proportion within any other diocese.'—Grey's Examination of Neale's *History of the Puritans*, vol. iv. p. 328. From the same authority it appears that most of the clerks deprived in 1662 had other callings, *e.g.* cobbling, gloving, skinning, bookselling, husbandry, and to these they generally returned.

Some of his clergy had come to him in the Tower for institution, in the early part of his imprisonment, and that many were faithful to him is evident from the fact they were expelled their livings for 'following Bishop Wren's fancies,' no other crimes being pretended against them.— *Annals of England*, p. 392.

—1,700 would probably be nearer the number—refused conformity.

'In other words, the Church of the Restoration had to begin her work with a clergy of whom at least three-fourths were aliens at heart to her doctrine and her discipline. To the politician this result was most satisfactory; to the Church little short of disastrous.'[1]

One of the earliest appointments made at the Restoration was that of Dr. Bruno Ryves[2] to be Dean of Windsor and Registrar of the Garter. In the August of 1660, Christopher Wren went to Windsor, and solemnly delivered to the Dean the three registers and the note books of the Order of the Garter, which Dean Wren had, with so much difficulty, recovered and hidden carefully until, at his death, he transferred the charge to his son. Dean Ryves gave a written acknowledgment to Christopher that he had safely received the books, and the service his father had done in preserving them was fully admitted. Gresham College had been cleansed and set in order after the Restoration, and Christopher resumed his lectures there, which were largely attended.

[1] See an interesting article, *The Church of England in the Eighteenth Century*, in the *Church Quarterly Review*, July, 1877, p. 321, *et seq.* It is not however quite accurate to say '*none* were ordained,' for Bishop Duppa held secretly 'frequent ordinations of young loyal church scholars,' among whom was Tenison, afterwards Archbishop of Canterbury.—*History of the Book of Common Prayer*, Lathbury, p. 296.

[2] Dr. Bruno Ryves, Dean of Chichester in 1642, was in the city during Sir William Waller's siege, and left a description of the sack of the cathedral and robbery of its plate by the commander and his troops. Dean Ryves was fined 120*l.* and deprived.—*Memorials of the See of Chichester*, p. 286.

After one of these lectures given in November, Lord Brouncker, Mr. Robert Boyle, Dr. Goddard, Dr. Petty, Dr. Wilkins, Sir Robert Moray and others withdrew with Wren to his room, where they discussed a project for a philosophical College or Society. It was not an entirely new idea, for it had been a favourite scheme of Evelyn's, also of the poet Cowley's.[1] It was not a matter to be arranged in one sitting, and accordingly they settled to meet weekly in Wren's rooms after his lectures, and agreed that for incidental expenses each should pay down ten shillings and subscribe a shilling weekly. A list was made of between thirty and forty probable members, among them those previously mentioned, and Christopher's old friend Sir C. Scarborough, Dr. Seth Ward, Matthew Wren, Cowley, Sir Kenelme Digby, Mr. Evelyn and others. Sir Robert Moray undertook to explain the project to King Charles, and brought back a gracious message that he well approved of it, and would be ready to give it every encouragement. One of the first orders of the Society was that Wren should at the next meeting of the Society bring in his account of the pendulum experiment, with his explanation of it: this experiment related to 'the determination of a standard measure of length by the vibration of a pendulum.'[2]

[1] Abraham Cowley, born 1618; educated at Westminster; was the intimate friend of Lord Falkland and of the poet Crashaw. Cowley followed Henrietta Maria to Paris, remaining steadily loyal. He died 1667.

[2] *History of the Royal Society* (by C. R. Weld), p. 96. Galileo is said to have first discovered the use of the pendulum as a measure of time, while watching the oscillations of the bronze lamp in the cathedral at Pisa. A pendulum clock was long reckoned a 'rarity.' Bishop Seth

There followed experiments for the improvement of shipping, in which Wren worked with Dr. Petty and Dr. Goddard. It was a question to what mechanical powers sailing, especially when against the wind, was reducible; 'he showed it to be a wedge; and he demonstrated how a transient force upon an oblique plane would cause the motion of the plane against the first mover. He made an instrument that mechanically produced the same effect and showed the reason of sailing to all winds.'

But to give all Christopher's experiments would be to write over again the already well-told history of the Royal Society. It had few more assiduous members.

In 1661, Christopher resigned his Gresham Professorship, in order to accept the Savilian Professorship of Astronomy, at Oxford.[1] It had been held by Dr. Seth Ward, who was soon afterwards made Bishop of Salisbury in succession to Bishop Hyde. Shortly after his appointment, Christopher had a command from the King to make him a lunar globe, according to the observations made with the best telescopes. He constructed one 'representing not only the spots and

Ward presented one, made by Fromantel, to the Society in 1662, in memory of his friend Mr. Laurence Rooke, late Astronomy Professor at Gresham College.

[1] Founded 1619 by Sir Henry Savile. He required that the Professor should explain the Ptolemaic and Copernican and other modern astronomical systems, should teach and read on Optics, Dialling, Geography and Navigation. He was to be of any nation in Christendom, provided he was of good reputation, had a fair knowledge of Greek, and was twenty-six years of age. If an Englishman he must have taken his M.A. degree. The choice of a professor was to lie with the Archbishop of Canterbury, the Lord Chancellor, the Chancellor of the University, the Bishop of London, the principal Secretary of State, Chief Justices, the Lord Chief Baron, and Dean of Arches. *Oxford*, vol. ii. p. 188. Ayliffe.

various degrees of whiteness on the surface, but the hills, eminences, and cavities moulded in solid work.' This curious toy was highly admired, placed in the King's cabinet at Whitehall, and esteemed a great 'rarity.'

In this year Wren took his degree as Doctor of Civil Laws, Oxford, and received a similar honour from the University of Cambridge. King Charles purposed paying a visit to Oxford, and the Philosophical Society both there and in London resolved to give him an entertainment. Lord Brouncker wrote from London to Wren to consult him. Wren wrote back :—

'My Lord,—The Act and noise at Oxford being over, I retir'd to myself as speedily as I could to obey your Lordship and contribute something to the collection of Experiments designed by the Society, for his Majesty's Reception. I concluded on something I thought most suitable for such an occasion; but the stupidity of our artists here makes the apparatus so tedious that I foresee I shall not be able to bring it to anything within the time proposed. What in the meanwhile to suggest to your Lordship I cannot guess.' . . . 'Geometrical problems, and new methods, however useful, will be but tasteless in a transient show.' He enumerates various things which he had thought of and rejected: 'designs of engines, scenographical tricks, designs of architecture, chymical experiments, experiments in anatomy, which last are sordid and noisome to any but those whose desire of knowledge makes them digest it.' 'Experiments of Natural Philosophy are seldom pompous, and certainly Nature in the best of her works is apparent enough in obvious things, were they but curiously observed; and the key that opens treasures is often plain and rusty, but unless it be gilt it will make no show at Court.'

He proposed to show an experiment with a 'weather wheel to measure the expansions of air.' Another—'no unpleasing spectacle—of seeing a man live without new air as long as you please;' this was to be effected by an instrument of Wren's invention which cooled, percolated, and purified the air. Also 'an artificial eye truly and dioptrically made as big as a tennis-ball.'

'My Lord,' the letter ends, 'if my first design had been perfect I had not troubled your Lordship with so much Tattle, but with something performed and done. But I am fain, in this letter, to do like some chymist who when Projection (his fugitive darling) hath left him threadbare, is forced to fall to vulgar Preparations to pay his Debts.'

The King appointed Wren as assistant to Sir John Denham, the Surveyor-General of Works. Sir John had been appointed by Charles I., in reversion during the lifetime of Inigo Jones, surveyor at that time, and had succeeded, at Inigo Jones's death, to what was then but a barren honour. Evelyn, who had a dispute with Sir John about the placing of Greenwich Palace in that very year, says: 'I knew him to be a better poet than architect, tho' he had Mr. Webb[1] (Inigo Jones's man) to assist him.' Of this Charles II. was probably aware, and anxious to supply his deficiency. That his choice should have fallen upon Wren, unless Evelyn's friendship suggested it, is remarkable, as, until then, Wren seems to have made no special study of architecture. No doubt the practical experience learned in the details of the assistant-surveyor's work was afterwards very serviceable to him. He appears to have had a most retentive memory as well as a very quick eye and power of apprehension. In spite, however, of these calls on his time he was assiduous at the Society's meetings.

The death of Laurence Rooke, his friend and fellow-labourer, threw more work on his hands. Rooke was succeeded in the Geometry Professorship by Isaac Barrow, afterwards a well-known divine who, in his first Latin oration, eulogised the Savilian Professor as 'formerly a prodigy of a boy, now a miracle of a man, and a genius among mortals. Lest I should appear to speak falsehood, it will be enough for me to name to you the most ingenious and excellent Christopher Wren.'[2] It was a high compliment, but Barrow knew that his audience would heartily re-echo it. It is to be hoped that Barrow's lectures were somewhat shorter than his sermons, which, fine as they are, were not always listened to with patience. 'On one occasion, when he was long preaching in the Abbey on a holiday, the servants of the Church, who

---

[1] He married Inigo Jones's daughter.
[2] *Lives of the Gresham Professors*, Ward, p. 97.

on those days showed the tombs and effigies in wax of the Kings and Queens to the common people, fearing to spend that time in hearing which they might more profitably employ in receiving, caused the organs to blow until they had blowed him down.'[1]

On March 25, 1663, the Society was finally incorporated by a charter from the King, with a preamble written by Christopher Wren, explaining its objects. The style of the preamble is far more florid than is usual in Wren's writing: it has in it the exultation of one who is accomplishing a long-cherished scheme. One paragraph is evidently intended as a defence against certain attacks which were made upon the English philosophers as they had been in past times against Galileo :—

'Not that herein we would withdraw the least ray of our influence from the present established nurseries of good literature and education, founded by the

[1] Isaac Barrow, born 1630. He was so little studious as a boy, and so fond of fighting, that his father used often solemnly to wish that if it should please God to take one of his children it might be his son Isaac. When, however, in 1677, he did really die, the Lord Keeper (Lord Nottingham) sent his father a message of condolence, importing that 'he had but too great reason to grieve, since never father lost so good a son.' Dr. Isaac Barrow, Bishop of Man, 1663, and S. Asaph, 1669, was his uncle. *Life of Dr. Barrow*, vol. i. p. ix., ed. 1830. Among his poems is the following, which seems to be incomplete :—

> AD. DD. CHR. WREN.
> Ad te, sed passu tremulo vultuque rubenti,
> Fertur ad ingenii culmen, opella levis,
> Nec quid vult aliud (quid enim velit haud tibi notum)
> Quam ut justum authoris deferat.—*Ib.* vol. viii. p. 541

piety of our royal ancestors and others, and whose laws which as we are obliged to defend, so the holy blood of our martyred Father hath especially endeared to us, but, that we purpose to make further provision for this branch of knowledge likewise, Natural Experimental Philosophy.' . . . 'Taking care as in the first place for Religion so next for the riches and ornaments of our kingdoms, as we wear an Imperial Crown in which flowers are alternately intermixed with the ensigns of Christianity.'

King Charles, the Duke of York, and Prince Rupert, always a lover of experiments, were among the first members of the Society, and its beginning was prosperous enough; but Court favour has always created some envy. It happened that in the self-same year Butler,[1] then secretary to Jeremy Taylor's friend, Lord Carbery, published his famous 'Hudibras.' It created a great sensation; the Court read it, the town read it; Pepys, hearing 'the world cry it up so mightily, tried twice or three times reading to bring himself to think it witty.' It was in everyone's mouth, and Butler naturally thought himself sure of promotion. None, however, came to him, and he directed his bitter wit against those more fortunate than himself, the members of the new Royal Society, and Bishop Sprat in particular, in a poem called 'The Elephant in the Moon,' which opened as follows :—

[1] Samuel Butler, born 1612, died, it is said, in great poverty, and was buried in S. Paul's, Covent Garden, 1680.

> ' A learn'd Society of late,
>   The glory of a neighbouring state,
>   Agreed upon a summer night
>   To search the moon by her own light,
>   To take an invent'ry of all
>   Her real estate and personal.
>
>   .   .   .   .
>
>   To observe her country how 'twas planted,
>   With what she abounded most or wanted,
>   And make the proper'st observations
>   For settling of new plantations,
>   If the Society should incline
>   T' attempt so glorious a design.'

With sharp touches indicating the various Members of the Society the satire continues, telling how they see in the moon, through the telescope, marvellous things, and an appearance of an immense elephant; they agree that a record must be made, and during the discussion who is to write it, one of the servants peeping through the telescope discovers that a *mouse* has got in between the two glasses! It, and a swarm of small flies, are the causes of the mysterious phenomena, the vast beast, the marching and countermarching armies which have been so learnedly explained![1]

The Society does not seem to have paid much attention to the poet, and the experiments went on as usual. A different task was presently offered to Wren by the King. When he married Catharine of

---

[1] Wren's lunar globe will be remembered. *Vide supra*, p. 125.
The satire made some sensation and caused La Fontaine to write *Un Animal dans la Lune*, in which, courtier like, he pays a compliment to Charles II., and hints at the happiness of England at peace and able to give herself 'à ces emplois,' while France was at war with Holland, Spain, and the Empire.

Portugal, he received Tangiers, Tripoli, and Bombay as part of her dowry. Tangiers was reckoned as a very important place to the English, whose sailors were still constantly harassed by the Moorish pirates, and the fortifications of the town were a pressing care. King Charles offered, through Matthew Wren, then Lord Clarendon's secretary, a commission to Christopher Wren, as one of the best geometricians in Europe, to survey and direct the works at the mole, harbour, and fortifications of Tangiers, offering him an ample salary, leave of absence from his Professorship, and a reversionary grant of Sir John Denham's office. Flattering though the offer was, Christopher declined it on the ground of his health, and begged the King to command his duty in England.

He no doubt judged wisely, and the refusal gave no offence at Court. Perhaps the leave of absence might not have been easily obtained, for the following letter from Dr. Sprat shows that Wren was already embarrassed by the difficulty of being in two places at once :—

'My dear Sir,—I must confess I have some little Peek against you—therefore am not much displeased, that I have this occasion of telling you some ill news. The Vice-Chancellor did yesterday send for me to inquire where the *Astronomy Professor* was, and the reason of his absence so long after the beginning of the *term*. I used all the arguments I could for your Defence. I told him that *Charles the Second* was King of *England, Scotland, France* and *Ireland*; and that he was by the late *Act of*

Parliament declared absolute Monarch in these his dominions : and that it was this mighty Prince who had confined you to *London*. I endeavour'd to persuade him that the drawing of lines in *Sir Harry Savill's* school was not altogether of so great a concernment for the benefit of Christendom as the rebuilding of *St. Paul's* or the fortifying of *Tangier* ; (for I understood those were the great works in which that extraordinary Genius of yours was judg'd necessary to be employ'd). All this I urged, but after some Discourse, he told me, that he was not now to consider you as *Dr. Bayly*[1] (for so he ow'd you all Kindness) but as *Vice Chancellor*, and under that Capacity he most terribly told me that he took it very ill you had not all this while given him any Account of what hinder'd you in the Discharge of your Office. This he bid me tell you, and I do it not very unwillingly because I see that our Friendships are so closely ty'd together that the same Thing which was so great a Prejudice to me (my losing your Company all this while here) does also something redound to your Disadvantage. And so, my dear Sir, now my Spite and Spleen is satisfied, I must needs return to my old Temper again, and faithfully assure you that I am with the most violent Zeal and Passion, your most affectionate and devoted Servant,

'THO. SPRAT.'

Wren had also employment at Cambridge, of a kind he would have been loth to put in other hands.

---

[1] Dr. Richard Bayley, President of S. John's College.

His uncle, the Bishop of Ely, had instantly on his release determined to give a chapel to Pembroke Hall, Cambridge, where he had been a scholar under Launcelot Andrewes,[1] and he employed his nephew as his architect. Upon this work and its endowment the Bishop expended 5,000*l.*, the first money he received after his release. His personal habits were austerely simple; for the last twenty years of his life he drank no wine, and only ate off a wooden trencher, practising fasting and abstinence with great strictness. He had never spent any of the revenues of his see upon his children, and now he made the chapel his heir, bestowing upon it an estate at Hardwick in Cambridgeshire.

The chapel, which has a peculiar interest as Wren's first architectural work, is built in the classical style he was to make famous in England, and bears his mark in its beautiful proportions, the richness of its stucco ceiling and the pannelled wood-work. The plain glazing of the windows and a something of bareness about the whole, are probably to be accounted for by the necessity of limiting the expense to a fixed sum. Its first stone was laid May 13, 1663, by the Master, Dr. Frank, acting for Bishop Wren, who was not present.[2]

It was probably at the same time that Wren executed some repairs in Ely Cathedral which had

---

[1] Bishop Andrewes bequeathed 332*l.* to the library of Pembroke College.

[2] Some alterations have recently been made at Pembroke, in which, under the late Sir G. Scott's orders, the chapel has been lengthened by about 20 feet, the stucco of the exterior stripped, and the red brick pointed.

suffered, like every other grand church, from the fury of the Puritans. Bitter indeed must have been the regret with which the surviving clergy returned to find the fabrics of their churches plundered and laid waste, and their flocks scattered or corrupted.

CHAPTER VI.
1664–1667.

REPAIR OF S. PAUL'S—SHELDONIAN THEATRE—THE PLAGUE—A LETTER FROM PARIS—CONSECRATION OF PEMBROKE CHAPEL—FIRE OF LONDON—BISHOP WREN'S DEATH—HIS FAMILY.

>Yet, London, Empress of the Northern Clime,
> By an high fate thou greatly didst expire,
>Great as the world's, which, at the death of time,
> Must fall, and rise a nobler frame by fire
>   *Annus Mirabilis*, ccxii. **Dryden.**

CHAPTER VI.

THE repairs of S. Paul's Cathedral could not be delayed. Wren, as Sir John Denham's assistant, was greatly occupied about the matter, which was one of no ordinary difficulty. The responsibility was really his, for Sir John went out of his mind, and though he recovered, probably did but little business.

When Inigo Jones built his portico, he cased the nave with Portland stone, and rebuilt the north and south fronts. In doing so he pared down the original pointed architecture, until little of its beauty or character remained. His work had in its turn been damaged by the Puritans, who set up booths in the portico, and dug sawpits in the cathedral inclosure. Besides these injuries Christopher Wren's accurate eye detected graver faults in the original design, some of which he enumerates. 'The pillars of the nave, though eleven feet in diameter, were only cased with stone, and filled up with rubbish inside. The roof was always too heavy for them, so that they are bent outwards on both sides, so that the roof already cracked will finally fall in.' He proposed to substitute a roof[1] of 'a light,

---

[1] For an account of the great rarity of stone roofs see Fergusson's *Illustrated Handbook of Architecture*, vol. ii. p. 879. It is said that Wren used often to look at the beautiful roof of King's College Chapel, Cambridge, and say he would build such another if anyone would tell him where to put the first stone.

thin shell of stone, very geometrically made.' The tower leant much to one side, and was propped with arches and buttresses, so as to block the view from the west end. Upon this tower, which he despairingly calls 'a heap of deformities,' there had been formerly a tall, thin, wooden spire, which was destroyed by lightning. For this he wished to substitute 'a dome or rotunda, and upon the cupola for outward ornament, a lantern with a spring top to rise proportionately.' He hints that when the dome was finished the rest of the cathedral should be harmonised with it, almost impossible though the task appeared. He expected great difference of opinion, and that 'some would aim at a greater magnificence than the age would afford, and some might fall so low as to think of piecing up the old fabric here with stone, there with brick, and covering all faults with a coat of plaster, to leave it still to posterity as an object of charity.' The miserable state of the building is implied in the epitaph of its Dean, Dr. Barwick, who in 1664, 'Inter sacras Ædis Paulinæ ruinas reponit suas (utrasque resurrecturas securus) '.[1]

Another work upon which Wren was engaged was the Sheldonian Theatre at Oxford. Sheldon, who succeeded Archbishop Juxon in the see of Canterbury in 1663, was determined to free S. Mary's Church from the profane uses to which it was put when the various 'Acts' were kept there, and any kind of jesting

---

[1] 'Among the sacred ruins of S. Paul's Church laid down his own (sure that both will rise again).' Sancroft, afterwards Archbishop of Canterbury, succeeded him.

and buffoonery was considered allowable. He had had experience of Wren in the discussions about S. Paul's, and now engaged him as architect. The building is too well known to need a description; the roof was reckoned a triumph of skill because of 'the contrivance of supporting the same without the help of any beam, it being entirely kept up by braces and screws; and is the subject of an excellent mathematical treatise by that prodigy of the age, Dr. Wallis.'[1] It was six years building, and cost 25,000l. Evelyn, with whom Wren had often discussed the plans, went to Oxford on purpose to be present at the opening on July 9, 1669.

'In the morning,' he says, ' was celebrated the Encenia of the New Theater . . . . it was resolved to keep the present Act in it and celebrate its dedication with the greatest splendor and formalitie that might be, and therefore drew a world of strangers and other companie to the Universitie from all parts of the nation. The Vice Chancellor, Heads of Houses and Doctors, being seated in magisteriall seates, the Vice Chancellor's chaire and deske, Proctors etc. covered with Brocatall (a kind of Brocade) and cloth of gold; the Universitie Register read the founder's grant and gift of it to the Universitie upon these solemn occasions. Then followed Dr. South, the Universitie's orator, in an eloquent speech which was very long and not without some malicious and indecent reflections on the Royal Society as underminers of the Universitie, which was very foolish

[1] *Oxford*, vol. i. p. 473. Ayliffe.

and untrue, as well as unseasonable. But, to let that pass from an ill-natured man, the rest was in praise of the archbishop and the ingenious architect.'

Dr. Plot, the historian of Oxfordshire, who was a member of the Royal Society, in his quaint book gives a careful technical description of the construction of the theatre by Wren, and his assistant, 'Richard Frogley, an able carpenter.'

During the years that the theatre was building Wren did not intermit his attendance at the Royal Society; amongst other inventions he produced a machine for drawing in perspective, which was exhibited at one of the meetings.

A frightful interruption came to these and to all other pursuits in London. In 1665, the plague, which had more than once afflicted England, broke out with fearful force in London, where the dark narrow streets with their houses meeting overhead, and the foul state of the entire town, gave every encouragement to its ravages. Pepys, who stayed in London all through the worst time of the plague, gives many a record of this visitation.[1]

'*June 7th.*—The hottest day that ever I felt in my life. This day, much against my will I did in Drury Lane see two or three houses marked with a red cross upon the doors and "Lord have mercy upon us!" writ there; which was a sad sight to me, being the first of the kind that, to my remembrance, I ever saw.

'*August 16th.*—To the Exchange, where I have

[1] *Diary*, vol. ii. p. 273, *et seq.*, ed. 1828.

not been a great while. But Lord! how sad a sight it is to see the streets empty of people and very few upon the 'Change! Jealous of every door that one sees shut up lest it should be the plague, and about us two shops in three, if not more, generally shut up.

'*September 3rd* (Lord's Day).—Up; and put on my coloured silk suit very fine, and my new periwigg, bought a good while since, and durst not wear because the plague was in Westminster when I bought it; and it is a wonder what will be the fashion after the plague is done as to periwiggs, for nobody will dare to buy any haire for fear of the infection, that it had been cut off the heads of people dead of the plague. My Lord Brouncker, Sir J. Minnes and I up to the Vestry' (he was then at Greenwich) 'at the desire of the justices of the peace, in order to the doing of something for the keeping of the plague from growing; but Lord! to consider the madness of the people of the town who will, because they are forbid, come in crowds along with the dead corpses to see them buried; but we agreed on some orders for the prevention thereof. Among other stories, one was very passionate, methought, of a complaint brought against a man in the town for taking a child from London from an infected house. Alderman Hooker told us it was the child of a very able citizen in Gracious Street' (Gracechurch Street), 'a saddler, who had buried all the rest of his children with the plague, and himself and his wife being now shut up and in despair of escaping, did desire only to save the life of this little child; and so prevailed to have it received stark naked into the arms of a friend who brought it, having put it into fresh clothes, to Greenwich, where upon hearing the story we did agree it should be permitted to be received and kept in the town.'

So the days went on and the grass waved in Whitehall Court, and to quote Pepys again: 'Lord! how everybody's looks and discourse in the streets is of death and nothing else, and few people going up and down, that the town is like a place distressed and forsaken.'

None but those whom absolute necessity kept in London stayed in the infected air; the works at S. Paul's were stopped; all meetings and lectures ceased, with good reason, since to gather people together was but to spread the infection.

Christopher Wren profited by the cessation of his London work, to travel abroad. Before going he had much to settle; to help Mr. Evelyn find a tutor, 'a perfect Grecian and more than commonly mathematical,' for his son. This youth went two years later, at the age of thirteen, to Trinity College, Oxford, 'being newly out of long coates.'

Wren's Oxford Professorship, and his works, both there and at Cambridge, required to be set in good order before he could go. At Oxford he was engaged on the repairs of Trinity College, for his friend Dr. Bathurst.[1] On June 22, 1665, Wren writes to them as follows :—

[1] Dr. Ralph Bathurst, born 1620, educated at Coventry and Oxford.

'My honoured Friend,—I am convinced with Machiavel or some unlucky fellow, 'tis no matter whether I quote true, that the world is generally governed by words. I perceive the name of a quadrangle will carry it with those whom you say may possibly be your benefactors, though it be much the worse situation for the chambers, and the beauty of the college, and of the particular pile of building. If I had skill in enchantment to represent the pile, first in one view, then in another, I should certainly make them of my opinion; or else I will appeal to Mons. Mansard or Signor Bernini, both of which I shall see at Paris within this fortnight.

'But, to be sober, if anybody, as you say, will pay for a quadrangle, there is no dispute to be made; let them have a quadrangle, though a lame one somewhat like a three-legged table.' . . .

Some technical details for the builder follow, and then:

'You need not use any apologies to me, for I must beg you to believe you can command me in things of greater moment, and that I love to serve you as your most faithful and affectionate Friend and Servant,

'CHRISTOPHER WREN.'

The College was repaired by Sir Thomas Pope, it having been left in a very ruinous condition, but the

Was ordained, but during the rebellion maintained himself by the practice of medicine. He was a fellow of the Royal Society, and in 1688 its president. He was president of Trinity from 1644 till his death in 1704. He was Dean of Wells, and was offered the bishopric, but refused it as taking him from his college and hindering the improvements he was making there. Evelyn speaks highly of his preaching and his admirable parts and learning.'

ornamental part is due to Dr. Bathurst, aided by munificent Archbishop Sheldon and other old members of the College.

He was making considerable additions to Trinity College at Cambridge : to this date belongs the library, which he added to the beautiful western Quadrangle known as Nevile's Court.

'A building,' said Wren, in a letter to the Master of Trinity, 'of that consideration you go about, deserves good care in the design and able workmen to perform it ; and that he who takes the general management upon him may have a prospect of the whole, and make all parts inside and outside correspond well together.'

Very full directions and six drawings follow, explaining the plan and its details.

'I suppose,' he ends, 'you have good masons ; however, I would willingly take a farther pains to give all the mouldings in great ; we are scrupulous in small matters and you must pardon us, the architects are as great pedants as critics and heralds.'

It was not until midsummer that Wren was able to start on his journey : he went at once to Paris to the Earl of S. Albans, the English ambassador, to whom he had letters. Lord S. Albans had lived at Paris in great ease and luxury all through the Rebellion, far more so, Evelyn indignantly says, than had the King. He was supposed to be privately married to the Queen Dowager, Henrietta Maria. He was what was then called a great virtuoso, a friend of

Cowley and of other wits, and entertained Wren with much courtesy and hospitality. Wren's name was, in itself, a sufficient introduction to the scientific men and philosophers of the city, in whose society he took great pleasure.

He had long been a Member of the Order of Freemasons, and had distinguished himself by the attention he gave to the lodges under his care : at the time of his journey to France he was Deputy Grand Master under Earl Rivers ; no doubt he availed himself to the full of the opportunities which Freemasonry afforded him for observing the details of the work and becoming acquainted with the workmen, the architects, and the sculptors, whom Louis XIV. had brought in great numbers to Paris.

It would have been interesting had Wren left us a record of his impressions of Paris from a political point of view. It was the brief interval of peace between England and France before the war of the Netherlands. Louis XIV., climbing upwards to the zenith of his brilliant reign, keeping the supreme power in his own hands since Mazarin's death (in 1661), with the wise Colbert for his financier, surrounded by all the great captains, statesmen, wits and artists who made up the 'Siècle de Louis XIV.,' must have been a very interesting subject for the observation of a philosopher like Wren, whose youth had been passed among terrible political storms. There is, however, but one slight hint in his journal, but one suggestion that he discerned the true value of much of the glitter and veneer of universal, if temporary, success. Pascal, with whom he had corresponded, and between whose brief career and his own there is a curious resemblance, had died three years before Wren took his one foreign journey.

The 'Académie Royale des Sciences,' which had just received the formal sanction of Louis XIV., had begun much like the English Royal Society, by small meetings and conferences at Paris amongst scientific men, and in these conferences, Pascal, while very young, had taken a brilliant place. His father, Etienne Pascal, when he found it a vain attempt to withhold mathematical science from his son, cultivated the boy's genius to the utmost, beyond, perhaps, what the very feeble physical frame could bear.

One cannot doubt that Wren was introduced to this society, and took an interest in its discussions, though his attention seems most of all to have been given to architecture.

In a journal written for a Dr. Bateman, the friend who gave him the letters to Lord S. Albans, he says:

'I have busied myself in surveying the most esteemed Fabrics of Paris, and the country round; the Louvre for a while was my daily object where no less than a thousand hands are constantly employed in the works; some in laying mighty Foundations, some in raising the stories, columns, and entablements &c. with vast stones, by great and useful engines, others in carving, inlaying of marbles, plaistering, painting, gilding &c., which altogether makes a School of Architecture, the best probably at this day in

Europe. The college of the Four Nations,[1] is usually admired, but the Artist had purposely set it ill-favouredly that he might shew his wit in struggling with an ill-convenienced situation. An Academy of Painters, Sculptors, Architects and the chief Artificers of the Louvre, meet every first and last Saturday of the month. Mons. Colbert, Surintendant, comes to the works of the Louvre every Wednesday, and if business hinders not, Thursday. The Workmen are paid every Sunday duly. Mons. Abbé Charles introduced me to the acquaintance of Bernini,[2] who showed me his designs of the Louvre, and of the King's Statue. Abbé Bruno

---

[1] Wren refers to the University of Paris, which was divided into four faculties—arts (letters and science), theology, civil and canon law, and medicine. The faculty of arts was divided into four *nations*. That of France divided again into five provinces or tribes, that of Picardy divided in the same way, that of Normandy, and that of Germany which was divided into two tribes, that of the continents (divided into two provinces), and that of.the islanders, which included Great Britain and Ireland.— *Dictionnaire Historique de la France*, par L. Lalanne.

[2] Gio. Bernini was born at Naples 1598 and was a great sculptor as well as architect. He made a bust of Charles I. of England after a picture by Vandyke. When the bust was carried to the king's house at Chelsea his Majesty with a train of nobles went to view it, and as they were viewing it a hawk flew over their heads with a partridge in his claw which he had wounded to death. Some of the partridge's blood fell on the neck of the bust, where it always remained without being wiped off. This bust, with the picture from which it was taken, is thought to have perished in the fireat Whitehall, 1697.—*Biographical History*, vol. ii. p. 88. Grainger.

Bernini was splendidly received at Paris and employed in several works of sculpture, among which was a bust of Louis XIV., probably the one to which Wren refers. His design for the Louvre was accepted, and he had just begun to work it out at the time Wren wrote, but Colbert and the two Perraults stirred up so many difficulties that Bernini abandoned the task, and the Louvre was left in the hands of Claude Perrault. Bernini returned to Rome and died there in 1680.

keeps the curious rarities of the Duke of Orleans' library, well filled with excellent Intaglios, medals, books of Plants and Fowls in miniature. Abbé Burdelo keeps an Academy at his house for Philosophy every Monday afternoon. But I must not think to describe Paris, and the numerous observables there in the compass of a short letter. The King's Houses I could not miss, Fontainbleau has a stately wildness and vastness suitable to the Desert it stands in.

'The antique mass of the Castle of S. Germains and the hanging gardens are delightfully surprising (I mean to any man of judgement), for the pleasures below vanish away in the breath that is spent in ascending. The Palace, or if you please the Cabinet, of Versailles call'd me twice to view it; the mixtures of brick, stone, blue tile and gold make it look like a rich livery: not an inch within but is crowded with little curiosities of ornaments: the women as they make here the language and fashions and meddle with Politics and Philosophy, so they sway also in Architecture; works of Filgrand and little Knacks are in great vogue; but Building certainly ought to have the attribute of Eternal and therefore the only thing uncapable of new Fashions. The masculine furniture of *Palais Mazarine* pleased me much better, where is a great and noble collection of antique Statues and Bustoes, (many of porphyry), good Basso-relievos; excellent pictures of the great masters, fine Arras, true Mosaics, besides *pièces de*

Raport[1] in compartiments and pavements, vases of porcelain painted by Raphael, and infinite other rarities. The best of which now furnish the glorious appartment of the Queen Mother at the Louvre which I saw many times. After the incomparable villas of Vaux and Maisons, I shall name but Ruel, Coutances, Chilly, Essoane, St. Maur, St. Mande, Issy, Meudon, Rincy, Chantilly, Verneuil, Liancour, all which, and I might add many others, I have surveyed, and that I might not lose the impressions of them, I shall bring you all France on paper. Bernini's design of the Louvre I would have given my skin for; but the old reserved Italian gave me but a few minutes' view; it was five designs on paper, for which he hath received as many thousand pistoles. I had only time to copy it in my fancy and memory, and shall be able, by discourse and a crayon, to give you a tolerable account of it. I have purchased a great deal of taille-douce, that I might give our countrymen examples of ornaments and grotesques, in which the Italians themselves confess the French to excel. I hope I shall give you a very good account of all the best artists of France; my business now is to pry into trades and arts. I put myself into all shapes to humour them; it is a comedy to me, and though sometimes expenseful, I am yet loth to leave it.' There follows a long list of what he calls 'the most noted artisans within my knowledge or acquaintance,' in which is many a famous name, Bernini, Poussin, Mignard, Mansard,

[1] *i.e.* Mosaic.

&c., and then he says, 'My Lord Berkeley returns to England at Christmas, when I propose to take the opportunity of his company, and by that time to perfect what I have on the anvil—observations on the present state of architecture, arts, and manufactures in France.'

With the great men Latin was probably the common tongue, but with the artizans he must have talked in French, and have either possessed or acquired no small mastery of the language and of the technical terms of their various trades. The 'observations' were either never hammered into the shape Wren wished, or else were subsequently lost or copied by someone else, as frequently happened to one so careless of his own fame as was Wren. In January 1666, the English Ambassador was recalled from Paris, and the war began between England, and the Netherlands with France for their ally.

Pembroke Chapel was meanwhile completed, and ' being beautified with splendid and decorous furniture and amply endowed with an annual revenue, was upon the feast of S. Matthew' (the Bishop's patron saint) ' 1665, solemnly consecrated and dedicated by Bishop Wren in person and by his Episcopal authority to the honour of Almighty God. A noble and lasting monument of the rare piety and munificence of that great and wise Prelate and in every point accorded to his character, which was so well known that the sole nomination of the founder was a sufficient account of the magnificence of the foundation. Before evening service the exterior or outer chapel and the cloister leading to it (a new fabrick of Sir R. Hitcham's foundation) were by his Lordship also consecrated for places of sepulture for the use of the Society, together with a cell or vault at the East end of the chapel under the altar for a dormitory for his Lordship.'[1]

Bishop Wren must have looked with joy on the completion of his thankoffering, and may have guessed, as he surveyed its beautiful proportions, that he had set his nephew, its young architect, on the road to fame. Very little is told us of the latter years of Wren's Episcopate; one or two stories are given in the 'Parentalia' and then contradicted, but it seems he kept his old firmness. In 1662 he held the second Visitation of his Diocese and the articles of inquiry and directions show no change in his opinions and no deference to Puritan notions. It was by a stretch of his power as Visitor that he admitted Dr. Beaumont to be master of Peterhouse, though the college had nominated two other deserving persons, of whom Cosin was one. The choice proved, in the end, a very wise one. He could be lenient also when he thought it right, and admitted several Fellows of Jesus College who came to him, in some fear of a refusal, for institution. He 'was very fair and civil towards them, despatched them without the usual height of the fees and persuaded them to studiousness and peace against all

[1] Wood. *Athenæ Oxonienses*, vol. i. p. 735. He used certain peculiarities in the Act of Consecration which have been repeated at he consecration of the addition to the chapel, March 25, 1881.

animosities.' So says a contemporary letter quoted in the 'Parentalia.'

Wren had come home at Christmas to find London comparatively free from the plague, and people gradually returning. The Royal Society, whose meetings had of course ceased during the infection, busied themselves in investigations as to the plague, and the possible methods of preventing it. It still raged in the country, and especially at Cambridge, driving Isaac Newton from his lectures there to the garden at Woolsthorpe in Lincolnshire, where the idea of the law of gravitation first occurred to his mind.

The repair of S. Paul's was again discussed and commissioners appointed in 1666, among whom were Evelyn, Wren, Dean Sancroft, and the then Bishop of London, who was Humphrey Henchman, the early friend of George Herbert.

On August 27th they inspected the cathedral. Two of the commissioners, Mr. Chichley and Mr. Prat, evidently wished to do as little as possible, declaring, when the nave was proved to lean outwards on both sides, 'it was so built for an effect of the perspective,' and proposing to repair the steeple on its old foundations. Wren thought very differently, insisted on new foundations, renewed his former proposal of 'a noble cupola' which was strongly supported by Evelyn, who had never forgotten the grandeur of S. Peter's just completed when he went to Rome as a young man in 1644. They retired to the Deanery to give their opinions in writing, promising to send estimates of the cost of their several plans. Six days later a new disaster overwhelmed London and solved the question of repairing the cathedral. On the night of September 2nd the Fire of London began; for three days and four nights it burned unchecked, having gained such strength during the first panic that it could not be beaten back, the sparks constantly kindling new centres of flame.

'All the skie,' says Evelyn,[1] 'was of a fiery aspect, like the top of a burning oven, and the light seen above forty miles round about for many nights. God grant mine eyes may never behold the like who now saw 10,000 houses all in one flame; the noise and crackling and thunder of the impetuous flames, the shrieking of women and children, the hurry of people, the fall of towers, houses and churches, was like an hideous storme, and the aire all about so hot and inflam'd that at last one was not able to approch it, so that they were forc'd to stand still and let the flames burn on, which they did for neere two miles in length and one in bredth. The clowds also of smoke were dismall and reached upon computation neere fifty-six miles in length. Thus I left it this afternoone burning, a resemblance of Sodom, or of the last day.

'*Sept.* 4.—The burning still rages and it was now gotten as far as the Inner Temple; all Fleet Streete, the Old Bailey, Ludgate Hill, Warwick Lane, Newgate, Paules' Chaine, Watling Streete now flaming and most of it reduced to ashes; the stones of Paules flew like granados, the mealting lead running

[1] *Diary*, September, 1666.

downe the streetes in a streame and the very pavement glowing with fiery rednesse so as no horse nor man was able to tread them and the demolition had stopped all the passages so as no help could be applied. The Eastern wind still more impetuously driving the flames forward. Nothing but the Almighty power of God was able to stop them, for vaine was the help of man.'

At last the people were roused to take some steps. King Charles, who showed on this occasion great courage and presence of mind, got by water to the Tower and insisted on the houses near being blown up so as to prevent the flames from reaching the powder magazine.

Pepys gives a vivid account of the dismay and confusion; the goods removed and removed again as the fire reached what had been thought to be places of safety; the rain of fire drops, and the ever-new places in which the fire broke out, and his own difficulties of getting anything to eat but the cold remains of his Sunday's dinner! On September 17 he went by water to Greenwich—' seeing the City all the way, a sad sight much fire being in it still.' S. Paul's suffered terribly; the Portico was split and rent, nothing but the inscription remaining, of which each letter was perfect. The heat had calcined the largest blocks of stone, the Portland stone flew off wherever the flames touched it; the lead roof (no less than six acres by measure [1]), melted and fell in, and carrying everything with it in its fall, broke into S. Faith's, the crypt below the choir,

[1] Evelyn's *Diary*, September, 1666.

where the books belonging to the Stationers' Hall had been carried for safety. They caught fire and continued burning for a week. The altar and roof above it, though of lead, remained untouched, and one Bishop's tomb.[1] When at length the fire burnt out, the city was a 'ruinous heap,' the air still so hot as almost to singe the hair of those who sought amongst the ruins for some remains of former wealth. In the fields all round were two hundred thousand people of all classes equally destitute, silent from the very greatness of their calamity and asking no relief. The King did his utmost for them, and a proclamation was made for the country to come in and refresh them. Most fortunately the weather was warm and fair.

For a few days their stupor lasted, when it was broken into by a general alarm that the Dutch were in the river burning all the shipping. When this was at length appeased, the people flocked back to what had been the city, and either set up little sheds where their houses had been or took refuge with friends whose dwellings were uninjured, so that in four days' time of the hundreds who had thronged the fields not one remained. To rebuild the city was an urgent necessity, and while the flames were in parts still burning Wren and Evelyn had both made plans for a new city and presented them to the King. Wren's was the first shown to King Charles, and though there is much resemblance between it and that of Evelyn, yet Wren's

---

[1] That of Robert de Braybrook (Bishop of London 1382 and 1405). The tomb of Donne (Dean of S. Paul's 1621-1631) was not entirely destroyed.

is evidently the more useful, as well as the finer plan of the two, and was the one which the King accepted. All persons were agreed that to allow the old, narrow, filthy streets, with their magazines of oil and rosin, and their wooden houses touching each other overhead, to be put back was only to insure another plague and another fire, but the manner of rebuilding was in as great dispute as was the origin of the fire. Pepys believed that it was caused by the Dutch, who in the following year did venture into Chatham and burnt several men-of-war as they lay at anchor there; but the popular idea was that it was caused by the French and the Roman Catholics, and there were plenty ready to swear that they had seen foreigners kindling the flames in fresh places by throwing fire-balls into the houses. Some said it was done by the Puritans, and very few appear to have accepted the theory, probably the true one, that it was caused by the over-heating of a baker's oven.

Christopher Wren began his work by having the ruins cleared away. It was no easy task, especially as every now and then the flames would break out anew when the air reached the cellars where they had been smouldering. But it was a mere matter of necessity, as until this was done it was not possible to pass to and fro or take the necessary levels and measurements. He also repaired a portion of the west end of S. Paul's, which best permitted it, for divine service. It was employment enough for one man, but as the evenings grew longer, in the intervals of elaborating his plans for the new city, he returned to the Royal Society and attended all its meetings.

Improvements in building naturally occupied much of the Society's attention. Mr. Hooke produced a scheme for a better method of brick-making;[1] new models for the London granaries were required, and Wren gave an account of those at Dantzic.

On April 24, 1667, his uncle, the Bishop of Ely, died, at the age of eighty-one, at Ely House, in Holborn, which had probably been his chief abode, though he left it on occasions for the work of his diocese and for the consecration of the chapel at Pembroke Hall. Back to his well-loved University, and to the resting-place he had prepared for himself underneath the altar of the chapel, the Bishop's remains were slowly borne during the first bright days of May, attended by 'his children, his alliance, and his family.' The Heralds' College conducted the funeral with full dignity and solemnity. When they reached Cambridge the Vice-Chancellor and the whole university met the procession, which was headed by Rouge Dragon, Pursuivant-at-arms, carrying the silver-gilt Crozier, and Norroy, King-at-arms, carrying the silver-gilt Mitre, both of which, as well as a pair of massive silver altar candlesticks, the Bishop had provided a year before. On May 9, with the same attendance,

---

[1] The bricks, which were temporarily used in the building of S. Paul's, were of so good a quality that Richard Jennings, Wren's master carpenter, bought and transported them by water to Henley-on-Thames (his native town), and with them built a house a mile from Henley, which, bearing the name of 'Badgemore,' is still to be seen. The bricks of which it is built are often admired.

which included 'twenty-four scholars of S. John's, Peter House, and Pembroke who were his relations,'[1] the coffin was borne to Pembroke Chapel from the Registry, at the end of the Regent's Walk, where it had lain in state for two days, and after Evening Service had been said was laid in a 'coffin of one fair whole stone,' in the vault of the chapel. Dr. Pearson pronounced a Latin oration over it, recalling the chief events of the Bishop's long and troubled life, describing his high-minded character, his resolute self-denial, and contrasting his conduct in never seeking, or by the least word asking, for promotion, but rather being besought to accept it, with those who gaped for church preferment, and rather snatched honours than received them. Dr. Pearson dwelt on his liberality to the University, on his never enriching his family out of the revenues of the sees he had ruled; and paid a warm tribute to the courage and faith with which he had fought for the Church, and either alone, or amongst very few, had understood her discipline and dared to revive it.

Of the four sons who survived the Bishop, Matthew, the eldest, early attracted notice by an answer to Harrington's 'Commonwealth of Oceana' and by a pamphlet 'Monarchy asserted,' a vindication of a former work written in 1659. He was highly thought of by the Royalists, and was a member of the Parliament which met in 1661. He was Lord Clarendon's secretary, remained loyal to him during his unmerited disgrace, and was then taken by the Duke of York as

[1] *Desiderata Curiosa*, p. 545. Peck.

his secretary. Matthew remained with the Duke until 1672; when he died and was buried in the vault at Pembroke Chapel. He had taken a share in most of the political events of his day, always with honour and credit. Thomas, the next brother, left the profession of medicine, received holy orders, and was given the Rectory of Littlebury in Essex by his father; a preferment that he held until his death in 1680. Bishop Wren also made him Archdeacon of Ely. He was a great musician and a member of the Royal Society. The two younger sons, Charles and William, were both Oxford scholars, and received degrees at the Restoration. Charles sat for Cambridge in the Parliament of 1685, called by James II. on his accession. All these three younger sons received degrees in 1660, with many others who had been ejected by the Parliamentary Visitors in 1648-9. William Wren, who was made a knight, was a barrister of the Middle Temple, and enjoyed the questionable advantage of Judge Jeffreys' acquaintance. Jeffreys, then Lord Chancellor, writing to Pepys[1] in 1687, says:—

'My most Hon^{ed} Friend,—The bearer, Capt. Wren, came to mee this evening, with a strong fancy that a recommendation of myne might at least entitle him to your favourable reception; His civillities to my brother and his relation to honest Will Wren, and you know who else, emboldens me to offer my request on his behalfe. I hope he has served our M^r. well, and is capable of being an object of the King's favour in his request; however, I am sure I

[1] Pepys' *Diary*, vol. v. p. 326.

shall be excused for this impertinency, because I will gladly, in my way, embrace all opportunities wherein I may manifest myselfe to be what I here assure you I am, Sir,

'Your most entirely affectionate
'Friend and Servant,
'JEFFREYS, C.'

William Wren died in 1689 and was buried in the Temple Church. There is no mention of the marriage of any of the Bishop's children, and respecting the daughters I can find no record whatever, so it seems that that branch of the Wren family died out. Captain Wren was probably one of the Durham Wrens, or of those who lived at Withibrook in Warwickshire and are mentioned by Dugdale.

CHAPTER VII.

1668-1673.

PATCHING S. PAUL'S—SANCROFT'S LETTERS—WREN'S EXAMINATION OF S. PAUL'S—SALISBURY CATHEDRAL—LONDON AS IT MIGHT HAVE BEEN—LETTER TO FAITH COGHILL—WREN MARRIES HER—TEMPLE BAR—S. MARY-LE-BOW—ARTILLERY COMPANY—GUNPOWDER USED TO REMOVE RUINS.

Methinks already from this chymic flame,
    I see a city of more precious mold,
Rich as the town which gives the Indies name,
    With silver pav'd, and all divine with gold.

Already, labouring with a mighty fate,
    She shakes the rubbish from her mounting brow,
And seems to have renewed her charter's date,
    Which heaven will till the death of time allow.
Dryden, *Annus Mirabilis*, ccxciii.

CHAPTER VII.

AFTER the death of Bishop Wren, Christopher was a frequent attendant at the Royal Society, where several experiments were made of raising weights by means of gunpowder, a matter which Wren was anxious to investigate before trying to remove the mass of ruins which had been S. Paul's. Much very tedious work of carting away rubbish and opening roadways still pressed on Wren and his assistants before even the necessary levels could be taken and adjusted or any building could be begun.

In spite of Wren's previous statement, and that of Evelyn and Sancroft, in spite of the immense additional damage which the conflagration had caused, attempts were still made to patch up the remains of S. Paul's Cathedral.

As has been said, something was done in order to make it possible to hold Divine Service in the ruins, and there Sancroft ministered, and there possibly he preached before the King on the occasion of the solemn fast held for the fire on October 10, 1666.[1] Parts of the sermon rise to real eloquence, and he admonishes King Charles and his luxurious Court

---

[1] 'Lex Ignea, or the School of Righteousness.'—*Life of Sancroft*, vol. ii. p. 355. Doyley.

with singular courage and directness. So matters remained with the Cathedral until the spring of 1668.

Wren was at Oxford, delivering his Astronomy Lectures, when he received the following letter from the Dean of S. Paul's:[1]

'What you whispered in my ear, at your last coming hither, is now come to pass. Our work at the west end of S. Paul's is fallen about our ears. Your quick eye discerned the walls and pillars gone off from their perpendiculars and I believe other defects too, which are now exposed to every common observer. About a week since, we being at work about the third pillar from the west end on the south side, which we had new cased with stone, where it was most defective almost up to the chapiter, a great weight falling from the high wall, so disabled the vaulting of the side aisle by it, that it threatened a sudden ruin so visibly that the workmen presently removed, and the next night the whole pillar fell, and carried scaffolds and all to the very ground.

'This breach has discovered to all that look on it two great defects in Inigo Jones' work; one that his new case of stone in the upper walls (massy as it is) was not set upon the upright of the pillars, but upon the core of the groins of the vaulting; the other that there were no keystones at all to tie it to the old work; and all this being very heavy with the Roman ornaments on the top of it, and being already

[1] *Life of Sancroft*, vol. i. p. 141. Doyley.

so far gone outwards, cannot possibly stand long. In fine, it is the opinion of all men, that we can proceed no farther at the west end. What we are to do next is the present deliberation, in which you are so absolutely and indispensably necessary to us that we can do nothing, resolve on nothing without you.' . .
'You will think fit, I know, to bring with you those excellent draughts and designs you formerly favoured us with ; and, in the mean time, till we enjoy you here, consider what to advise that may be for the satisfaction of his Majesty and the whole nation, an obligation so great and public, that it must be acknowledged by better hands than those of
'Your affectionate Friend and Servant,
'W. SANCROFT.'

Wren seems to have been unable to come up to London, and to have written an answer to Dean Sancroft reiterating his opinion, while the attempt at repairs continued.

At the beginning of July Sancroft wrote to him again :—

Sir,—Yesterday my Lords of Canterbury, London, and Oxford met on purpose to hear your letter read once more, and to consider what is now to be done in order to the repairs of S. Paul's. They unanimously resolved, that it is fit immediately to attempt something, and that, without you, they can do nothing. I am therefore commanded to give you an invitation hither in his Grace's name, and the rest of the commissioners, with all speed, that we may prepare something to be proposed to his Majesty (the design of such a quire, at least as may be a congruous part of a greater and more magnificent work to follow); and then, for the procuring of contributions to defray this, we are so sanguine as not to doubt of it, if we could but once resolve what we would do, and what that would cost; so that the only part of your letter we demur to, is the method you propound of declaring first what money we would bestow, and then designing something just of that expense: for quite otherwise—the way their lordships resolve upon, is to frame a design, handsome and noble, and suitable to all the ends of it, and to the reputation of the city and the nation; and to take it for granted that money will be had to accomplish it: or, however, to let it lie by, till we have before us a prospect of so much as may reasonably encourage us to begin.

'Thus far I thought good to prepare you for what will be said to you when you come, that you may not be surprised with it: and, if my summons prevail not, my lord the Bishop of Oxford hath undertaken to give it you warmer, *ore tenus*,[1] the next week, when he intends to be with you, if, at least, you be not come towards us before he arrives, which would be a very agreeable surprise to us all, and especially to your very affectionate, humble Servant,

'W. SANCROFT.'

Wren obeyed this intreaty, came up from Oxford,

---

[1] i.e. by word of mouth.

THE STATE OF S. PAUL'S. 169

made a thorough examination of the Cathedral, and wrote a report for the commissioners.

'What time and weather,' he says, 'had left entire in the old and art in the new repaired parts of this great pile of S. Paul's, the calamity of the fire hath so weakened and defaced, that it now appears like some antique ruin of two thousand years' continuance, and to repair it sufficiently will be like the mending of Argo-nairs,[1] scarce anything at last will be left of the old.' He enumerates the various 'decays' of the building from the date of the fire in Queen Elizabeth's reign which burnt the whole roof and caused 'the spreading out of the walls above ten inches from their true perpendicular'—up to the last fire, of which he says—'The second ruins are they that have put the restoration past remedy, the effects of which I shall briefly enumerate.

'First, the portico is nearly deprived of that excellent beauty and strength which time alone and weather could have no more overthrown than the natural rocks ; so great and good were the materials, and so skilfully were they laid after a true Roman manner. But so impatient is Portland stone of fire that many tons are scaled off and the columns flawed quite through.'

Then follows an account of the injuries to the rest of the building, but as they have been already touched on in the extracts from Evelyn's Diary and Sancroft's letters, they shall not be repeated here.

[1] Probably a misprint for 'Argo-navis,' referring to the frequent repairs of the Argo.

'Having shown in part,' he continues, 'the deplorable condition of our patient, we are to consult of the cure, if possible art may effect it. And herein we must imitate the physician, who, when he finds a total decay of nature, bends his skill to a palliative to give respite for the better settlement of the estate of the patient. The question is then, where best to begin this sort of practice; that is to make a new quire for present use.'

The only part of the cathedral where this could be safely and easily done was at the eastern end of the nave :—

'Since,' he said, 'we cannot mend this great ruin, we will not disfigure it, but that it shall still have its full motives to work, if possible upon this or the next ages: and yet prove so cheap, that between three and four thousand pounds shall effect it all in one summer.

'And, having with this ease obtained a present cathedral, there will be time to consider of a more durable and noble fabric, to be made in the place of the lower and eastern parts of the Church, when the minds of men, now contracted to many objects of necessary charge, shall by God's blessing be more widened, after a happy restoration, both of the buildings, and the wealth of the city and nation. In the meantime to derive, if not a stream, yet some little drills of charity this way; or, at least, to preserve that already obtained from being diverted, it may not prove ill-advised to seem to begin something of the new fabric. But I confess this cannot well be put in execution without taking down all that part of the ruin; which whether it be yet seasonable to do we must leave to our superiors.'

Many meetings and much discussion ensued, and Wren's opinion at last prevailed; the King issued an order in council for taking down the walls at the east end, the old choir, and the tower, and for clearing the ground in order to lay a fresh foundation. While this was being done, Wren prepared sketches and designs for a new S. Paul's. He had also an engagement out of London: his friend Dr. Seth Ward, the Bishop of Salisbury, an active member of the Royal Society, asked Wren to survey his beautiful cathedral, which had suffered much in the civil wars, and lately by lightning and tempest.

Though the architecture of the cathedral was not of the kind which he considered the best, Wren had too fine a taste, too quick an eye for beauty of form, not to admire it heartily, and in his report he pronounced that 'the whole pile was large and magnificent, justly accounted one of the best patterns of the age wherein it was built.' He praised the pillars and mouldings, 'the stately and rich plainness' to which the architect had trusted. He made a thorough examination of the whole, especially the spire, which had declined to the south-west, and had caused great alarm. Wren was of opinion that the architect had not laid as sufficient foundations, especially under the pillars, as he should have done, considering the marshy nature of the soil, the frequent inundations, the great weight that the pillars had to bear, and that they themselves were too slight, particularly those under the spire.

To prevent further mischief to the spire, he ordered some timbers in it, and in the tower, to be cut away, and put in bands and braces of iron wrought by anchor smiths who were accustomed to great work for ships. He then had a plummet dropped to the pavement, from the highest possible part of the spire, the height of which he reckoned at 404 feet from the ground, to see exactly what the decline was, and ordered this trial to be repeated at certain times to see if the decline increased.

When, nearly 200 years later, Mr. Wyatt made the trial, he found that the decline was unaltered, so true had Wren's science proved.

Both this year and the previous one had, so far as London was concerned, been taken up by the business of levelling, marking out streets, and adjusting the claims of such as had had houses in the city before the fire. Wren had laid before the King and Parliament a model of the city as he proposed to build it, with full explanations of the details of the design; the model probably does not exist, but the ground-plan has been preserved, and suggests a London very different to the present one.

The street leading up Ludgate Hill, instead of being the confined, winding approach to S. Paul's that it now is, even its crooked picturesqueness marred by the viaduct that cuts all the lines of the Cathedral, gradually widened as it approached S. Paul's, and divided itself into two great streets, ninety feet wide at the least, which ran on either side of the Cathedral, leaving a large open space in which it stood. Of the two streets, one ran parallel with the river until it reached the Tower, and the other led to the Exchange, which Wren meant to be the centre of the city, standing in a great piazza, to which ten streets, each sixty feet wide, converged, and around which were placed the Post Office, the Mint, the Excise Office, the Goldsmiths' Hall, and the Ensurance, forming the outside of the piazza. The smallest streets were to be thirty feet wide, 'excluding all narrow, dark alleys without thoroughfares, and courts.'

The churches were to occupy commanding positions along the principal thoroughfares, and to be 'designed according to the best forms for capacity and hearing, adorned with useful porticoes and lofty ornamental towers and steeples in the greater parishes. All churchyards, gardens, and unnecessary vacuities, and all trades that use great fires or yield noisome smells to be placed out of town.'

He intended that the churchyards should be carefully planted and adorned, and be a sort of girdle round the town, wishing them to be an ornament to the city, and also a check upon its growth. To burials within the walls of the town he strongly objected, and the experience derived from the year of the plague confirmed his judgment. No gardens are mentioned in the plan, for he had provided, as he thought, sufficiently for the healthiness of the town by his wide streets and numerous open spaces for markets.

Gardening in towns was an art little considered in his days, and contemporary descriptions show us that 'vacuities' were speedily filled with heaps of dust and refuse.

The London bank of the Thames was to be lined with a broad quay, along which the halls of the city companies were to be built, with suitable warehouses in between for the merchants, to vary the effect of the edifices.

The little stream whose name survives in *Fleet* Street was to be brought to light, cleansed, and made serviceable as a canal one hundred and twenty feet wide, running much in the line of the present Holborn Viaduct.[1]

These were the main features of Christopher Wren's scheme, and had he been allowed to accomplish it, we can imagine what the effect of London might have been without its noisome smells, without its dark crooked lanes, without its worst smoke, its river honoured not only with the handsome quay it has at length obtained, but with a line of beautiful buildings and fair spires, and above all S. Paul's, with an ample space around it, giving free play to its grand proportions. Wren, with a perfect knowledge of his own powers, which he considered as dispassionately, and knew as accurately as any matter of mathematical

[1] In 1672 a bridge, with a beautiful arch resembling those that cross the canals at Venice, was built over 'the Ditch,' opposite Bridewell Hospital. One or two other bridges were built, and the stream made navigable, but apparently not 'cleansed,' which in time rendered it a nuisance. The bridges were taken down and the stream reduced to a drain in 1765.—*Ann. Reg.*, 1765, p. 136.

science, was ready to undertake and perform his scheme to the uttermost.

The difficulties were however considerable : there were the endless quarrels about property, the reluctance to part with an old site, and, chief difficulty of all, the utmost hurry of rebuilding in order to house the people before the approaching winter.

Pepys[1] says that in April 1667 :—

'Moorefields have houses two stories high in them, and paved streets, the city having let leases for seven years, which will be very much to the hindering of the building of the city ; but it was considered that the streets cannot be passable in London till the whole street be built; and several that had got ground of the city for charity to build sheds on, had got the trick presently to sell that for 60*l.* which did not cost them 20*l.* to put up ; and so the city being very poor in stock, thought it as good to do it themselves and therefore let leases for seven years of the ground in Moorefields.'

Thus Wren had by no means clear ground on which to work, and an opportunity was forfeited, which, *absit omen*, may never recur, of making London one of the beautiful cities of the world.

Important sanitary improvements were, however, made : the houses were not built of wood ; the principal streets were less narrow ; and, above all, the lingering contagion was burnt away. Nothing less would probably have availed ; but the fire was a cleansing one, and

---

[1] *Diary*, vol. iv. p. 8.

left behind it this blessing, that though more than two hundred years have elapsed the plague has not, as yet, reappeared.

The Custom House of London was one of the first buildings to be restored, and Wren began it in 1668. It was a stately stone edifice, built in three sides of a square, with an open court in front. The same fate befell this building which had overtaken its predecessor; in 1719 it was burnt down.

Besides all these architectural and scientific cares, Wren had business of his own on hand, and was at this time engaged to be married to a lady four years younger than himself, whom probably he had known for some time. His bride was Faith, daughter of Sir Thomas Coghill and Elizabeth his wife, who lived at Bletchingdon in Oxfordshire. Sir Thomas was sheriff of the county in 1633, and was knighted at Woodstock in that year, the same in which King Charles was crowned in Scotland. Sir Thomas was a grandson of Marmaduke Coghill,[1] of Coghill, Knaresborough. He married, in 1622, Elizabeth Sutton, the heiress of Horsell and some lands in Surrey. Faith, their daughter, was born on March 17, 1636, and baptized in the same month at Bletchingdon by her relation the Rev. John Viell, the then rector. It seems likely that Wren made her acquaintance while both were children when staying with his sister Susan and her husband,

---

[1] The Coghills of Glen Barrahane, county Cork, are descended from the elder branch of this family. Captain Coghill, who died with Lieutenant Melville, having carried off the colours from the battle of Isandula, January 1879, was the eldest son of the present head of the family.

Dr. William Holder, at Bletchingdon Rectory. It may have been Faith who comforted him when, on June 3, 1656, they laid Dean Wren in the chancel of Bletchingdon Church.

One letter to Faith Coghill from her lover, exists among the curious autographs of the 'Parentalia,'[1] its delicate, finished and yet firm writing, eminently characteristic of Christopher Wren: it is as follows—

'Madam,—The artificer having never before mett with a drowned watch, like an ignorant physician has been soe long about the cure that he hath made me very unquiet that your commands should be soe long deferred; however, I have sent the watch at last and envie the felicity of it, that it should be soe neer your side, and soe often enjoy your Eye, and be consulted by you how your time shall passe while you employ your hand in your excellent workes. But have a care of it, for I put such a Spell into it that every Beating of the Ballance will tell you 'tis the pulse of my Heart which labours as much to serve you and more trewly than the watch; for the watch I believe will sometimes lie, and sometimes perhaps be idle and unwilling to goe, having received so much injury by being drenched in that briny bath, that I dispair it should ever be a trew servant to you more. But as for me (unlesse you drown me too in my teares) you may be confident I shall never cease to be,

'Your most affectionate humble servant,
'CHR. WREN.

'June 14.

[1] Never before printed.

'I have put the watch in a box that it might take noe harm, and wrapt it about with a little leather, and that it might not jog, I was fain to fill up the corners either with a few shavings or wast paper.'

On December 7, 1669, Christopher Wren and Faith Coghill were married in the Temple Church in London. Of their married life there is absolutely no record; they probably lived chiefly in London, as Wren had a house in Scotland Yard, which went with the office of Surveyor-General.

One of Wren's early works was the rebuilding, on a somewhat larger scale, of the Royal Exchange. 'Charles II. went to the Exchange with his kettle-drums and trumpets to lay the first stone of the new building of the Exchange on the 23rd of October 1667.'[1] Wren's own wish had been, as has been said, to make it the nave or centre of the town, in which case he meant to contrive it after the form of a Roman Forum with double porticoes. Thwarted in this, he restored it as much as possible to what it had previously been, replacing the statue of Sir Thomas Gresham, the only thing in the building uninjured by the Fire. It is curious that this restoration should have begun just a hundred years from the time when Queen Elizabeth was feasted by Sir Thomas Gresham at his house, visited the new building, and caused it to be proclaimed 'the Royal Exchange' by the sound of the trumpet.

The rebuilding was very quickly performed, though

[1] Pepys' *Diary*, vol iv. p. 241.

at considerable cost.[1] Readers of the *Spectator*[2] will remember Addison's fine description of the Exchange, and 'the grand scene of business which gave him an infinite variety of solid and substantial entertainments.'

Next came Temple Bar, which was begun in 1670, and finished in 1672. It was built of Portland stone, and had in its four niches statues of James I. and Anne of Denmark on the west side, Charles I. and Charles II. on the other.[3] Blackened and defiled as it was, and disfigured by the neighbouring houses, it was one of the picturesque, characteristic buildings of London, now disappearing with alarming rapidity, and had seen many a generation pass in triumph or in sorrow under its archway. The thanksgiving for the Prince of Wales's recovery (1872) was the last historical spectacle with which Temple Bar was connected. On that occasion the City was moved to wipe off some of the smoke of two hundred years, and to let Temple Bar be seen somewhat as it must have been when the great architect finished it, as the entrance to a city which, in spite of all drawbacks, might be fairly called his creation.

Wren attempted to prosecute his design for the quay along the northern bank of the Thames, but the ground was being rapidly encroached upon by buildings, some few of which were tolerable, but the greater

---

[1] This building was destroyed by fire 1838, and rebuilt from designs by Mr. Tite 1844.

[2] *Spectator*, vol. i. No. 69.

[3] They were the best work of John Bushnell, an eccentric and half-crazy sculptor, who died in 1701.

part unsightly. Various interests;—the immense water traffic, doubled, one can believe, at a time when the city streets were still impassable; the uncertain support given by the King—all combined to defeat his plan. Could he now walk along that glorious achievement the Embankment, what would not his feelings be on seeing the hideous buildings which it has revealed!

The Surveyor-General's office was one which entailed endless work. There was not a street laid down, hardly a house built, in any part of the town, without the surveyor being first consulted;—now about 'a parcel of ground bought by Colonel Panton' (the present Panton Street, S.W.); now about the houses pulled down for the safety of Whitehall during the Fire. —Into every case Wren made careful inquiry, visiting the places himself, and insisting on the buildings being of stone or brick, with proper paving in the streets, and having a due regard to health.

In spite of his care several wretched buildings were put up in places which, as a few surviving names testify, were then fields near the City.

When Wren found that the owners persisted in erecting such shabby buildings he presented a petition to the King, as follows:—

'To the King's Most Excellent Majesty. The humble petition of Christopher Wren, sheweth. That there are divers buildings of late erected, and many foundations laid, and more contrived in Dog's Fields, Windmill Fields, and the fields adjoining to Soe

Hoe,[1] and several other places without the suburbs of London and Westminster; the builders whereof have no grant nor allowance from Your Majesty, and have therefore been prohibited and hindered by your petitioner as much as in him lieth. Yet, notwithstanding, they proceed to erect small and mean habitations which will prove only receptacles for the poorer sort, and the offensive trades, to the annoyance of the better inhabitants, the damage of the parishes already too much burthened with poor, the rendering the government of these parts more unmanageable, the great hindrance of perfecting the city buildings, and others allowed by Your Majesty's broad seal; the choking up the air of Your Majesty's palace and park, and the houses of the nobility; the infecting or total loss of the waters which by many expenseful drains and conduits, have formerly been derived from these fields to Your Majesty's palace of Whitehall and to the mewes; the manifest decay of which waters (upon complaint of your serjeant plumber) the office of Your Majesty's works by frequent views and experiments have found.

'May it, therefore, please Your Majesty to issue a royal proclamation, to put stop to these growing inconveniences and to hinder the buildings which are not already or shall not be licensed by Your Majesty's grant; and effectually to empower your petitioner to restrain the same or otherways to consider of the

---

[1] 'Soe Hoe' became a favourite residence. In November 1689, Evelyn came up 'with his family to winter at Soho in the Great Square.' Some handsome houses are still standing.

premises as in Your Majesty's wisdom shall seem most expedient.

'And your Petitioner, &c.'

The petition was considered by the King in council, a proclamation was issued, and full powers were given to the surveyor, backed by commands that he should take effectual care that the proclamation was obeyed. This Wren was very ready to do : with all his gentleness and courtesy he had inherited much of Bishop Wren's firmness, and had no intention of swerving from his point.

The churches of the City began to rise gradually. Pepys says :[1]—

' It is observed, and is true, in the late fire of London, that the fire burned just as many parish churches as there were hours from the beginning to the end of the fire ; and next that there were just as many churches left standing as there were taverns left standing in the rest of the City that was not burned, being, I think, thirteen in all of each : which is pretty to observe.'

There has been much dispute as to whether or not Wren repaired S. Sepulchre's Church. Mr. Elmes and others declare that he repaired it in 1671, but Mr. Hoby, one of its churchwardens, who made a careful study of all the parchments and papers belonging to S. Sepulchre's, gives it as his deliberate opinion that—

' The church was not destroyed, but very much injured, by the Fire of London, in 1666. The inhabitants

[1] *Diary*, Jan. 31, 1667-8.

would not wait until Sir C. Wren could attend to them, but repaired their own church, and did it so badly that a long time elapsed before he would grant the certificate necessary to enable them to obtain the money from the commissioners.'[1]

As has been said, such unauthorised building and patching took place pretty frequently, and all that recent researches have brought to light goes to prove that Wren had very little to do with S. Sepulchre's.

S. Mary le Bow, with its proverbial bells,[2] was begun in this year and finished five years later, on a very old foundation. The first S. Mary's was built by William the Conqueror,[3] on marshy land, and stood upon arches of stone, whence the church took the name of S. Maria de Arcubus or le Bow. The 'great bell of Bow' was, in 1469, ordered by the common council to be rung at nine o'clock every evening, and money was left for this object; when the church was burnt in the Great Fire it had twelve very melodious bells hung in its steeple. When Sir Christopher came to rebuild the church he found an older foundation to work upon than even that in 1100. In clearing the ground he came upon a foundation firm enough to build upon, which on examination proved to be the 'walls, with windows and pavement, of a Roman temple.' Upon these walls he built the body of the church, but for its beautiful steeple it was necessary to buy the site of an

---

[1] *Restoration of the Church of St. Sepulchre, London.* A. Billing.

[2] It is said that in the children's game of 'Oranges and Lemons, say the bells of S. Clement's, &c.' the best peals of bells in London are enumerated. I do not know the date of the game.

[3] *Repertorium*, vol. i. p. 437-440. Newcourt.

old house and to advance about forty feet to the line of the street. Here the workmen dug through about eighteen feet of made earth, and then, to Wren's surprise and their own, came to a Roman causeway of rough stone firmly cemented, about four feet thick, underneath which lay the London clay.

With this foundation Wren was content and built up what has ever ranked as one of his finest churches. A good judge of architecture has pronounced that the steeple is 'beyond all doubt the most elegant building of its class erected since the Reformation .... there is a play of light and shade, a variety of outline, and an elegance of detail, which it would be very difficult to match in any other steeple.'[1]

The Arches Court of Canterbury derived its name from this church, where, until the fire, its sittings were held. The court then sat at Exeter House in the Strand, then at Doctors' Commons, and finally in Westminster Hall.

The vane which completes the spire is the City dragon, with a cross on either wing, curiously chased in gilt copper.

The ancient Church of S. Christopher le Stocks in Threadneedle Street suffered severely in the Fire, only the mere shell of the building remaining; it had been made a storehouse for a quantity of papers hastily rescued from some merchant's office and placed in S. Christopher's, where they perished and greatly damaged the church. It had been lately repaired and was endowed with 20*l.* in trust ' for a minister to read divine

---

[1] *Hist. of Modern Architecture.* Fergusson, pp. 306-307.

service there daily at 6 o'clock in the morning for ever. 50*s.* each yearly to the clerk and the sexton for their attendance, and 5*l.* yearly to provide for lights in winter time.' In 1671, Wren finished the repairs of the church, carefully preserving its pinnacled Gothic tower; in 1696 he further adorned the interior. It is curious that the first church which came under Wren's hands should have been one dedicated to his patron saint; curious also that this should have been the first of the churches destroyed by those who should have been their guardians. S. Christopher's was literally sacrificed to Mammon; it was destroyed for the enlargement of the Bank of England in 1781.

In 1669 Wren appears in a new character as a member of the Honourable Artillery Company. He was admitted at their festival on August 17, when the company marched in state to a church in Broad Street, probably one of the many temporary ones put up after the Fire, and rewarded Dr. Waterhouse for his sermon with three of the newly-coined guinea pieces. A great banquet in the Clothworkers' Hall in Mincing Lane, where the Duke of York, Prince Rupert, the Archbishop of Canterbury and many other distinguished persons were present, concluded the festival.[1] It is hardly conceivable that Wren could have found time to be more than an honorary member, but scattered notices here and there of observations made when 'firing off my piece' seem to point to his having attended the drills of the company.

[1] *Hist. of the Honourable Artillery Company.* Captain Raikes, vol. i. p. 194.

One wishes there was a portrait extant of Sir Christopher in his uniform, wearing the red-plumed high hat which appeared on gala days!

In 1673 Wren resigned the Savilian astronomy professorship, to which the pressure of his architectural work made it impossible he should any longer attend. No doubt it was with great regret that he gave up the post, with all its curious speculations, its boundless possibilities of discovery, and turned himself from the study of the heavens to the dust and turmoil, the endless difficulties and petty quarrels, which thwarted him at every step of his London labours.

In truth, the pressure of business was enormous. Not a moment could be spared while the population of the City had neither churches, places of traffic, nor houses to dwell in; and the architect, whose plan had been marred, had to do the best he could in the midst of every kind of incongruity.

The futile attempts to patch up S. Paul's were in 1673 at last abandoned, and Wren ordered the ground to be cleared that new foundations might be laid. A great mass of material for building had had to be disposed of while the repairs were going on.

The Archbishop of Canterbury, the Bishops of London, Winchester, and Oxford, and the Lord Mayor, were commissioners for the repair of S. Paul's; from them Wren obtained an order that—

'The clerk of the works shall be required to dispose of
and sell the stone, chalk, timber and free stone for,
and towards, the rebuilding of the parochial churches
and to *no other use whatsoever*, as he shall be directed,

at merchantable rates to the masons and carpenters that build the said churches by order of Sir Leoline Jenkins (judge of the Admiralty Court), Dr. Sancroft, and Dr. Wren, or any two of them.'

The money thus collected was put aside for the fabric of the Cathedral.

Though much of the old material was removed in this manner, and yet not diverted from its proper purpose, the ground was by no means clear. Wren, appointed under the Great Seal, architect of S. Paul's, and one of the commissioners in the new commission for its rebuilding, had to take down by degrees what portions of the old building were still standing.

Warped and cracked as they were, the walls, eighty feet high and five thick, were yet strong enough to make the process of pulling down both difficult and tedious. Wren determined to avail himself of the knowledge he had acquired in the Royal Society's recent experiments in raising weights by means of gunpowder. Houses, it is true, had been blown up in several places during the Fire in order to protect the Tower of London and Whitehall, but the use of gunpowder to raise a definite weight, and throw it a fixed distance and no farther, was a novel experiment. When the labourers reached at last the old central tower, the walls of which were two hundred feet high, they were afraid to go up to the top, as they had done elsewhere, and work with their pickaxes, while those below shovelled away the stones and mortar that they threw down into separate heaps.

This was the time for Wren's experiment.

With great precautions, and the use of eighteen pounds of gunpowder only, he blew up the northwestern angle of the tower, so contriving it that, while he raised more than three thousand tons weight, it was not scattered and no damage was done, though the shock made the neighbours imagine it to be an earthquake.

Encouraged by this success, Wren had another mine prepared, but unluckily was obliged to go out of town himself and to leave it in the charge of his next officer.

The man, thinking to improve upon his master, increased the quantity of powder, caused an explosion which shot stones far and wide, and though no lives were lost, terrified the City, all the more that an old superstition declared that the tower of S. Paul's and the City of London would fall together.

Forbidden, owing to the panic thus caused, the use of this modern method, Wren betook himself to ancient times, and devised a gigantic battering ram, with a great spike at one end. Thirty men, fifteen on each side, worked the ram against one place in the wall, Wren watching and encouraging them when, disheartened by a day's work without visible result, they were ready to give up in despair. On the second day the wall fell.

Wren made great use of this machine and 'pleased himself that he had recovered so notable and ancient an engine.'

CHAPTER VIII.

1672-1677.

BIRTH OF HIS ELDEST SON—S. STEPHEN'S, WALBROOK—S. BENNET FINK—PLANS FOR S. PAUL'S—THE EXCAVATIONS—SON CHRISTOPHER BORN—DEATH OF FAITH, LADY WREN—SECOND MARRIAGE—CITY CHURCHES—THE MONUMENT—TOMB OF CHARLES I.—REMAINS OF THE LITTLE PRINCES IN THE TOWER.

K. Rich. But didst thou see them dead?
Tyr. I did, my lord.
K. Rich.   And buried, gentle Tyrrel?
Tyr. The chaplain of the Tower hath buried them,
    But where, to say the truth, I do not know.
                        Richard III., Act 4, scene 3.

CHAPTER VIII.

EARLY in October, 1672, Christopher Wren's eldest son was born, and baptized by the name of Gilbert, at S. Martin's-in-the-Fields, a very different-looking building from the present S. Martin's with its stately portico. Wren and his wife lived in the house in Scotland Yard, and, avoiding the uneven, difficult streets, could daily go by water, then the favourite way of transit for a Londoner, to examine and superintend his works in the city. Later on Wren built himself a little house of red bricks in the yard of the Falcon Inn at Southwark, and watched from its window the progress of S. Paul's and of his other buildings in the city.

Besides the churches already begun, three new ones were taken in hand that year. S. Mary-at-Hill[1] was only partially destroyed by the fire. Upon it Wren first tried his plan of a domed roof, and succeeded in making it, at any rate within, a beautiful little church. S. Michael's, Cornhill, of which only the tower was left

[1] To this church and parish belongs the honourable distinction of having successfully resisted the encroachments of the railway company which recently attempted to desecrate the church. 'The City Church and Churchyard Protection Society'—alas! that any such society should be needed—which fought this battle, must have the best wishes of any biographer of Christopher Wren.

standing, was rebuilt that year; its situation threw a great difficulty in the architect's way, as it could only be lit from one side; this difficulty Wren overcame and produced an interior [1] equally light and good. The tower was taken down in 1722, and rebuilt from designs of Wren's. These designs were taken from the tower of Magdalen College at Oxford, and instance Wren's power of producing a bold, rich effect in a style of architecture altogether foreign to his taste.

Perhaps the most beautiful of all Wren's churches is S. Stephen's, Walbrook, begun at this same time, and finished seven years later. The outside, cramped by its situation, and overshadowed by tall houses, is not handsome, but within, the church is as original as it is graceful and beautiful:—

'The circular dome, placed on an octagonal base supported by eight pillars, was an early, and long a favourite, mode of roofing in the East . . . Wren, however, is the only European architect who availed himself of it . . . . he certainly has produced the most pleasing interior of any Renaissance church which has yet been erected.' [2]

So great was the fame, and such the charm of the building that when the great sculptor Canova [3] visited England, and was asked should he ever wish to return to the country? he answered, 'Yes, that I might again see S. Paul's Cathedral, Somerset House, and S. Stephen's, Walbrook.'

---

[1] The interior has been lately altered.

[2] *History of Modern Architecture.* Fergusson, p. 307.

[3] Antonio Canova, born 1757, died 1822. He had come to England to see the Elgin Marbles.

In the midst of so much work it is not wonderful that, for the moment, Wren's diligent attendance at the Royal Society slackened somewhat, though at the end of 1672 his name occurs among those of the Society who cordially welcomed Isaac Newton to their fellowship. Wren bestowed especial praise on Newton's invention of a refracting telescope. Friends they appear always to have remained, and their dispositions were not unlike, though the travels and varied experiences of Wren's early years had quickened his faculties, and prevented that entire absorption in one idea which is evident from many stories about Isaac Newton. As, for instance, when one of Newton's philosophical friends abroad—

'Sent him a curious prism, at that time a rarity in England, it was taken to the Custom House and Newton claimed it. The officers asked him to set some value upon it that they might regulate the duty. Newton, rating the prism by his own idea of its use and excellence, replied, "The value is so great I cannot ascertain it." They pressed him again to set some estimate on it, but he still replied, "I cannot say what it is worth, for the value is inestimable." The honest Custom House officers took him at his word, and made him pay an exorbitant duty for the prism, which he might have taken away upon only paying a rate according to the weight of the glass!"[1]

[1] *History of the Royal Society*, p. 237. Weld. The anecdote is taken from an article in an old *Gentleman's Magazine*, written professedly by one who knew Sir I. Newton.

The Royal Society was at this time put to serious inconvenience, as more than half of the members failed in paying their weekly money. Wren, who, as might be expected, was one of those who paid most punctually, was re-elected a member of the council, and agreed to serve on a committee for this special matter.

The death of his friend and cousin, Matthew, in the summer of 1672, was a grief to him, as well as a loss to the Royal Society, of which he had been a member from its beginning. On the 20th of November, 1673, Wren received the well-earned honour of knighthood from King Charles at Whitehall. No details of any kind respecting the ceremony are to be found in the chary family record.

S. Bennet Fink, a very graceful and original composition despite the corner into which it was squeezed; and S. Olave's, Jewry, built of brick and stone with a good pinnacled stone tower, were begun at this period, and finished three years later. S. Dionysius, or, as it was commonly called, S. Dionis, Back Church Street, was one of the first completed; its Ionic eastern façade was in Wren's most classical style; the pulpit was carved by Grinling Gibbons. Its tower and steeple, according to a frequent custom of Wren's, were added some years later. S. Dionis has, alas! now been swept away, and its site, where the original church was consecrated in 1288, desecrated.[1] The beautiful little S. Bennet's has shared the same unholy fate. S. George's, Botolph Lane, built also in 1674, a handsome stone

[1] Destroyed 1876.

church with a vaulted roof and good oak fittings, though threatened, still fortunately survives.

Grinling Gibbons, whom Wren continually employed, was introduced to him by Evelyn, who found the young man in a cottage at Deptford carving a copy of Tintoretto's beautiful Crucifixion. Evelyn showed Wren the carving and besought him to give some employment to a man of such genius. This he gladly promised, and accordingly, many a little known city church is adorned with carvings so light and so graceful that it is hard to believe that they are cut out of wood.

Some works in stone Gibbons also did for Sir Christopher, but wood appears to have been the material he preferred. In 1674 Wren had the satisfaction of restoring Le Soeur's [1] beautiful statue of King Charles to its place at Charing Cross. In the Rebellion it had been overthrown by order of the Parliament, who directed that it should be broken up. John Rivet, a brazier in Charing Cross, purchased it, hid it in the vaults of S. Paul's, Covent Garden, and, to divert suspicion, sold bronze medals and knife-handles, professedly made from its metal. After the Restoration, he produced it intact, and, under Wren's direction, it was placed on its present pedestal, which was carved by Gibbons, whose handywork is easily recognised in the free, flowing lines of the deeply-cut carving, much as time, aided by London atmosphere,

[1] Hubert Le Soeur was a pupil of John of Bologna; he came to England in 1630. The statue of Lord Pembroke at Oxford, and that of King Charles, which has Le Soeur's name on the horse's hoof, are all that now remain of his works.

has eaten the very stone away. The poet Waller wrote an epigram[1] on its restoration, which, besides its intrinsic merit, is interesting in connection with the statue :—

> That the first Charles does here in triumph ride,
> See his son reign where he a martyr dy'd;
> And people pay that rev'rence as they pass,
> (Which then he wanted) to the sacred brass,
> Is not th' effect of gratitude alòne,
> To which we owe the statue and the stone.
> But heav'n this lasting monument has wrought,
> That mortals may eternally be taught
> Rebellion, though successful, is but vain,
> And kings so kill'd rise conquerors again:
> This truth the royal image does proclaim
> Loud as the trumpet of surviving Fame.

It was about this period that Wren rebuilt the theatre in Drury Lane, which had fallen a prey to its usual enemy, fire. It was reopened in 1674 with a play whose epilogue was written by Dryden. The 'old theatre in Salisbury Court,' as Horace Walpole calls it, was also built by Wren. During this time Sir Christopher, now formally appointed architect of S. Paul's with a modest salary of 200*l.* a year, had busied himself in designs for the future cathedral. Everyone, whether qualified or not, gave their opinion about the designs. The first, which was 'a fabrick of moderate bulk, but of good proportion, a convenient quire with a vestibule and portico, and a dome conspicuous above the houses,' was planned by Wren at a time when the Cathedral fund was very small, and the chances of increasing it appeared but slender. This design was rejected as deficient in size and grandeur.

[1] On the statue of King Charles I. at Charing Cross in the year 1674. E. Waller.

After this, in order to find out what style of building was really desired, Wren made several sketches 'merely for discourse sake,' and perceiving that the generality had set their hearts upon a large building, he designed one with which he was himself satisfied, considering it 'a design antique and well studied, conformable to the best style of Greek and Roman architecture.' The design was greatly admired by those who understood the matter, and they begged Sir Christopher to let them see it in a model.[1] Wren accordingly made a large one, apparently with his own hands, in wood, with all the intended ornaments properly carved. Its ground plan was that of a Greek cross, the choir was circular, it had a very short nave, and no aisles. Externally there was a handsome portico, one small dome immediately behind it, and over the centre of the cross a larger dome. Within it would have been as beautiful as it was original, with the eight smaller domes, not seen outside, encircling the central dome. The Duke of York on seeing the plan complained much of the absence of side oratories, such as are common in most foreign cathedrals, and insisted upon their being added. Sir Christopher knew that such a change would cramp the building and break the beauty of the design to a degree that went to his heart. He

[1] The model was long preserved in what was called the Trophy Room of S. Paul's. 'It unfortunately has suffered much from neglect, decay, and the uncontrolled mischief of visitors; that which was one of its noblest features, its long stately western portico, has entirely disappeared. The model was lent to and still remains in the Architectural Exhibition at South Kensington, on condition of repairing some of its reparable parts (a condition but imperfectly fulfilled).'—*Annals of S. Paul's Cathedral*, Dean Milman, p. 40.

shed tears in attempting to change the Duke's opinion. The latter was, as ever, obstinate, and the change had to be made.

The outside, with the two hollow curves joining the transepts with the nave, and the two different-sized domes, would probably have been disappointing; but one speaks with diffidence, for this was Sir Christopher's favourite design, the S. Paul's which he told his son he would most cheerfully have accomplished. When the time came for working out the design, it is very likely that he would have remedied many of the defects which critical eyes now see in the model; but no such opportunity ever came. Preparations were indeed made, in May 1674, for a building after this design; but the clergy were startled by the novelty of the plan, the circular choir, and the absence of aisles, and the architect was compelled to give up his cherished scheme. Several designs, none equal to the first, were produced by Sir Christopher, the large central dome appearing in each of them. Upon this feature he had determined, even in the days before the fire, when the old pointed choir still stood.

At length Wren grew weary of criticism and showed his designs no more to the public. King Charles decided on one,[1] and issued a warrant for its erection, stating that the duty on coal [2] amounted to a considerable sum, and saying:—

---

[1] An engraving giving a section of this very curious design is to be found at page 97 of Mr. Longman's exhaustive and interesting *Three Cathedrals dedicated to S. Paul's in London.*

[2] The fourth portion of the tax on coal granted for the public buildings of the City was given for the rebuilding of S. Paul's.

'Among the designs we have particularly pitched on one as well because we found it very artificial, proper and useful as because it was so ordered that it might be built and finished by parts.' The east end was to be begun first. Liberty was left to Wren 'to make some variations rather ornamental than essential as from time to time he should see proper,' and the whole was left to his management.

This design is wholly unlike the present Cathedral, and is inferior to any of Wren's other buildings. 'Artificial' in the modern sense of the word, it undoubtedly is. The west end much resembles old S. Paul's as Inigo Jones left it, and is poor and flat; there is a low flat dome, then a lantern with ribbed vaulting, surmounted by a spire something like S. Bride's, but thin and ungraceful. One feels that Wren must have been disgusted with the design when finished, and could only have done such a thing at a time when his genius was rebuked and harassed by vexatious limitations and interference. Accepted, however, the design was, and Wren, provided with funds and ordered to begin, shook off the fetters which had so cramped him, and by a series of alterations, which certainly reversed the King's order, being essential rather than ornamental, he by degrees worked out the plan of the beautiful S. Paul's which is the crown of London.

No objection seems to have been raised to these changes.

He had a large staff of workmen under him, and an assistant surveyor, John Oliver, who directed the workmen, measured the masons' work, bought in materials, and examined the accounts; a clerk of the works, Laurence Spenser, who overlooked the men, saw that they did their work as directed, and made up the accounts; each of these was paid 100*l.* a year, half as much as the salary of the architect himself; a clerk of the cheque, Thomas Russell, who called over the labourers three times a day, and kept them to their business. Besides these, there was the master-mason,[1] Thomas Strong, the master-builder of S. Stephen's, Walbrook, frequently employed by Wren, and the master-carpenter, Richard Jennings; all were carefully chosen, and were devoted to Sir Christopher, whose great genius, gentle disposition, and steady equable mind made him much beloved and respected.

On June 21, 1675, the first stone of S. Paul's was laid by Sir Christopher and his master-mason, not by King Charles, as is sometimes said.[2]

In the previous year Wren had lost his son Gilbert, who was buried in S. Martin's on March 23. In the February following another son was born and baptized by the name of Christopher. This son survived his father and began the collection of letters, papers, and miscellaneous facts about the Wren family which was afterwards published under the name of 'Parentalia; or, Memoirs of the Wrens.' It is, in truth, little but a heap of materials amongst which each fact has to be sought for and its proper place ascertained.

[1] Thomas was the son of Mr. Valentine Strong, a well-known master-mason of Hertfordshire; his six sons were all engaged in the same trade as himself. *Life of Sir C. Wren*, p. 316. Elmes.

[2] Sir C. Wren gave the mallet and trowel used on this occasion to the Freemasons' lodge of which he was master, then called after his name, now the 'Lodge of Antiquity, No. 21.'

It has been truly said that the accounts of the building of S. Paul's are meagre in the extreme. A little is, however, known. As Wren had foretold, there was much 'to be done in the dark;' the old foundations were not to be trusted, and immense excavations had to be made. In the course of this work, he discovered 'graves of several ages and fashions, in strata or layers of earth, one above another, from the British and Roman times.'

The 'Parentalia' describes 'a row of Saxon graves, the sides lined with chalk stones, below were British graves, where were found ivory and wooden pins of a hard wood, seemingly box, about six inches long; it seems the bodies were only wrapped up and pinned in woollen shrouds, which being consumed the pins remained entire. In the same row and deeper were Roman urns intermixed.'

Below this was hard 'pot-earth,' which Wren thought would be sufficiently firm to bear the great weight about to be laid upon it, but to ascertain its depth he had dry wells dug, and found it very unequal, in one place hardly four feet; he searched lower and found loose sand, then sand and shells; he speaks of them as sea shells, but it is now thought that they were probably river; below this again hard beach, and then London clay. He took great precautions when he laid any foundations here, fearing lest the sand should slip. The bed of sand is a danger still, for if pierced by a drain or other underground works the sand might run off, leaving a hollow under the pot-earth. The

Cathedral authorities are accordingly wisely jealous of any excavations near S. Paul's. When the north-east portion of the choir was reached, in digging the foundations a pit was found, from which all the pot-earth had been taken, containing many fragments of vases and urns, all of Roman pottery. This pit was a very serious difficulty, occurring as it did at the very angle of the choir.

Sir Christopher's assistants suggested to him to drive in piles of timber; but he knew that, though timber lasted well under water, yet in this case, where it would be half in dry and half in wet sand, it would rot in the course of time, and 'his endeavours were to build for eternity.' He dug down more than forty feet, till he came to the hard beach, below which was the London clay, and upon the beach built a pier of solid masonry ten feet square, till within fifteen feet of the ground, and then by turning an arch brought it level with the rest of his foundation.

The theory commonly received was that a temple of Apollo stood where Westminster Abbey now stands, and that the site of S. Paul's Cathedral was occupied by a temple of Diana. Wren, however, believed in neither legend. The temple of Apollo he thought was invented merely that the monks of Westminster might not be behind the Londoners in antiquities. In spite of the horns of stags, tusks of boars, and the like, said to have been found during former repairs of S. Paul's, in spite of an image of Diana dug up hard by and in the possession of Dr. Woodward,[1] he wrote to

[1] J. Woodward, the founder of the Cambridge Geological Professorship,

Bishop Atterbury[1] that he 'changed all the foundations of old S. Paul's, and rummaged all the ground thereabouts, and being very desirous to find the footsteps of such a temple, I could not discover any, and therefore can give no more credit to Diana[2] than to Apollo.'

In the September of 1675, when the work with which her husband's name is for ever connected was but little advanced, Lady Wren died, and was buried, as her son Gilbert had been, in the chancel of S. Martin's-in-the-Fields, leaving her husband with a baby son hardly seven months old. The 'Parentalia,' with characteristic carelessness, gives neither the date of her death nor the place of her burial.

No hint even is to be found of how this loss affected Sir Christopher, but whether it was from the desolate state of his home, or the helplessness of a widower left with an infant son, or from other causes, he was not long in marrying again. His second wife was Jane Fitzwilliam, daughter of the second Baron Fitzwilliam, her mother was an heiress, the daughter of Hugh Perry *alias* Hunter, a sheriff and alderman of London. Lord Fitzwilliam died in 1643, the same

was born 1665, published a series of curious geological speculations under the name of *A Natural History of the Earth*. In 1707 he published *An Account of Roman Urns and Antiquities lately dug up near Bishopsgate*, addressed to Sir C. Wren, whom, as I have said, he did not convince. Woodward was a Fellow of the Royal Society and the College of Physicians. He died 1728.

[1] Francis Atterbury, born 1662, made Dean of Westminster and Bishop of Rochester 1715; was a strong Jacobite, and was banished in 1723: died 1732.

[2] A stone altar was however found during some excavations in Foster Lane in 1830, at no great distance from the Cathedral, with an image of Diana about which there can be no misapprehension, as it closely resembles the Diana of the Louvre.—*Annals of S. Paul's*, p. 7.

year that he had succeeded to his father, and the widowed Lady Fitzwilliam died twenty-seven years later at 'Dutchy House in the Savoy,' the family house; so Jane Fitzwilliam had been some years an orphan when she was married to Sir Christopher in the Chapel Royal at Whitehall, on February 24, 1676-7.

In this year Wren rebuilt S. Magnus, London Bridge,[1] which having escaped one 'most dismal fire' in 1633, was destroyed by the Great Fire of 1666. Sir Christopher rebuilt the church with Portland stone and oak timber, adding to it a picturesque tower with a cupola and a peal of ten bells. London Bridge, then covered with little houses and shops, would, Sir Christopher foresaw, require alteration, and he, anxious that S. Magnus should not suffer when the time came, proposed to leave space by it for a footway. The churchwardens overruled him. The improvement Wren expected has since been made, and when the workmen came to make a pathway under the portico they discovered to their great surprise that Sir Christopher had made the necessary arches, though bricked up, and left them to be in readiness for the change which he foresaw, though the churchwardens of S. Magnus did not. The state of London Bridge was very unsatisfactory; constant repairs were needed, and to shoot the narrow arches and not be swamped by the fall of the water was no easy feat. Wren had a plan for saving repairs and improving the water way by wide Gothic

---

[1] Jack Cade's instruction to his followers on reaching London was 'Up Fish Street, down *S. Magnus* corner. Kill and knock down, throw them into the Thames.' *Henry VI.*, part ii. act iv. scene 8.

arches, taking away every other arch, and making the two into one, which would reduce the fall to nine inches at the most. This seems to have remained a scheme only.

S. Mildred's in the Poultry was also begun in this year, a small stone church with a tower and cupola. It was destroyed in 1872,[1] and the details of its removal are instructive as well as painful, and may well be contrasted with the account of the manner of removing the remains of old S. Paul's.[2]

S. Stephen's, Coleman Street, on the site of an old Jewish synagogue, is of the same date; it is a neat small church mostly built of stone, with a curious old

[1] The following interesting anecdote was related to one of the Honorary Secretaries (Mr. Wright) by a member of the Society (Mr. Fytche):—'Walking one fine summer morning in June 1872 down to the Mansion House, on reaching the Poultry I was surprised to see a man on the top of the tower of S. Mildred's Church hammering away at the stones with a crowbar; so, finding the door open, I went up the stairs of the tower and said to my friend of the crowbar, "Why, you are pulling the church down!" "Ay," says he, "it's all to be down and carted away by the end of July." "I suppose it's going to be rebuilt elsewhere!" "*Built* anywhere? No; my master has *bought* it." "Who is your master?" "Don't you know him? Mr. So-and-So, the great contractor." "What's he going to do with it?" "Do with it? Why, he's twenty carts and forty horses to lead it away to his stoneyard, and he's going to grind it up to make Portland cement!" So I asked him of the crowbar to show me round the church. "Would your master sell the stones instead of grinding 'em up?" I asked. "Sell 'em? Yes, he'll sell his soul for money!" So I made an appointment for his master to come up to the Langham Hotel next morning, and we agreed about the purchase—he to deliver the stones at a wharf on the Thames, and they were brought down in barges and landed at the head of a canal on the east coast of Lincolnshire, and are now lying in a green field near my house, called S. Katherine's Garth, from an old Priory of S. Katherine, which formerly stood there, and which I hope some day to rebuild as my domestic chapel.'—*Report of the City Church and Churchyard Protection Society*, 1880.

[2] *Vide supra*, p. 186-7.

stone carving, in high relief, of the Last Judgment, over the door leading to the churchyard.

S. Lawrence, Jewry, 'that new and cheerful pile,'[1] is a large well-proportioned building in the Corinthian style, with a tower and spire, built in the following year. It had been repaired by the parishioners in 1618, and boasted among its vicars three who had become bishops: Edward Reynolds, Bishop of Norwich, one of those who, during the Rebellion, sided strongly with the Presbyterians, and conformed at the Restoration; Dr. Seth Ward, Bishop of Exeter and Salisbury, who has been mentioned before; and Wren's other scientific friend, Dr. Wilkins, Bishop of Chester, who was buried in the chancel of S. Lawrence's Church in 1672.

S. Lawrence's possesses some excellent stone carving of fruit, possibly from Gibbons' chisel.

S. Nicholas, Coleabbey, was built this year by Sir Christopher on the site of a church so ancient that it stood some feet below the street, and was entered by steps descending down to the floor; its most recent addition was in Richard II.'s reign, though the whole building was repaired in 1630. Wren's is a well-proportioned brick and stone church with a square tower and short fat steeple. S. Mary's, Woolnoth, was only repaired by Sir Christopher; it was afterwards rebuilt entirely by his clerk and pupil, Nicholas Hawksmoor,[2]

---

[1] Evelyn's *Diary*, May 28, 1682.

[2] Nicholas Hawksmoor, born the year of the fire, became Wren's pupil in 1683 and helped him in many of his works. Hawksmoor built several churches under Queen Anne's Act; they are original, but heavy, and not always in good taste. He died 1736.

in 1719. S. Mary's, Aldermanbury, a fine bold stone church, its nave and aisles divided by well-sculptured columns; and S. Michael's, Queenhithe, belong also to this busy year. S. Michael's, standing close to the river, built of stone with plenty of space and room in it; its slender graceful spire ever beckoning to the swarming river and riverside population, might, one would have imagined, have been invaluable in zealous hands, but it has been swept away and the opportunity is lost.

It was also in 1677 that Sir Christopher completed the column generally known to Londoners as 'the Monument.' He began it in 1671; but the work had been much hindered by the difficulty of getting blocks of Portland stone of sufficient size. There had been great debate about the ornament for the summit. Wren wished it to be a large statue, as 'carrying much dignity with it, and being more valluable in the eyes of forreigners and strangers.' It was to be fifteen feet high, cast in brass, at a cost of 1,000*l*. The expense was one reason why this was given up, and the present ornament, a flaming vase of gilt bronze, substituted. Cibber[1] carved a basso-relievo on one side, representing King Charles in a Roman costume, protecting the ruined city. The four dragons at the base were carved by Edward Pierce,[2] a sculptor and architect who frequently worked for Wren. The other three sides have Latin inscriptions, of which one is an account

[1] Caius Cibber, born 1630. The statues of Melancholy and Madness at Bedlam were his greatest works : died about 1700.
[2] He did much of the work of S. Clement Danes under Wren's directions, and made a bust of Sir Christopher, now at All Souls : died 1698.

of the fire, accusing the *furor Papisticus* as its cause; a brief inscription in English, lower down on the pedestal, repeats the same charge against the 'treachery and malice of the Popish faction.' Sir Christopher had written a Latin one for the column, which spoke of the fire as originating in a humble house, and briefly recounted its ravages; he added, as he was well entitled to add, that the city was rebuilt 'not with wood and mud as before, but with edifices, some brick and some stone, and adorned with such works that it was seen to rise fairer from its ruins far than before.' As he wrote, he must have given a sigh of regret to the perfection of his unused plan.

The accusation against the Romanists appealed powerfully to the inveterate prejudices of the multitude. It was accordingly insisted upon and ordered to be put up. James II. had the inscription effaced, but in William III.'s reign it was re-cut deeper than before, and so remained to justify Pope's well-known lines:—

——London's column pointing to the skies,
Like a tall bully lifts the head and lies.[1]

It is a curious retribution that the Monument designed by so great an architect as Wren, to commemorate such an event as the burning of London, and the singular courage and energy of its citizens, is now more generally connected in men's mind with falsehood and calumny than with a great historical event.

The column was at first used, as Wren had intended it should be, as a place for certain experiments of the Royal Society; but the vibration of the column

[1] *Moral Essays*, Ep. iii.

during the ceaseless traffic of London proved too great to allow of the experiments being successfully carried on. Evelyn, with much sense, wished that the column had been placed where the fire ended, and a 'plain lugubrious marble' where it began; and says:—

' I question not but I have the architect himself on my side, whose rare and extraordinary talent and what he has performed of great and magnificent, this column and what he is still about and is advancing under his direction, will speak and perpetuate his memory, as long as one stone remains upon another in this nation.'[1]

The King had proposed to Sir Christopher a very congenial piece of work. The remains of Charles I., which had been hastily buried in S. George's Chapel at Windsor, were to be removed to what was known as the tomb-house at the east end of the chapel, re-interred there with the solemn service that had been denied to them before, and a grand tomb built over them. Lord O'Brien proposed in the House of Commons a grant of money for the purpose, and the House voted 70,000*l.* to be raised by a two months' tax. Sprat, Bishop of Rochester, preaching before the Commons on the following day, the anniversary of King Charles's death, alluded to the tardy honour done 'by that much-desired, long-expected vote.' Sir Christopher prepared designs for a splendid monument.

It was to take the form of a Rotundo with a beautiful Dome and Lantern, and a Colonnade with-

[1] *Of Medals*, p. 162, ed. 1697. Evelyn.

out, like that of the Temple of Vesta at Rome. Mosaic work was to be freely used, black and white marble and gilded brass; the cupola was to be painted in fresco. In the central niche fronting the entrance was the King's monument. Four statues, emblems of heroic virtues, standing on a square plinth, and pressing underneath the prostrate figures of Rebellion, Heresy, Hypocrisy, Envy and Murder, support a large shield, on which is a statue erect of King Charles in modern armour, over his head a group of angels bearing a crown, a cross, and branches of palm. Two designs were made, one for brass work, one for marble: one design is drawn by Grinling Gibbons, whom Wren meant to employ for the carving. The other is by Wren himself, drawn with extraordinary care, in delicate pen and ink, and they yet remain with his note upon them. 'Alas! for the state of the times! —not yet erected.' The failure of his design was a great annoyance to Wren, who was most anxious to have paid this tribute to the King's memory.

Why the plan was never executed it is hard to say. Charles II. kept the designs for some time and then returned them, begging Wren to keep them carefully; but the moment for their use never arrived.

Though he was not allowed to honour King Charles, curiously enough, it fell to Wren's lot to provide a tomb for two other murdered Princes of England.

Some repairs were being made in the Tower of London under the orders of Wren, who was at that time repairing what is known as the White Tower, one of the oldest parts of the fortress. As the workmen were removing some stairs which led from the Royal lodgings to S. John's Chapel, they came upon a wooden chest, which proved to contain the remains of two children, exactly corresponding in age and state of decay with the date of the murder of Edward V. and his brother Richard Duke of York in 1573. The place also corresponded in every respect with the traditions respecting the murder :[1] it was said to have been done in the Bloody Tower—the spot where the bones were found is but seventy yards distant; they were always said to have been buried in consecrated ground by the Priest of the Tower—the place where the remains were was just within S. John's Chapel. The discovery caused considerable interest, and was fully represented to the King, who desired that the bones should be laid, under the Surveyor's directions, in Henry VII.'s Chapel in Westminster Abbey in a white marble coffin with a suitable monument. Wren designed a pedestal and urn of white marble surmounted by twin crowns and palms. No doubt the monument accords better with the taste of the age in which it was erected than with that of the building in which it is placed, but it has an interest of its own. By the King's wish a mulberry-tree was planted on the spot where the bones were discovered, but subsequent buildings at the Tower destroyed the tree, and even its stump has perished.

[1] For an interesting account of these see *The Tower of London*, by Lord de Ros, p. 417.

CHAPTER IX.

1677-1682.

EMMANUEL COLLEGE—GREENWICH OBSERVATORY—BIRTH OF JANE AND WILLIAM WREN—S. BARTHOLOMEW'S—PORTLAND QUARRIES—DR. AND MRS. HOLDER—DEATH OF JANE, LADY WREN—POPISH PLOT—PAPIN'S DIGESTER—SIR J. HOSKYNS— ALLHALLOWS, BREAD STREET—PALACE AT WINCHESTER.

Who taught that heaven-directed spire to rise?—POPE, *Moral Essays.*

CHAPTER IX.

GREAT as was the pressure of Wren's London work, he did not confine himself to that city alone, but in 1677, we find him at Cambridge, busied with buildings there. The beautiful chapel of Emmanuel College, which still stands unaltered as he left it, was Sir Christopher's work in that year. More than thirty years before, Bishop Wren, when Bishop of Ely, had instanced amongst the irregularities to be amended at Cambridge the absence of a chapel at Emmanuel College,[1] and it well became his nephew to supply this lack. Sancroft had first set the plan on foot, and when he was removed in 1665 to S. Paul's—a removal so costly that, little knowing, he consoled himself by thinking the next would be to his grave—his successor, Dr. Breton, continued his work.

A picturesque cloister runs north and south across

[1] It was founded in 1584 by Sir Walter Mildmay, a great supporter of the Puritans.
In Bishop Corbet's poem, *The Distracted Puritan*, the hero says:—

> 'In the house of pure Emmanuel
> I had my education,
> Where my friends surmise
> I dazel'd my eyes
> With the sight of Revelation.'

Evelyn, who visited it in September 1655, says: 'That zealous house .... the Chapel (it was but a room) is reformed *ab origine*, built N. and S. as is the Librarie.'

the façade built of stone instead of the brick with stone dressing as Wren at first intended; within the chapel the rich stucco ceiling, the pannelling and wood carving, the tall columns which support a pediment behind the altar, as well as the bold metal scroll-work of the altar rails, all show Wren's hand and eye. In the manuscript list of Wren's architectural works in the 'Parentalia' the Chapel of Queen's College at Oxford is assigned to him as built at about this time; but it does not appear in the more accurate printed list, and is not generally reckoned amongst his works.

The Observatory at Greenwich, known by the name of Flamsteed House, was being completed. It was built at the suggestion of Sir Jonas Moor, the Surveyor-General of the Ordnance, for the purpose of ascertaining the motions of the moon and the places of the fixed stars, in order, if possible, to discover accurately the longitude at sea.[1] Wren, confessedly one of the best astronomers in England, was on the commission for building the Observatory, and was its architect. Greenwich was chosen as the site at his suggestion; the King, who took a great interest in the project, allowed 500*l.* towards it, and Sir Christopher used in the work some spare wood, iron, and lead from the Tower Gatehouse, and the bricks taken from Tilbury, the fort built by Elizabeth to repel the Spanish Armada.

The Observatory was begun in June, 1675, and roofed in at the Christmas of the same year, and Flamsteed shortly afterwards installed there.

[1] *Vide infra*, p. 331-3.

The Museum at Oxford, known as the Ashmolean, was Sir Christopher's work in 1677. It contained a collection of objects of natural history which was then reckoned a very good one: it had been collected by John Tradescant, and bequeathed by him to Mr. Elias Ashmole, the historian of the Order of the Garter, who made the whole over to the University, endowing a lecture upon them.

The collection contained several curious specimens of Roman, Indian, and other weapons, some clothing made of feathers; among other 'rarities,' a 'toad included in amber,' and a 'habit of feathers from the Phœnix wing as tradition goes.'[1] Ashmole was of the Royal Society and a student of astrology.

In the November of this year, Sir Christopher's only daughter Jane was born, and was baptized at S. Martin's, probably by the Rev. William Lloyd, then the vicar, who bore the high character of 'an excellent preacher, a man of great integrity and piety, one who thoroughly understood all the parts of his function and had a mind fully bent to put them in execution.' Wren's fourth and youngest child was born in June, 1679, and baptized, also at S. Martin's, by the name of William. Sir Christopher's good friend Evelyn was one godfather, the other was Sir William Fermor, the head of an old Cavalier family of Northamptonshire, whose father, all but ruined in the civil wars, survived to attend as one of the Knights of the Bath at Charles II.'s coronation. Sir William, who was by his mother's side first cousin to Lady Wren, was a friend of

[1] Evelyn's *Diary*, September 17, 1657, and July 23, 1678

Evelyn's, whose tastes he shared. He was created Lord Lempster[1] by William and Mary. The other sponsor was Lady Newport, daughter of the Earl of Bedford, and wife of the Lord Treasurer, Lord Newport, who, greatly distinguished by his loyalty and his suffering in the Civil War, was made Comptroller of the Household, and in 1672 Lord Treasurer, an office which he held under the two succeeding monarchs.[2] Lord Newport was a friend both of Wren and of Evelyn, and entertained them, Prince Rupert, and others at his house, where he had a fine collection of pictures.

Wren began five of his churches in this year: one was the little square church of SS. Anne and Agnes, Aldersgate, with its four Corinthian columns and decorated ceiling.

'There is a constant tradition in the parish that SS. Anne and Agnes were two sisters who first built this church at their own charge,'[3] but at what date is not said. It once bore the name of 'S. Anne-in-the-Willows,' from the willow-trees that grew hard by.

S. Bartholomew's, Bartholomew Lane, near the Exchange, had been consumed all but its old square tower, which must have been a striking object standing up tall and fire-scathed amongst the ruins. To this tower Wren added a sort of crown of open arches, but he carefully preserved the tower, itself a curious relic

---

[1] His son Thomas was created Earl of Pomfret by George I., 1721; the title is extinct.

[2] He appeared for the seven bishops on their trial, greatly angering King James thereby. He voted for William and Mary, and was by them created Earl of Bradford, 1694.

[3] *Repertorium*, vol. i. p. 276. Newcourt.

of London before the fire. Internally it was a handsome basilican church, effective from the good keeping and harmony of all its parts. Its date of consecration went back to the beginning of the fourteenth century. Bishop Miles Coverdale[1] was buried there. Alas! that all must be written in the past tense! The church has been destroyed because its site was wanted for the Sun Fire Office! It is a cruel fate, having been rebuilt after the Great Fire to be destroyed for a Fire Insurance Office.

S. Michael's, Bassishaw, or Basinghall, taking this name from the great merchant family of Basing, several of whom were sheriffs, and others lord mayors of London, was rebuilt of brick and stone with a curious little stone spire.

S. Swithin's in Cannon Street is reckoned a model of excellence in construction; it is of stone with a tower and spire, and domed roof; the curious relic known as 'London Stone,' is built into the church wall; it was formerly fixed in the ground in the street. Many different opinions have been advanced about it —that it was the centre of the City, which however it was not, being too near the river; that it was a place for tendering money before the Exchange existed; and, most prosaic of all, that it was set up by one named London Stone who lived there![2] All agreed that it had been there since the time of the Saxon kings.

S. Bride's, Fleet Street, was begun in this year, but not entirely finished until twenty years later; on it

[1] Born 1437. Assisted Tindal in translating and printing the Bible. Died 1568.
[2] *New View of London*, vol. i. p. 14. E. Hatton.

Wren lavished considerable care and skill, securing a spacious handsome interior, and a richly carved oak altar-piece. The bold tower and steeple,[1] with its graceful diminishing circles with their open arcades, are thought to rival S. Mary's, Bow, but the latter is perhaps the more poetical of the two.

The great work at S. Paul's was the while proceeding. In 1676 Compton, Bishop of London, issued an Address, urging the claims of the Cathedral, not on the citizens alone, but upon the country at large ; he insisted with some eloquence that all churches should as much as possible imitate the 'exceeding magnifical' temple of Solomon in their beauty and grandeur, and especially the cathedral of wealthy London. His address, his warm interest in the work, and that of Dean Sancroft, who was a contributor until driven from his archbishopric, brought many contributions : among them may be mentioned Morley, Bishop of Winchester, who gave 1,800*l.* ; Dr. John Fell, who gave 100*l.*, 'in lieu of his consecration dinner and gloves' when consecrated Bishop of Oxford, 1680 ; Bishop Ken, who gave the same sum at his consecration, 1685, also in lieu of the dinner and gloves ; Bishop Wilson, of Sodor and Man, who gave from the quarries of the island the dark stone steps which lead to the west doors. Though hampered often, the architect was never actually stopped by lack of money. He himself

---

[1] The steeple has been slightly lowered by Sir W. Staines in recent years ; it was 234 feet high. When this was done, it was discovered that an old hawk had inhabited the two upper circles, the open arcades of which were filled with masses of bird's bones, chiefly those of the city pigeons upon which he had preyed.

out of his scanty salary gave 50*l.* towards the expenses.

In a letter speaking of his progress in building S. Paul's he says, 'I have received a considerable sum, which, though not proportionable to the greatnesse of the work, is notwithstanding sufficient to begin the same—and with all the materials and other assistances which may probably be expected, will put the new quire in great forwardness.' The materials referred to are probably such parts of the old building as it was possible to use again; and it may here be said that Wren had the control of the quarries of Portland stone.[1] In 1669, King Charles issued a proclamation that—

> 'Whereas great waste had been for many years past made of our quarries in the Isle of Portland, . . . and the great occasion we have of using much of the said stone, both for the building and repairing our houses and for the repaire of S. Paul's, our pleasure is . . . that all persons forbeare to transport any more stone from our Isle of Portland without the leave and warrant first obtained from Dr. Christopher Wren, Surveyor of our Works, as hath been formerly accustomed in that behalf.'

Wren must have commanded an army of quarrymen in the little island, not then grim with convicts and with a prison; but nevertheless he had, as in the case of the Monument, not seldom to pause in his work before he could get blocks of the size he required. As the choir rose the time came in which the space

---

[1] There is a quantity of stone quarried for S. Paul's still lying at the back of the island, ready for transportation.

for the great Dome was to be marked out. The architect stood watching with some of his friends, and called to one of the workmen to bring him a stone to mark a special spot; when the man obeyed, Wren saw that the stone thus brought had an inscription upon it —the single word 'Resurgam.'[1] It was looked upon by Sir Christopher as a singularly happy omen, and he took great pleasure in telling the anecdote.

In the meantime a sharp controversy was going on within the Royal Society between Dr. Wallis and Sir Christopher's brother-in-law, Dr. Holder. Dr. Holder had a living in Hertfordshire and had received from Bishop Henchman a canonry in S. Paul's. In 1678 he brought out a book called 'The Elements of Speech' with an appendix concerning 'Persons deaf and dumb.' In this book he described the cure he had himself performed when at Bletchingdon of a young gentleman, Mr. Alexander Popham, the son of a certain Edward Popham, admiral in the service of the Long Parliament, whom, though born dumb, he had gradually taught to speak. The youth, taken away before the cure was quite finished, lost the lately acquired power of speech, but on being sent to Dr. Wallis recovered it; thereupon Dr. Wallis claimed

---

[1] *Anecdotes of Distinguished Persons*, vol. ii. p. 310. Seward. It is supposed to have been part of the gravestone of Dr. John King, Bishop of London, 1611-21,' called by King James 'the *King* of preachers.' 'He was a most solid and profound divine of great gravity and piety, and a most excellent volubility of speech.'—*Repertorium*, vol. i. p. 29. Newcourt. Bishop King preached at S. Paul's Cross before King James I. and all his Court when James the First began the restoration of the Cathedral under Inigo Jones. A quaint print of this scene still exists.—*Three Cathedrals of S. Paul*, p. 20. Longman.

the entire credit. In his book Dr. Holder took occasion to speak of the Royal Society as originating in meetings held at Oxford.

Upon this Dr. Wallis wrote a pamphlet entitled 'A Defence of the Royal Society in reply to some cavils of Dr. W. Holder.' The quarrel appears to have been a hot one, turning chiefly on the credit of curing Alexander Popham.

Wood, the antiquary,[1] speaks of Dr. Wallis 'as one that can make black white, and white black, for his own ends, and hath a ready knack of sophistical evasion (as the writer of these matters doth know full well),' and gives the credit to Dr. Holder. Wallis was little loved by any royalist because of his conduct in decyphering King Charles I.'s papers at Naseby.[2] In the 'Parentalia' are two finger alphabets, with two hands drawn in Indian ink, the fingers of which have different letters assigned to the different joints; one is an ordinary and simple way, the other, more elaborate, is entitled 'An arte to make the Dumbe to speake, the Deafe to heare. To speake amongst others unseen and unhearde. Learned in an howre.' Minute directions are given, but the system is so elaborate that it is very sanguine to think it could have been 'learned' under several hours. The writing is not like Christopher Wren's, and I think it must belong to Dr. Holder's scheme.

Mrs. Holder went on in her tranquil course, ministering to the poor around her. In early days she had

[1] *Fast. Oxon.*, vol. i. p. 139. Wood.
[2] *Vide supra*, pp. 77, 78.

made a careful study of such medical science as was then known. Barbarous as the surgery was, the remedial part of medicine appears to have been somewhat better understood. The circulation of the blood had very lately been discovered by Harvey; and whether it was the efficacy of the herbs and simples used, or the faith of the patients, or both, it is certain that many cures were made and much suffering alleviated. It is said of Mrs. Holder that 'she happily healed thousands.' She cured Charles II. of a hurt in his hand, whether in his early days of peril and wandering, or in later life, is not said. After the Restoration she was connected more or less with the Court, as her husband was subdean of the Chapels Royal, and she healed Queen Catharine and many of the Court. When one reads in Evelyn's or in Pepys' diary of the frightful remedies used: the 'hot fire pans' applied to the head in cases of apoplexy, the constant bleeding, the roughness of the entire treatment, one is thankful to think that they were occasionally ministered to by the gentler hand of a woman.

A taste for the science of medicine seems to have been common in the Wren family. Sir Christopher studied it at Oxford under Sir Charles Scarborough and drew the plates for Dr. Thomas Willis' 'Cerebri Anatome,' which was in great repute. His cousin, Thomas Wren, made it a matter of serious study, probably living by it as a profession at the time when Bishop Wren's imprisonment left his younger children penniless. The same honourable calling was chosen by Sir Christopher's grandson, Stephen Wren. Among all the patients whom good Mrs. Holder tended and cared for, in none could she have taken more pride than in the brother over whose sickly childhood she had watched, and whose fame she saw daily increasing. Nor was there any drawback to her delight: loving, gentle, modest, and courteous he had been as a boy, and the famous successful architect possessed those qualities still. In a corrupt age, all testimony leaves him spotless; in positions of great trust and still greater difficulty his integrity was but the more clearly shown by the attacks made against him; among the foremost philosophers of his age, he was a striking example that 'every good gift and every perfect gift is from above;' no child could hold the truths of Christianity with a more undoubting faith than did Sir Christopher Wren.

His personal appearance is only known to us from pictures: it seems he was 'thin and low of stature,' and it is recorded that when he was building a hunting palace at Newmarket for Charles II., the King came to see it, looked round, and was well satisfied with the general effect, but said he thought the rooms were too low. Wren, who knew the King well, and could hold his own when needful, looked up to the ceiling, and said quietly: 'Sir, I think they are high enough.'

On hearing this, King Charles stooped till he was the architect's height, crept about the room in this attitude, and said laughing, 'Ay, Sir Christopher, I think *they are high enough.*'[1]

The beautiful S. Stephen's, Walbrook, was finished

---

[1] *Biographical History of England*, vol. iii. p. 327. Noble.

in 1679, and the parishioners, aware that their church was a gem of no common order, offered 'a purse of twenty guineas to the Lady of Sir Christopher Wren, as a testimony of the regard that the parish has for the great care and skill that Sir Christopher Wren showed in the rebuilding of our church.'[1] Lady Wren did not long survive to share in her husband's fame and to sympathise in his work.

Early in October she died and was buried in S. Martin's-in-the-Fields, where Dr. Thomas Tenison[2] had succeeded Dr. Lloyd, when the latter was made Bishop of S. Asaph. He, too, was a hard-working parish priest, though neither so zealous nor so wholehearted a churchman as the former vicar. He communicated to Evelyn[3] his plan 'of erecting a library in S. Martin's parish for the public use, and desired his assistance with Sir Christopher Wren about the placing and structure thereof.' Dr. Tenison said that he had 'between thirty and forty young men in orders in his parish either governors to young gentlemen, or chaplains to noblemen, who being reproved by him on occasion for frequenting taverns or coffee-houses, told him they would employ their time better if they had books.' Wren fell readily into a scheme so con-

---

[1] *Lives of the Gresham Professors*, p. 104. Ward. The church has been lately cleansed, but the disfiguring pews most unfortunately still encumber the area.

[2] Thomas Tenison, Bishop of Lincoln and Archbishop of Canterbury; his endowments were munificent: died 1715.

[3] *Diary*, February 15, 1684. The very valuable library which Dr. Tenison founded was, alas! sold by Act of Parliament, 1861, and the proceeds ordered to be applied to middle-class education, which was hardly what the donor intended.

genial as this, and in a very few days the two friends were together at Dr. Tenison's making a drawing and estimate of the library to be begun in the spring of that same year.

In 1678, the nation was excited to absolute frenzy by the declarations of the infamous Titus Oates concerning the 'Popish Plot.' In the same spirit as that in which they had laid the burning of London at the door of the Romanists, the mob lent greedy, credulous ears to the tales of Oates, and were encouraged by Lord Shaftesbury and his party, who made political capital out of this madness. Looking back, it is difficult to understand how such manifest falsehoods could have obtained credit; but it should be borne in mind that only seventy-three years had passed since the Gunpowder Plot had all but succeeded, and despite its failure left a mark in popular feeling which, however obscured and travestied, remains to this day. That it was fresh in the minds of the Members of Parliament may be seen from their insisting that a guard should be placed in the vaults over which they sate.

Bedloe, Oates' villainous ally, having declared that an army of thirty thousand pilgrims was coming from Spain to join forty thousand who were ready to rise in London, the House of Lords insisted that a communication between the Spanish ambassador's house and that of his neighbour Mr. Weld should be secured. No less a person than Sir Christopher himself was to be despatched by the Lords' committee to see to this matter. Wren took the matter quietly enough; went with Mr. Edward Warcup, one of his assistants, and sent in a report stating that they had caused 'padlocks to be hung on all such dores as open out of Mr. Weld's house into the Spanish Embassador's house;' had then 'acquainted his Excellency Count Egmont, who with great civility gave permission for all things necessary to be done on his side.' They locked the doors on his side, barred some with iron, and handed over the keys to tne Clerk of the Parliament, which no doubt felt itself more secure after this precaution.

Evelyn, it is plain from passages in his diary, disbelieved and distrusted Oates, and Wren, who gave no heed to panics, was probably of the same opinion. One wishes that Pepys had not been compelled in 1669, by failing eyesight, to give up keeping his most amusing diary, that he might have recorded his impressions of this time of frenzy. He, however, was a sufferer by it, being clapt into the Tower on a charge of 'Popery, felony, piracy, and treason,' in 1679. The 'treason' charged seems to have been that he sent information to the French Court about the state of the English navy. The 'Popery,' from which he was certainly free, was probably thrown in to give a flavour suited to the times. It is an incredible charge, and Pepys, who defended himself in a spirited letter to the Duke of York, was discharged in the following February.

The Royal Society, despite all these storms, kept its even course. Wren, who had been Vice-President, was elected President in 1680. With all his work, he contrived to take the Chair frequently at the meetings. Their discussions were very varied:—observations with the barometer, ways of sounding the sea, the curve described by a granado shot into the air, an account of the anatomy of the otter, and its power of diving ;—Sir Christopher hereupon described the seal which was in S. James's Park, as having muscles by which it could contract and dilate its nostrils, and by such means sink itself and lie at the bottom of the pool made for it, for a great while together, and that it ate its food at the bottom of the river.

A new discovery by a French doctor named Papin[1] of a 'digester' for softening bones, caused much discussion at the Society. Wren inquired whether a contrary process to M. Papin's could not be devised to harden bones, but Papin could give no answer. Two years later M. Papin gave a supper to which several of the Society went. Evelyn says, it was[2]—

'All dress'd, both fish and flesh, in M. Papin's Digestors, by which the hardest bones of beef itselfe and mutton were made as soft as cheese, without water or any other liquor, and with lesse than eight ounces of coales producing an incredible quantity of gravy; and, for close of all, a jelly made of the bones of beef, the best for clearness and good relish, and the most delicious that I had seene or tasted. We eat pike and other fish bones, and all without impediment; but nothing exceeded the pigeons, which tasted just as if baked in a pie, all these being

---

[1] Denys Papin, born at Blois, was an M.D. of Paris; came to England, and in 1680 was elected a Fellow of the Royal Society. He died in 1710.
[2] *Diary*, April 12, 1684.

stewed in their own juice, without any addition of water, save what swam about the Digestor, as *in balneo*; the natural juice of these provisions acting on the grosser substances, reduced the hardest bones to tenderness; but it is best descanted with more particulars for extracting tinctures, preserving and stewing fruite, and saving fuel, in Dr. Papin's booke[1] published and dedicated to our Society, of which he is a member. . . . This philosophical supper caus'd much mirth amongst us, and exceedingly pleased all the company. I sent a glass of the jelly to my wife, to the reproch of all that the ladies ever made of the best hartshorn.'

The Royal Society had another foreign visitor, M. Chardin,[2] the Persian traveller. Sir Christopher, Sir John Hoskyns, and Evelyn[3] went to visit him when he arrived in England in 1680, and invited him to honour the Royal Society with his company. They found him dressed in his Eastern habit, speaking Latin, and understanding Greek, Arabic, and Persian from his eleven years of travel in those parts. He was a well-bred, modest man 'not inclined to talk wonders.' Chardin was a fair draughtsman and had besides taken two artists with him to draw landscapes, to measure

---

[1] *The New Digester, or Engine for the Softening of Bones*, 4to. A modification of Papin's 'digester kettle' still exists, and goes by his name, though used far less than it deserves.

[2] Born in Paris, 1643. The son of a Protestant jeweller, he went to Persia in search of diamonds, amassing a considerable fortune. He married in England in 1681, and died there 1735. He was buried at Chiswick, but his monument is in Westminster Abbey. 'Sir John Chardin. *Nomen sibi fecit eundo.*'—*Life of Sir C. Wren*, p. 419. Elmes.

[3] *Diary*, August 30, 1680.

and design the palaces and temples burnt at Persepolis. He was then on his way to France, but on his return promised to show the drawings. He returned, finding the persecution of the Protestants still hot in France, and Sir Christopher proposed him as a member of the Royal Society. His book, 'Travels of Sir John Chardin,' was published in London and is still in high esteem both for its special interest and the accuracy of its statements. Evelyn assisted him in engraving the plates and in the translation of the book. Charles II. made him a knight, and he was employed in Holland as the agent of the English East India Company.

At the meeting of the Royal Society on November 30, 1681, Wren was re-elected President and chose Sir John Hoskyns as Vice-president.[1] Sir John Hoskyns, who, like Wren, had been educated at Westminster, was a Master in Chancery highly thought of for his legal attainments and his integrity; he and Wren appear always to have been friends; and when Wren resigned the presidency, Sir John succeeded him. Tradition[2] says that Sir John 'affected plainness in his garb, walked in the street with a cudgel in his hand and an old hat over his eyes. That he was often observed to be in a reverie; but when his

[1] The friendship and connection with Sir Christopher is curious, for in 1837 Mr. Chandos Wren Hoskyns married Theodosia Anne Martha Wren, only surviving child of Christopher Roberts Wren, of Wroxall Abbey in Warwickshire, who was himself the great-great-grandson of Sir C. Wren, Mr. Chandos Hoskyns being the direct descendant of Sir J. Hoskyns mentioned above. To their only child, now the wife of the Rev. C. F. C. Pigott, Rector of Edgmond, Salop, and Prebendary of Lichfield, I am indebted for the use of many valuable family papers.

[2] *Biog. Hist.*, vol. iii. p. 371, vol. iv. p. 314. Grainger.

spirits were elevated over a bottle, he was remarkable for his presence of mind and quickness of apprehension and became a most agreeable and instructive companion.' It also says that he bore an irreproachable character.

The great western front of Christ Church, Oxford, was at this time occupying Wren's attention. Wolsey had laid the foundations of the gateway, but it had been left unfinished until Wren took it in hand and built the grand gateway and noble tower which are among the features of Oxford.

The churches which at this time were building in London were All Hallows, Bread Street; the original church dated back to the beginning of the thirteenth century. Lyndwode, the author of the 'Provincial Constitutions,' was rector there in 1418. The poet Milton was baptized there December 20, 1608. An inscription on a tablet at the west end of the church recorded this, and also Dryden's lines:—

> Three Poets in three distant ages born,
> Greece, Italy, and England did adorn;
> The first in loftiness of thought surpassed,
> The next in majesty; in both the last.
> The force of nature could no further go,
> To make a third she joined the other two.

Here also it is supposed that Sir Isaac Newton was buried, though the exact spot was not known.

Wren built on the old site a stone church of considerable beauty, whose tall pinnacled tower had a singular grace of its own. All, alas! destroyed, the ancient site desecrated, and the materials sold, no matter for what purpose.

S. Peter's, Cornhill, a small compact brick and stone church with a low tower and a key for its vane and camerated roof, was rebuilt in this year. Several small charitable legacies belong to this church: Sir B. Thorowgood settled three shops, at the west end of the churchyard, upon the parish for the maintenance of an organist to play on Sundays and Holydays for ever. In 1700 these shops were all three let for 24*l*.!

S. Clement Danes in the Strand, which had been patched up in 1674, was taken down and rebuilt, being finished in 1682. Sir Christopher, who received the moderate salary of 100*l*. for the rebuilding of the *City* churches, had nothing necessarily to do with S. Clement's, but yet, as is recorded on a marble slab on the north side of the chancel, he 'freely and generously bestowed his great care towards the contriving and building.' It stands in too frequented a place and is too well known to need description, and will, I think, be readily admitted to bear Wren's mark. Evelyn calls it 'that pretty and well-contrived church.' The steeple surmounting the tower was added by Wren's pupil Gibbs[1] in 1719. S. Antholin's, Watling Street, was entirely consumed by the fire, so that all its registers perished, a misfortune which happened to but few of the churches. Sir Christopher spent especial care upon it. The roof was a cupola adorned with rich festoons; the octagonal spire was built of freestone, with three circles of windows and considerably ornamented, was the chief feature of this beautiful little

[1] James Gibbs, a Scotch architect who built S. Mary-le-Strand, S. Martin's-in-the-Fields, &c.; born 1674, died 1754.

church. At the time of its building the spire was much remarked, and must have formed a pleasant contrast to the little neighbouring church of S. Augustine in the same street, with its tower cupola and small steeple, which was added in 1695. This church was finished in 1683 and survives S. Antholin's, which has shared the evil fate of All Hallows, Bread Street.

The hunting palace at Newmarket, of which mention has been made, was accidentally burnt down, and this made King Charles more anxious to have a palace in the ancient city of Winchester. Lands were bought for a park, a river was to have been brought from the downs with a thirty-foot cascade in the park, and a broad street planned to lead to the cathedral from the future palace. Wren designed a magnificent palace,[1] with a great cupola which would have been seen far out at sea, and laid the first stone on March 23, 1683. The work was much pressed forward both by King Charles and by the Duke of York, who frequently stayed at Winchester for a considerable time watching the progress of the building, and hunting in the forest. At such times the King was lodged in the Deanery and his train in the houses of the close, where most of them were sufficiently incongruous inmates. Ken, then a prebendary of the Cathedral, utterly refused to give a lodging in his house to the notorious Nell Gwynne.

Winchester had many associations for Wren, to whom the name of Lancelot Andrewes must have been a household word from childhood, and it is pleasant to

[1] *Life of Bishop Ken*, by a layman, ed. 1854, p. 186.

think that he at this time became acquainted with the saintly Ken. The palace, which was finished as far as the shell in 1685, was never used either by Charles II. or his successors, though Queen Anne made one visit to Winchester, and was so much struck with the situation and the shell of the building as it stood awaiting completion, the marble pillars sent by the Duke of Tuscany for the great staircase lying on the ground, that she resolved to finish it as a jointure house for Prince George, but his death and the cost of the great war made her give up the scheme. Sir Christopher seems to have hoped that George I. might finish it. It is, however, now used as a barrack.

Dr. Morley, Bishop of Winchester, had also engaged Sir Christopher's assistance; and having pulled down a part of the old episcopal palace, he began to build another; he died when but one wing was erected and left sufficient money to finish it. Bishop Mew, his successor, as the 'Parentalia' says, 'never minded it;' but it was finished, apparently not under Wren's auspices, by Sir Jonathan Trelawney. He became Bishop of Winchester in 1707; as Bishop of Bristol he was one of the famous 'Seven Bishops.'

CHAPTER X.

1681–1686.

CHELSEA COLLEGE—S. JAMES'S, WESTMINSTER—A HARD WINTER—CHICHESTER SPIRE—AN ASTRONOMICAL PROBLEM—A SEAT IN PARLIAMENT—MORE CITY CHURCHES—A CURIOUS CARVING.

If to do were as easy as to know what were good to do, chapels had been churches, and poor men's cottages princes' palaces.—*Merchant of Venice*, act i. scene ii.

CHAPTER X.

CHARLES II.'s gift of Chelsea College to the Royal Society had proved a gift of greater magnitude than they had been able to deal with, and the building had remained unused since 1669. Nor did their funds allow them to make use of Mr. Howard's donation of a piece of land, though the ever-ready Sir Christopher produced a design for it of some size, on the principle 'that a fair building may be easier carried on by contribution with time, than a sordid one.' At last, in 1681, he proposed the sale of Chelsea College back again to King Charles, and Wren and Evelyn undertook to manage what must have been rather a delicate transaction. During the negotiation Sir Stephen Fox came to Evelyn and proposed that the King should buy it, and build there a hospital for soldiers. The proposal came well from Sir Stephen, who, originally a chorister of Salisbury Cathedral, by the favour and help of Bishop Duppa first, and then by that of the King, and most of all by his own honesty and dexterity, became paymaster to the whole army and acquired an honest and unenvied fortune. The King agreed to the plan, and the matter was arranged by Wren, Evelyn, and Fox, who was a liberal benefactor to the college. The three men went across to Lambeth to their old friend

Sancroft and acquainted him with the plan, and received his approval.

Wren set instantly to work, and in August 1682 the foundations were being laid; the whole building was not completed until William and Mary's reign; but during all that time Wren's energy and care never flagged, but were extended even to the minutiæ of the regulations, all of which he drew up, for the health, comfort, and economy of the building. As architecture the building has been severely criticised; but when the worst is said, it still remains picturesque, cheerful and spacious, and a beautiful object as seen from the Thames.

The Royal Society continued its meetings at Gresham College, which it did not quit until, in 1710, the members purchased a house in Crane Court, which has only very lately been pulled down. The next year saw many of Wren's churches finished.

All Hallows the Great, in Thames Street, a plain brick and stone edifice with a strong square tower, was then completed: it, like by far the greater number of the City churches, had been repaired and beautified under the vigorous rule of Laud while Bishop of London. Thomas White, who came into the living a few months only before the Fire, was afterwards as Bishop of Peterborough one of the famous 'Seven Bishops.' At the time when Wren rebuilt the church the living was held by the learned church historian, Dr. William Cave.[1]

S. Mildred's, Bread Street, is another church be-

---

[1] He wrote *Primitive Christianity*, *Lives of the Fathers*, &c.; was a Canon of Windsor, where he died in 1713.

longing to this date. It is so hidden by the tall warehouses that have sprung up round it that it is but little known; but its red brick tower, tall spire, and, above all, its most light and graceful dome, are all after Wren's best manner. The destruction of this beautiful little church has actually been threatened, but it has been ably defended, and it is to be hoped it will not add another name to the black list of desecrated City churches.

A third church belonging to this year is S. James's, Westminster, then called 'in the fields,' from the large parish of S. Martin's, out of which it was taken. It was built principally at the expense of Henry Jermyn, Earl of S. Albans, Wren's Paris friend, who gave his name to Jermyn Street, where the church stands.

The proportions of S. James's and the technical skill displayed in building it, especially the construction of the roof, have been always admired. Wren, who was allowed but a moderate sum to expend upon it, was proud of having combined beauty with 'the cheapest of any form I could invent.'[1] When the church was newly done, with its bricks red instead of darkly grimed with smoke, with the handsome pillared entrance to the south aisle, a flight of steps leading up to it, which have vanished, leaving only as a mark the closed iron gates in the railings, without the strange excrescence that now does duty as a porch—its exterior must have been far more attractive than it is now; the little pinched steeple[2] is said, as indeed one

---
[1] *Vide infra*, p. 310.
[2] Newcourt says, 'A lofty spire was at first built, but the tower

would imagine, to be no building of Wren's. Within, Evelyn[1] gives us his description of the effect.

> 'I went to see the new church at S. James's elegantly built; the altar was especially adorned, the white marble inclosure curiously and richly carved, the flowers and garlands about the walls by Mr. Gibbons in wood; a pelican with her young at her breast, just over the altar in the carved compartment and border, invironing the purple velvet fringed with I.H.S. richly embroidered, and most noble plate were given by Sir R. Geere to the value (as was said) of 200*l*. There was no altar anywhere in England nor has there been abroad more handsomely adorned.'

The font, now well placed in a baptistery beneath the tower, is one of Gibbons' few works in marble. It represents Adam and Eve, two detached statuettes standing on either side of the Tree of Knowledge, the branches of which support a bowl whereon are finely cut in low relief the Ark of Noah, and the baptism of the Ethiopian Eunuch. With all this, and without the high, stiff indevout pews which now disfigure the church—pews that Sir Christopher did not put there, and to the presence of which in any of his churches he always strongly objected, it must have been a decidedly handsome edifice. The organ, built by Renatus Harris, was made for James II.'s timber chapel at the

---

not proving strong enough, it was taken down, and another sort of spire built.' It is said to be by Willcox, a carpenter.

[1] *Diary*, December 7, 1684.

camp on Hounslow Heath; after the King's flight Wren obtained the organ from Queen Mary for S. James's Church.

Dr. Tenison, who then held S. James's jointly with S. Martin's, obtained the timbers of the chapel and used them in erecting the chapel of the Holy Trinity in Conduit Street,[1] which was also included in the enormous parish of S. Martin. S. Bennet, Paul's Wharf,[2] was finished in this year; picturesque and characteristic in its red brick, stone carving, well suited to its situation, then less cramped and overshadowed than it is now.

Its rector, Mr. Peter Lane, had experienced all the greater perils that had lately befallen the City; presented to the living in 1662, he steadily ministered there through the terrible time of the plague, and was then burnt out by the Great Fire. He lived, however, to return and to minister for five years in the new church built by Sir Christopher. In this church Inigo Jones was buried, in the darkest days of the Rebellion.

The handsome Church of S. James's, Garlickhithe, with its curious columnated steeple, and its projecting clock surmounted by a figure, is also of this date.

It was well that Sir Christopher had been able to get even this much of his numerous works finished, for the winter of 1683-4 was of exceptional severity. On December 23 the Thames was frozen over; on January 9,

[1] It was private property and never consecrated, and has within the last few years been pulled down and the site used as a shop.

[2] *Repertorium*, p. 367. Newcourt. Now used by the Welsh congregation.

Evelyn[1] 'went crosse the Thames on the ice, now become so thick as to beare not only streetes of booths in which they roasted meate and had divers shops of wares, quite acrosse in a towne, but coaches, carts, and horses passed over.' Evelyn himself drove across it to Lambeth to dine with Archbishop Sancroft, who had succeeded Sheldon in 1677. 'London,'—says Evelyn a few days later in words which, alas, still describe but too vividly a genuine 'London fog,'—' by reason of the excessive coldnesse hindering the ascent of the smoke, was so filled with the fuliginous steame of the sea-coale that hardly could one see crosse the streetes, and this filling the lungs with its grosse particles exceedingly obstructed the breath so as one could scarcely breathe. Here was no water to be had from the pipes and engines, nor could the brewers and other tradesmen worke, and every moment was full of disastrous accidents.'

In addition to this dismal state of things 'the small pox was very mortal.'

For eight weeks no foreign posts reached the city, for 'the very sea was so locked up with ice that no vessell could stir out or come in.' It was not until April was advanced that there was any sign of spring. It was certainly no building weather, and must have sharply tried the rising Choir of S. Paul's. Sir Christopher made a journey to Chichester on the invitation of the old Bishop, Guy Carleton, to examine the spire of the Cathedral. The whole building had

[1] *Diary*, January 9, 1684.

suffered terribly under the wanton sack of Sir William Waller and his men, and required extensive repair.

Sir Christopher 'for about two hours viewed the tower at the north west angle both without and within, and above and below, and observed the great want of repairs especially in the great western tower; made his report; proposing to clear away the ruin of the fallen tower; to pull down the south western tower; to shorten the nave by one arch, and to substitute a fair built west end of his own.'[1]

He next examined the beautiful spire, well known as a landmark to sailors in the channel, sister spire to that most perfect one at Salisbury which he has preserved to this day. He adopted a different plan with the Chichester spire to that which he had formerly pursued, for he took down the top of the spire, and fastened to the finial within an immense pendulum of yellow fir wood, which in great gales preserved exactly the balance of the spire. This lasted till 1813, when the pendulum was repaired by Mr. Elmes, and so remained until, after a great gale in 1861, the spire fell in; it has since been rebuilt, and is now rather higher than it was formerly. The other part of Wren's scheme was not acted upon. At this time he built Fawley Court in Oxfordshire: the place had lain in ruins since the civil war, when it suffered, though the property of Sir Bulstrode Whitelock, even more from Cromwell's troops than from those of Prince Rupert. Sir Bulstrode's descendants sold the property to Mr. William Freeman, who pulled the ruins down and got Sir

---

[1] *Memorials of the See of Chichester*, p. 306

Christopher to build the present Court, with its four fronts, handsome hall, and characteristic festoons of flowers in the ceiling.

In this same year Wren was made Controller of the Works, for which he received a salary of 9*l.* 2*s.* 6*d.* a year; not a very magnificent sum considering that a good deal of petty work and cares went with the office. It was necessary to see that this person had not incroached on the castle stables, or that person on the castle ditch; to measure and plan, and settle little quarrels and disputes in a way infinitely tormenting, one would think, to a man who had already such enormous works to consider. But Wren's genius was a patient one, and had a great grasp of details; he dealt with point after point as it arose, and no one seems ever to have complained of his breaking an engagement or neglecting to settle their difficulties.

While this work was going on all London was startled by the tidings of Charles II.'s sudden illness and death, when all the luxury of the Court was at its height. With all his grave faults, the King's death caused considerable grief throughout England; to both Wren and Evelyn he had been always kind and friendly, and both looked with great anxiety to the reign of his successor.

The Royal Society certainly lost a steady friend in Charles II. and was soon to see its court favour fade away. It was, however, much occupied with a discussion between Newton and Robert Hooke concerning the planetary motions. The question was one which deeply interested Wren, and which hitherto he had not been able to answer. As he and Hooke were walking together—Wren, whom one can never imagine but with all the courtesy and refinement of a finished gentleman, and Hooke half a miser, utterly slovenly, and jealous of any rising fame—they were met by Dr. Halley, an astronomer of some note even then, who was struggling with this problem and confessed that he had hitherto failed.

Wren promised a book worth forty shillings to whoever should solve the problem, whereupon Hooke declared he understood it from Kepler's 'Law of Periods and Distances,' and would show his solution some day to Wren; this he never did, and very soon Newton published his 'Principia,'[1] in which he solved this problem, acknowledging freely that Wren and Halley had independently deduced the law of gravity from Kepler's second law. He had a great quarrel with Hooke, the less to be wondered at, as, excepting Sir Christopher, Hooke quarrelled with everybody and was a philosopher of the sourest type. In 1685 Sir Christopher was returned to Parliament for the borough of Plympton S. Maurice, in Devonshire, a Parliament in which his cousin Charles also sat. The elections in Devonshire are supposed to have been specially influenced by the Court.

The 'Parentalia' gives no hint even of what his politics were, whether he spoke often or how he voted. And yet it was a stormy time. The Parliament had not sat a month before Monmouth's brief rebellion began,

[1] The title of Newton's book is *Philosophiæ Naturalis Principia Mathematica*. The MS. is in the possession of the Royal Society.

to be bloodily quenched; public feeling was in a state of irritation and suspense, no one feeling sure what King James might not do. He did continue Wren unmolested in the S. Paul's commission, and the progress of the building was steady, though probably its architect thought with no light anxiety that it might be used for services other than those for which it was designed.

The same doubt may have clouded his satisfaction in the many churches which were finished in this and the immediately following years. S. Martin's on Ludgate Hill, closely wedged in by the neighbouring houses, with its little tapering spire, of which that of S. James's, Westminster, appears a caricature, should have had its place among the churches of the previous year. It harmonizes beautifully with the great dome of S. Paul's. Sir Christopher bestowed on the inside much of the ornament, the festoons and the carving, which its situation did not allow him to bestow on the outside; in those days it had daily services and may well have stood open, offering 'a shadow from the heat' to the incessant passers-by.

S. Alban's, Wood Street, is in the pointed style of architecture in which Wren's genius generally felt fettered, though, as in the case of S. Michael's, Cornhill, he sometimes dealt very successfully with it.

S. Mary Magdalene's, Fish Street,[1] is more after

---

[1] Matthew Griffiths, the favourite and the pupil of Dean Donne, held this living through the Rebellion, and being a hearty Episcopalian was sequestered, plundered, and twice imprisoned; he returned to London and read the Prayers of the Church in the obscure church of S. Nicholas

Wren's usual manner, with its good proportions, its highly ornamented round-headed windows, its stone balustrade and solid square stone tower, with the little steeple rising from it on seven steps. Within, carving in 'right oak' was bestowed with no sparing hand, especially in the altar-piece. And here one may say that, while defects in church arrangement, such as galleries, pews, and the like, are invariably laid on Sir Christopher and said to be the inevitable concomitants of his style, it should be borne in mind that in many and many an instance the churchwardens during the eighteenth century repewed and 'beautified' the churches which Wren had left as completed; in what style, and on what principle one can readily guess. It should be remembered also that an 'altar-piece,' as the old books call it, was an invariable part of his design. If there was rich carving, if there was black and white marble, he placed it there; the altar was the principal part of the church in his eyes, even though he did not often avail himself of the dignity given by a flight of steps. The close altar rails which are now not admired, were, it must be remembered, ordered by Archbishop Laud to protect the Holy Table from profanation, and were always so placed by Wren.

Olave's,* hard by his own church, to the poor Cavaliers; for this he suffered seven violent assaults and five imprisonments; the last for preaching before General Monk a strong Royalist sermon before Monk had declared himself. Mr. Griffiths was speedily released and restored to his benefice.

---

* S. Nicholas Olave was burnt to the ground and the parish incorporated with that of S. Nicholas Coleabbey.—Newcourt's *Rep.*, p. 305.

S. Mary Magdalene's included the parish of S. Gregory, the little church which nestled by old S. Paul's, so that Fuller described the Cathedral as 'the mother church, having a babe in her arms.'[1]

S. Bennet's, Gracechurch Street, or Grasschurch Street, as it was really named, from a herb market formerly held hard by, is, or rather was, of the same date. It was well placed at the corner of two streets, and stood boldly out with a tall tower crowned with a cupola and slender spire; the interior was full of carving and ornament. S. Bennet's is, however, a thing of the past; the building is gone, the site desecrated, and the memory of such an edifice alone survives in the names of the streets which formerly led to and now usurp its place.

The little plain Church of S. Matthew, Friday Street, close pressed by neighbouring houses, is the last completed in this year. Obscure as the street where it stands may have been, it was full of associations for Wren. In Friday Street was the house where his aunt Anna lived, and where his uncle Matthew 'lay,' when summoned to that memorable conference with Bishop Andrewes. Hard by in the parish of S. Peter's, Eastcheap, now incorporated with that of S. Matthew, Christopher's merchant grandfather had lived and died, and there his own father had been born. S. Peter's churchyard was preserved, and its single plane-tree is carefully protected.

[1] It would seem from the S. Gregory's vestry books that Sir C. Wren put up at the request of the parishioners 'a wooden tabernacle' for the use of both parishes. It was set up in S. Paul's Churchyard, and taken down after a time as interfering with the building of the Cathedral.

S. Matthew's has a less pleasant association: the living was for a time held by the notorious Henry Burton,[1] the friend and ally of Prynne. Burton was at first designed to accompany the Prince of Wales to Spain, but doubts of his principles arising, he was rejected and dismissed from his attendance as the Prince's chaplain. This formed one strong motive for the bitter spite he bore to the church of his ordination. It is likely also that he stirred Prynne's malice against Bishop Wren, who appears to have been Burton's successor in the vacant chaplaincy.

The lesser details of the Surveyor-General's work must this year have been a burden. There were complaints from Winchester, where the sudden stoppage of the buildings and plans for the palace caused great inconvenience; a complaint from Catherine Barton, the beautiful niece of Sir Isaac Newton, widow of Colonel Barton, who sold her farm to Charles II., and by the trickery of the agent never received her money; and a complaint of the same kind from Sir Richard Tichbourne's son. Sir Christopher examined both these cases carefully, and compelled the agent to submit, and to satisfy the parties. Then there were troubles with the Duke of Buckingham and the 'chaos' he had made in Spring Gardens, that chaos so vividly described in 'Peveril of the Peak.' Nobody but Wren could give the estimates for the new stables at S. James's Palace, or order the new planting at Hampton Court and in Greenwich Park, or secure

---

[1] *Repertorium*, p. 475. Newcourt.

the proper tithes for the Rector of S. Thomas's, Winchester.

Again, there was Verrio the painter's account for work done at Whitehall and Windsor to be examined. For the chapel at Whitehall Verrio demanded 1,250*l*., and, says Wren, 'I suppose when the rest of the ceiling and walls are finished, as they ought to be, it may fully deserve it.' The whole bill was 2,050*l*., of which Verrio had received already more than 1,400*l*., so that he may be reckoned as fortunate.

It is not wonderful that in 1686, Wren attended no meeting of the Society. Two churches were finished this year: S. Clement's, East Cheap, and S. Mary's, Abchurch, in Cannon Street.

S. Clement's, with its square tower and balustrade, has within a great deal of fine oak carving, and its ceiling adorned with one great circle with an outer line of curious fretwork. Bishop Pearson was rector before the Fire, and the famous treatise on the ~~Nicene~~ Creed is dedicated to his parishioners there.

S. Mary's, with its quaint little round windows and flat-topped roof, is not externally beautiful, but within it is one of the gems which Wren bestowed on out-of-the-way nooks: its cupola[1] is gracefully supported on eight arches and pendentives, the east end is rich with Gibbons' carving of festoons of fruit, palm leaves and a pelican in her piety. Much handsome work has also been bestowed on the inside doorcases.

Wren's promise to Evelyn to employ Gibbons was certainly redeemed; for, besides the works which

---

[1] *Walks in London.* A. Hare, vol. i. p. 331.

have been glanced at, Gibbons was busied on the stalls of S. Paul's choir, where, darkened but uninjured by time, his work stands out in all the peculiar grace and tenderness which his chisel could give to wood. The angels which cluster beneath the great organ seem themselves to be taking part in the music which flows from it, and are as unlike as possible to the lumps of marble or wood with which other hands too often deform a church, and which the old guide-books term 'Cupids'!

Still, it is a physical impossibility that all the work which bears Gibbons' name is by him and him only.

The fame of the Cathedral, its architect, and its carvings, was widely spread, and brought many from the country to seek for work on the new building. Of one of these a curious account remains.[1] A young man, named Philip Wood, of Sudbury, Suffolk, who had great skill in carving, came up to London to make, if he could, sufficient fortune to enable him to marry the daughter of his patron, a retired London merchant named Haybittle. After long waiting in London, without work, till his money was all but spent, he, remembering the rich wood-work which abounded in the churches of his native Suffolk, bethought himself that in the Cathedral, whose progress he daily watched, 'they would surelie put carvings.' The foreman to whom he spoke repulsed him, saying 'We want no carpenters here.' Undiscouraged, the young man

[1] For this anecdote (taken from MS. in the British Museum) I am indebted to a number of the *British Workman* for 1877. It is, I think, the foundation of Mr. J. Saunders' graceful story of *Jasper Deane*.

came again day after day for a week, till at length Sir Christopher noticed him, and learning from the foreman that he was 'a country fellow who troubled them to give him some of the carving to do,' beckoned to Wood to come and speak to him. As the young man approached full of hope, he said, 'Friend, you want carving work—what have you been used to carve?' At this critical, long-desired moment the poor youth lost his presence of mind, and instead of mentioning the 'sundry figures of lions and elephants' that he had carved for Mr. Haybittle's house, stammered out, 'Please your worship, I have been used to carve troughs.' 'Troughs!' said Sir Christopher; 'then carve me as a specimen of your skill, a sow and pigs (it will be something in your line), and bring it to me this day week. I shall be here.' So he went away, with a smile at the presumption which could aspire to step straight from such work to that of adorning S. Paul's.

Distracted at his own folly and the loud laughter of the workpeople, Wood rushed back to his lodging, and but for the kind advice of his Quaker landlady, would have given up all for lost. She wisely told him to take Wren at his word and carve the best sow and pigs that he could make.

He obeyed her exactly, spent his last guinea on a block of pear-wood, and wrought with all his might to get it ready by the appointed day. Sir Christopher was showing the building to a party of friends, but as soon as he saw Wood with his carving hidden in an apron, he beckoned him forward. Wood produced his carving; Wren looked at it a moment in silence, and then said, 'I engage you, young man; attend at my office to-morrow forenoon.' Shortly afterwards he came to Wood again and said, 'Mr. Addison [1] wishes to keep your carving, and requests me to give you ten guineas for it;' then with his gentle courtesy, he added, 'Young man, I fear I did you some injustice, but a great national work is entrusted to me, and it is my solemn duty to mind that no part of the work falls into inefficient hands. Mind and attend me to-morrow.' Wood was employed for seven years in the Cathedral, and received considerable sums of money; and it is pleasant to know that he did marry Hannah Haybittle.

Thus some of his work is in S. Paul's, and to him London streets were indeed paved with gold. Yet one cannot but think sadly, for one who thus succeeded, what numbers then and now come full of hope, to the great city, and without help or friends lose their all, and are left without even the means of returning. To the number of these the House of Charity, which occupies one corner of Wren's once handsome Soho Square, can bear but too true a testimony.

[1] Probably the father of the great writer.

CHAPTER XI.
1687–1696.

PARLIAMENT DISSOLVED—CHURCH BUILDING—ACQUITTAL OF THE SEVEN BISHOPS—JAMES II.'S FLIGHT—WILLIAM AND MARY—COLLEGE OF PHYSICIANS—HAMPTON COURT—GREENWICH HOSPITAL—RICHARD WHITTINGTON—S. PAUL'S ORGAN.

S

> Be it enacted then
> By the fair laws of thy firm-pointed pen,
> God's services no longer shall put on
> A sluttishness for pure religion;
> No longer shall our churches' frighted stones
> Lie scattered like the burnt and martyr'd bones
> Of dead devotion.
> *On a treatise on Charity.* RICHARD CRASHAW.

CHAPTER XI.

WREN's parliamentary career was soon interrupted, for King James dissolved, in 1687, an assembly which had done so little to forward his views.

Church building went on apace. S. Andrew's, Holborn, which, though the fire had not reached it, was in a ruinous state, was rebuilt and made a large handsome stone church, with an interior very like that of S. James's, Westminster. The tower was merely repaired and not rebuilt.

Christ Church, Newgate, on the site of the old Franciscan Monastery of Grey Friars, had formerly been a magnificent edifice: the choir only was rebuilt by Wren, and sufficed to make a large parish church, which was filled with handsome carving; a graceful pillared steeple was added in 1704.

S. Margaret Pattens,[1] in Rood Lane, was finished in 1687 : built of brick and stone with a tall tower and graceful spire, and much enriched by carving within. Its existence has been threatened, but it stands out an honourable, though fortunately not at all a solitary example, of a well-worked, and therefore well-filled, City

---

[1] The name is often supposed to originate in the patten-makers who are said to have lived near, but its origin is more probably ' S. Margaret *with the Paten.*'

church, and it is to be hoped may defy its threatened destroyers.

Early in the following year came the trial of those Seven Bishops who refused to publish in church the King's declaration of liberty of conscience.[1]

It was perhaps the most unwise thing that James II. ever did, and as the Bishops passed to the barge that was to take them to the Tower, rank upon rank of kneeling people besought their blessing. It was an event to move Wren greatly : he could remember when a child hearing of Archbishop Laud's imprisonment, and the long years of Bishop Wren's captivity were frequently cheered by his nephew's visits to the Tower. Most of those who now passed to that ill-omened abode were his friends or acquaintance. Bishop Turner of Ely was on the S. Paul's Commission ; Bishop Lloyd of S. Asaph while rector of S. Martin's had baptized Wren's daughter and youngest son ; Bishop White he had known in the days when he was rector. Bishop Ken at Winchester, and Archbishop Sancroft had been for years his steady friends.

[1] 'Not,' says Evelyn (*Diary*, May 18, 1688), ' that they were averse to the publisheing of it for want of due tendernesse towards Dissenters . . . but that the Declaration being founded on such a dispensing power as might at pleasure set aside all laws ecclesiastical, it appeared to them illegal and . . . . a point of such consequence that they could not so far make themselves parties to it as the reading of it in church during the time of Divine Service would have done.' They were sent to the Tower June 8, for refusing to give bail for their appearance. They refused on the ground that to do so would have prejudiced their peerage. The bishops were Francis Turner of Ely, William Lloyd of S. Asaph, Thomas Ken of Bath and Wells, John Lake of Chichester, Sir Jonathan Trelawney of Bristol, Thomas White of Peterborough, and William Sancroft, Archbishop of Canterbury.

If he failed in dignity at one crisis, there is abundant material in Sancroft's letters, and in the rest of his life, to show he must have been a charming companion and capable of inspiring sincere affection.

They remained in the Tower about a week, and on June 29 were triumphantly acquitted. The story of their acquittal has been told once for all by Lord Macaulay and need not be re-told here. London was full of illuminations, the favourite device being seven candles—the tallest central one representing the archbishop—and all the newly-hung bells of the city were set ringing. Wren had private sorrows to hinder him from entering into the public rejoicing: his only surviving sister, Susan, died just at this time, and Wren must have been watching by her on the very day of the Bishops' acquittal. A little later, he, and her husband, Dr. William Holder, brought her body to the crypt of S. Paul's and laid her there. The epitaph, on a marble monument, is written with all the diffuseness of style common to those of that time, but is touching from its real affection.

The crypt of S. Paul's was of course the part of the building first finished. Long ago Wren had spoken of 'the quantity of work to be done in the dark,' and it certainly proved enormous. The crypt of S. Paul's is one of the largest and most intricate that exists, extending under the entire church, not the choir only, as is the case in S. Peter's at Rome. The dimness of a London atmosphere renders it hard to get much effect of light and shade, but on a clear day the curious twilight effect is striking. There are all the tombs which were preserved from the old cathedral, there are now the remains of some of our greatest dead, and there is the Church of S. Faith, the floor of which is now being slowly covered with a beautiful mosaic.[1]

When, however, Sir Christopher laid his sister there, all was empty and not fully complete; the cluster of pillars and arches that sustain the great dome with their massive strength must have been but newly finished.

Only one church was completed by Sir Christopher in this troubled year, that of S. Michael, Crooked Lane; a handsome stone church with a stately tower and spire. It contained the tomb of a famous city worthy, Sir William Walworth:

> Who with courage stout and manly might
> Slew Wat Tyler in King Richard's sight.[2]

This association had no value in the eyes of the Corporation of London, with whom it might have weighed: they were as indifferent to this lesser reason as to the infinitely higher claim of consecrated ground, and in 1830 the church was swept away for the new London Bridge.

All through the year the relations between King James and his people were growing more and more strained. Messages were passed and repassed between many of the high officials and the Prince of Orange, and in their dread of the Church of Rome, the people forgot what they had suffered under the tyranny of

---

[1] The mechanical part is done by the women convicts of Woking Gaol.

[2] *New View of London*, vol. ii. p. 423.

the Puritan sects. Hurry and confusion were everywhere; as the year advanced the Prince of Orange's landing was hourly reported on all parts of the coast. Too late King James took some of the measures which, taken earlier, might have saved all; and on November 5, 1688, the Prince landed at Brixham in Torbay.

For some time all was confusion and all private business was suspended. Early in the next year a convention was called of the Lords and Commons, and the crown offered to William and Mary. The Queen's behaviour, the absence of even the show of feeling for her father, were much remarked on at the time and are a great stain on her memory. A Parliament was called on the 13th of February, to which Sir C. Wren was returned for the borough of New Windsor. His election was set aside for a technical error in the manner of his return, but he was instantly re-elected. It is evident from this that he took the new oath of allegiance, probably holding, with Evelyn and other honourable men, that King James had abdicated and that therefore the throne was vacant. The S. Paul's commission was renewed, and amid all the changes the work there went on; making in its steady, undeviating progress, its unity of design, a fair type of the growth of the spiritual church, despite the sharp contrast apparently existing between the peaceful, regular growth of the material edifice, and the hindrances and trials that beset the spiritual one. Those were the days when some of the best and most learned churchmen, unable to reconcile the contradiction of the two oaths, lost high office, honours, and all prospects of worldly success by becoming 'non-jurors.' It should be borne in mind that it was on no doctrinal ground that they left the Communion of the Church in England, but simply because, considering James II. still as King, they could not honestly take an oath of allegiance to William as his successor, or attend services where an usurper was prayed for as the rightful sovereign.

It was a most grievous blow to the Church, by no means recovered from the struggle with Puritanism or from the semi-Puritan clergy she had been constrained to accept. Yet, in the midst of all these misfortunes, thus much at least was gained; men were forced to understand the true grounds of their position and to learn, as the Church in Scotland learnt by a sharper lesson, that State aid, and State protection, are not among the essentials of the Church. The misfortune of so many friends, and especially that of good Archbishop Sancroft, must greatly have moved Wren, and it is provoking that his grandson has given no intimation of his ancestor's views, not even saying on which side he voted in the Convention Parliament, which offered the crown to William and Mary.

Wren certainly knew how to manage his Windsor constituents. He had erected from time to time several buildings there, among which was the Town Hall, built upon arches, with a wide vaulted space below, which is now used as the Corn Exchange.

When all was finished, the mayor and corporation came in state to inspect the new building, and to stamp with their approval another of the great architect's works. Much seems to have been approved of, but one member of the municipality declared in alarm that the room above the vaulted space was inadequately supported and would one day fall in.

In vain Wren, who had built vault after vault and knew to a nicety what weight each of his arches would bear, explained the perfect security of the upper room; the anxious man could not be pacified and the architect promised to put two columns below. He did so, and the alderman was calmed, little knowing that Sir Christopher's columns when complete had about half an inch of space between themselves and the ceiling they were supposed to support! Wren must many a time have laughed to himself when he passed that way.

Two other buildings of his, one of which is called 'the Bank House,' stand in Windsor not far from what are known as 'The Hundred Steps.' There is another house there of his design, now used by the freemasons and the volunteers. Wren sent his eldest son to Eton, where the boy was at this time, and afterwards to Pembroke College, where his name alone was a recommendation.

In 1689 Wren finished building the College of Physicians in Warwick Lane; as far as the confined space would admit, the front was handsome, but the dome and its ornament provoked the satire of Garth in the opening lines of his 'Dispensary':[1]

---

[1] Canto i. Samuel Garth, a physician of some fame, who provided for Dryden's funeral in Westminster Abbey. Died 1718.

> Not far from that most celebrated place,[1]
> Where angry justice shows her awful face,
> Where little villains must submit to fate
> That great ones may enjoy the world in state;
> There stands a dome majestic to the sight,
> And sumptuous arches bear its oval height;
> A golden globe, placed high with artful skill
> Seems, to the distant sight, a gilded pill.

Whatever its exterior defects may have been, the theatre within was arranged with masterly skill so as to enable all the students to see and hear during the lectures and demonstration. The difficult science of acoustics was one to which Wren gave much attention, and his churches are, in this respect, very successful. The Physicians retained the college Wren built for them until very recent times, when they moved into the present building which does not adorn Trafalgar Square.

Not all the Halls belonging to the City Companies perished by the fire, though many suffered severely. Wren, and Jarman, the City Architect, rebuilt and repaired some seventy-nine of them.[2]

Of these, a large number have been altered or pulled down, but a few may be mentioned.

The Mercers' Hall in Cheapside; the Grocers', a portion of which was long used by the Bank of England; the Haberdashers', where the rich ceiling was its great ornament; the Tallow Chandlers', with its interior colonnade and its fountain; the Apothecaries', one of the largest in the City; the Stationers'; and, last but not least, the Alderman's Court adjoining Guildhall,

---

[1] Newgate.   [2] See Appendix ii.

rebuilt almost immediately after the fire; a very handsome room, rich in carving, and finely proportioned.

S. Edmund the King, in Lombard Street, was finished this year. The necessities of the site caused Wren to build it north and south, the altar being at the north end. The front to Lombard Street, the only part of the outside visible, is of stone and very picturesque with its belfry and little domed spire. The interior has been lately re-arranged with a wise treatment of the old work and carving. The 'marble font possesses, like that of S. Mary Abchurch, a very beautiful canopied cover; it is in two stages, the lower being domed, and above are four seated figures of the Cardinal Virtues; it is railed in and is on the west side of the church.'[1]

S. Margaret's, Lothbury, belongs to the same date, and was rebuilt of stone. Some years later Wren bestowed much rich wood carving on the interior. He chose the Corinthian style for this building and handled it with considerable skill.

Queen Mary, who had the Stuart love for genius, was invariably gracious and even friendly to Wren, with whom she held many a conversation on matters of art and science. He considered her to be very well versed in all these subjects and enjoyed discussing them freely with her. Queen Mary was much charmed with the situation of Cardinal Wolsey's old palace of Hampton Court, and engaged Wren to make alterations there. The old buildings were accordingly in part pulled down and two sets of royal

[1] R. I. B. A. Sessional Papers, 1876-7, p. 162.

apartments built; Queen Mary, though she amused herself with planning the gardens and making suggestions, had yet the wisdom to defer to Wren's better taste and knowledge. Her husband, with characteristic obstinacy, insisted on his own ideas, thereby dwarfing the cloisters and marring much of the architecture. It is, however, fair to say that King William always owned that the defects [1] were his, the merits, Wren's; and these merits are very great, as anyone who knows the fine old palace with its rich red brick, its arcades, and the quaint formal gardens will readily allow. He built, at about the same time, the Pavilion and Ranger's House in Bushey Park.

Kensington Palace was also under Wren's hands. It had been the property of Lord Chancellor Finch, and was sold by his son to William III. Wren added another story to the old house, which forms the north front of the palace, and also built the south front. The defect of the building as seen at the end of the long avenue of Kensington Gardens is its want of height, but on a nearer approach this fault is much diminished. King William was in the midst of his Irish campaign while the work went on, but found time to send back repeated inquiries as to its progress, and complaints when that did not answer his expectations. There, five years later, Queen Mary died, to the regret of all her subjects, and even of her cold-hearted husband.

Nor were these the only palaces which Wren

[1] Horace Walpole says that Wren's descendant assured him that Sir C. Wren had prepared a far better design for Hampton Court which Queen Mary preferred, but it was overruled by William III. This may only mean the cloisters, as Walpole is not accurate.—*Anec.*, vol. iii.

contrived for Queen Mary. That of Greenwich had been begun by Inigo Jones for Henrietta Maria, and a wing had been built for Charles II., but it had been left unfinished. Wren, who knew Greenwich well from his visits to the Observatory, and who took a great interest in sailors, observing the entire lack of any refuge for them in illness, proposed to Queen Mary the magnificent plan of making the palace into a seaman's hospital. The Queen willingly entered into the idea, and proposed to add to the Queen's House, as it was called, so as to make it a dwelling for herself, at the same time. Evelyn, Sir Stephen Fox and others, came readily into the scheme and contributed liberally. Wren's contribution, though not in money, was a liberal one also; for he gave his time, labour, skill and superintendence, despite his innumerable other works.

The plans were prepared and money collected, but nothing was actually done until some years later.

Wren's eldest son had in the meantime finished his Eton and Cambridge career and had obtained, by his father's interest, the post, which must surely have been a sinecure! of Assistant Deputy Engrosser. He does not seem to have inherited any of the brilliant genius of his father, though apparently of very fair abilities and with much taste for antiquities. Far more like Sir Christopher was his daughter Jane, who shared his tastes and studies and took a vivid interest in his work. She added to her other accomplishments that of being a very skilful musician. She was never married, but remained all her life her father's affectionate companion.

Wren's old friend, Dr. Bathurst of Trinity College, Oxford, appealed to him, in the spring of 1692, for help in the buildings which were still going on there.

> 'Worthy Sir,—When I sent Mr. Phips (the surveyor of the buildings) to wait on you with a scheme of our new building, he told me how kindly you was pleased to express your remembrance of me, and that you would send me your thoughts concerning our design; and particularly of the pinnacles, the which as they were superadded to our first draught, so I must confess I would be well content to have omitted with your approbation. The season for our falling to work again will now speedily come on; which makes me the more hasten to entreat from you the trouble of two or three lines in relation to the promises whereby you will farther oblige,
>
> 'Sir, your old friend, and ever faithful servant,
>
> 'R. BATHURST.'

Wren's answer comes promptly, and shows his generous readiness to help the schemes of others, no matter how pressing his own work was.

> 'Sir,—I am extremely glad to hear of your good health, and, what is more, that you are vigorous and active, and employed in building. I considered the design you sent me of your Chapel which in the main is very well, and I believe your work is too far advanced to admit of any advice: however, I have sent my thoughts, which will be of use to the mason to form his mouldings.

'He will find two sorts of cornice; he may use either. I did not well comprehend how the tower would have good bearing upon that side where the stairs rise. I have ventured a change of the stairs, to leave the wall next the porch of sufficient scantling to bear that part which rises above the roofs adjoining.

'There is no necessity for pinnacles, and those expressed in the printed design are much too slender.

'I have given another way to the rail and baluster, which will admit of a vase that will stand properly upon the pilaster.[1]

'Sir, I wish you success and health and long life, with all the affection that is due from,

'Your obliged, faithful friend, and humble servant,

'CHRISTOPHER WREN.

'P.S. A little deal box, with a drawing in it, is sent by Thomas Moore, Oxford carrier.'

In the same year the Church of S. Andrew by the Wardrobe[2] was finished; recent alterations in the city have benefited this building; it now stands well above a flight of steps, with its square tower, and the red brick which contrives to be red and not black, and stone dressings.

Two years later Wren rebuilt All Hallows, Lombard

---

[1] This plan was adopted. Dr. Bathurst died in May 1704 at the age of 86.

[2] So called from being in the street where formerly was a strong tower where several kings, and Queen Philippa, Edward the Third's wife, lodged, also called the Queen's Wardrobe, as the building near S. Andrew's was the King's Wardrobe.—*New View*, vol. ii. p. 427.

Street, on an ancient foundation: outside it is one of his plainest and most solid churches, inside he spent upon it much rich work and curious carving both in stone and wood.

S. Michael Royal, College Hill, belongs to this same date, and was built under Wren's directions by Edward Strong, his master-mason. It is a well-lit, handsome church with a tower at one corner, and contains an altar-piece of singular beauty, carved by Grinling Gibbons in 'right wainscot oak.' The old church was founded and made a collegiate church of S. Spiritus and S. Mary by no less a person than Sir Richard Whittington, three times Lord Mayor of London (1397, 1406, 1419), whose fame, with that of his cat, survives in the well-known story. He founded also another college, known as the Whittington College, and endowed it with a divinity lecture 'for ever.' Edward VI., however, suppressed both the colleges and the lecture, though the Whittington College was allowed partially to survive as almshouses for poor men. Whittington[1] was buried in this church, but his monument perished in the Fire.

In the following year Wren added a well-proportioned, peculiar steeple, the gift of the parishioners, to the little stone Church of S. Vedast[2] in Foster Lane,

---

[1] 'The said Sir R. Whittington, as he was three times Lord Mayor, was as often buried in this church; first, by his executors under a fine monument; second, by the avaricious parson for the riches he hoped to find; and a third time by his friends, to interr him in lead under his monument as at first.'—*New View*, p. 428.

[2] 'S. Vedast was Bishop of Arras, A.D. 484, a man of great holiness and charity. Once he met with a cruel bear prowling in the ruins of an old Christian church; at his command the bear departed into the

a church to which a painful interest now attaches from the recent persecution and imprisonment of its rector, the Rev. T. P. Dale.

The church was decorated, as was Wren's custom, with fret-work, carving, and stucco, but is not otherwise remarkable.

S. Mary's, Somerset, or Somers'hithe, was likewise finished in this year: a stone church with two aisles surmounted by a handsome cornice and balustrade; its great feature was the beautiful pinnacled tower, which, though the church is gone, still stands a perpetual memorial of that reckless disregard of God's honour, which has counted any common want, any farthing of money, of more importance than the claims of His service, or than gifts solemnly offered to Him.[1]

The Cathedral meanwhile grew slowly, though many a hindrance annoyed its architect. The Parliament took part of the fabric money and applied it to the expenses of King William's wars, so that, as Sir Christopher complained, his wings were clipt and the Church was deprived of its ornaments.[2] The organ was

wilderness and never returned there again. S. Vedast is usually pictured with a bear.'—*Repertorium*, Newcourt, vol. i. p. 563.

[1] Fourteen churches (eleven of which were built by Wren) have been destroyed since 1781; during which time the increase of the City population has been by hundreds of thousands. The only attempt at an apology for this destruction has been based on the fact that on *Sundays* the City is empty. On so poor a plea as this the churches have been closely shut throughout the other days of the week, their incumbents have lived far away, leaving their parishioners uncared for; and then, when a grudgingly given Sunday service has been poorly attended, have hastened first to close and then to help in destroying the buildings which reproached them; and have called it 'thinning the City churches.'—See on this subject, *Sessional Papers*, 1876-7, R. I. B. A.

[2] *Three Cathedrals*, Longman, p. 151.

T

another annoyance. Sir Christopher's wish and intention was to place the organ where it now is, on either side of the choir, in order to leave the vista clear from the west door to the altar, which in his design stood grandly raised under a handsome canopy. This was overruled, and the organ was to be placed in a gallery cutting right across the entrance of the choir With his wonted philosophy, Wren bent his mind to reducing as much as possible the injury to the architectural effect, by keeping the pipes as low as he could. But in the builder of the organ, Bernard Smith, or 'Father' Smith, as he is called, Wren had a difficult person to deal with. Far from lowering the pipes, Smith made them higher than in his estimate, so that the case and ornaments had to be enlarged, and Sir Christopher complained bitterly that the Cathedral 'was spoilt by that box of whistles.' The rival organ builder, Renatus Harris, if indeed he was the author of an anonymous paper, called 'Queries about the S. Paul's Organ,'[1] was not sparing in his criticisms. One query asks 'Whether Sir C. Wren

> wou'd not have been well pleas'd to have receiv'd such a proposal from the organ builder of S. Paul's, as shou'd have erected an organ, so as to have separated twenty foot in the middle, as low as the gallery, and thereby a full and airy prospect of the whole length of the church, and six fronts with towers as high as requisite?'

This question is easy enough to answer, and fortunately Wren's wishes have been at last fulfilled by

---

[1] *Documents illustrating the History of S. Paul's*, p. 165-72.

that division of the organ, which now leaves the desired clear view from the great western doors to the altar. Harris, in 1712, proposed to erect a great organ over the west doors of the Cathedral, 'study'd to be in all respects made the most artful, costly and magnificent piece of organ-work that ever has hitherto been invented. The use of it will be for the reception of the Queen, on all publick occasions of thanksgivings for the good effect of peace or war, upon all state days, S. Cecilia's Day, the entertainment of foreigners of quality, and artists, and on all times of greatest concourse etc., and by the advice and assistance of Sir C. Wren, the external figure and ornaments may be contrived so proportionable to the order of the building, as to be a decoration to that part of the edifice and no obstruction to any of the rest. . . . . Sir Christopher Wren approves it.' Alas! at that time Wren's approval was enough to determine the majority of the commission to reject any plan thus sanctioned, and Renatus Harris's grand design survives on paper alone.

CHAPTER XII.

1697–1699.

OPENING OF S. PAUL'S CHOIR—A MOVEABLE PULPIT—LETTER TO HIS SON AT PARIS—ORDER AGAINST SWEARING—PETER THE GREAT—S. DUNSTAN'S SPIRE—MORNING PRAYER CHAPEL OPENED—WESTMINSTER ABBEY.

Home-keeping youth have ever homely wit.
Two Gentlemen of Verona.

CHAPTER XII.

ONE serious trouble and hindrance in all public works was the state of the coinage. The money had been so clipped and defaced, that no coin was worth its professed value, and for some time the expedients used by the Government failed to lighten the pressure. In paying such an army of workmen as those employed about S. Paul's, the inconvenience must have amounted to positive distress. Scattered here and there through Evelyn's diary are many references to the 'great confusion and distraction' it occasioned.

A sudden subsidence of a large part of the ground at Portland, close to the quarries set apart for Wren's use, caused an inconvenient delay in bringing the stone to London, but yet the work progressed, and on December 2nd, 1697, the choir was opened for service.

It was the occasion of the thanksgiving for the peace of Ryswick, which, though it brought little glory to England, was yet heartily welcomed as the close of a long and exhausting war.

King William went to Whitehall, and heard Bishop Burnet's flattering sermon, while Bishop Compton preached for the first time in the new S. Paul's. No report of his sermon has come down to us. The choir was not yet enriched with the carvings of

Gibbons; but the pulpit appears to have been very remarkable in its way: Sir Christopher had placed it *on wheels*, perhaps with a design of using it afterwards, for services under the dome, not unlike those we are now familiar with.

A pulpit on wheels was a novelty, which gave rise, we can well believe, to many squibs, one of which has been preserved.

A faithful copy of the Verses, lately fastened upon the pulpit of S. Paul's Choir.

TO THE ARCHITECT UPON HIS HAPPY INVENTION OF A PULPIT ON WHEELS FOR THE USE OF S. PAUL'S CHOIR.

This little Structure (Excellent Sir Kit)
Holds forth to us that You bestowed more Wit
In Building it than on all Paul's beside;
This shows the *Principles*, that but the *Pride*
Of its *Inhabitants;* True Sons of *Saul*,
For he (Good Man) *became All things to All*,
That by all Sorts of Means he might gain some.
They too for *Gain* would follow him to *Rome*,
This *Passively Obedient* thing will go as
They'd have it, or to *Mecca, Rome*, or *Troas*;
All one to it, if forward Hawl'd or back,
'Twill run a Holy Stage for *Will* or *Jack*;
And truckle to and fro' 'twixt Cause and Cause,
Just as Strongest Pull of *Interest* draws.
But if the Pulpit be a Vital Part
O' th' *Church*, or as the Doctors say her Heart,
Why don't you fix *that* also on a Rock
And let the Steeple Roost the *Weather-Cock?*
Where if a Puff of Strong Temptations blow,
It might remind the Staggering Saints and *Crow.*
Improve the Thought, Dear Sir, and let St. Paul's
Wise Fane be this new Going Cart *for Souls.*[1]

It hardly needs the hint that these lines were

---

[1] Given in *Documents illustrating the History of S. Paul's*, p. 157.

affixed to 'the *Dean's* side of the pulpit,' to read in them a bitter satire on Dean Sherlock, whose sudden change of front relative to the non-jurors, and acceptance of the Deanery of S. Paul's, laid him open to the grave suspicion of having acted from interested motives, and stirred up much vehement animosity. A spirited, if not an impartial, account of this controversy, is given by Lord Macaulay.[1]

Sir Christopher's remarkable invention appears to have survived the laughter against it, and to have remained in the Cathedral until 1803.

The vaults of S. Paul's were opened shortly after this thanksgiving to receive the body of Dr. White, the non-juring Bishop of Peterborough, whose funeral was attended by Bishop Turner, Bishop Lloyd and forty nonjuring clergymen.

At the beginning of the following year, as soon as travelling was possible, Wren sent his son Christopher to Paris ; not indeed with the intention of his making that grand tour which a few years later was supposed to finish a young gentleman's education, but that he might acquire a little experience and knowledge of the world. The young man, evidently, had other ideas, spent a good deal of his money, and then wrote home to his family a letter complaining in true English fashion, of the climate and the cookery of France, and asking leave to continue his journey to Italy. Sir Christopher's reply has been preserved ; and in its folio sheet and brown ink exists in the ' Parentalia.'

[1] *History of England*, vol. iv. p. 44-51. Sherlock was born 1641, died 1707.

It is, I think, so charming as to double one's regret that so very few of his letters have been preserved.

[1] 'Whitehall, March 7.

'My dear Son,—I hope by this time you are pretty well satisfied of the condition of the climate you are in; if not, I believe you will ere Lent be over; and will learne to dine upon sallad; and morue with egges will scarce be allowed: if you thinke you can dine better cheape in Italy you can trie, but I think the passing of the Alpes and other dangers of disbanded armies and abominable Lodgings will ballance that advantage; but the seeing of fine buildings I perceive temptes you, and your companion, Mr. Strong, whose inclination and interest leades him, by neither of which can I find you are mov'd; but how doth it concerne you? You would have it to say hereafter that you have seen Rome, Naples and a hundred other fine places; a hundred others can say as much and more; calculate whither this be worth the expence and hazard as to any advantage at youre returne. I sent you to France at a time of businesse and when you might make your observations and find acquaintance who might hereafter be usefull to you in the future concernes of your life: if this be your ayme I willingly let you proceed, provided you will soon returne, for these reasons, the little I have to leave you is unfortunately involved in trouble, and your presence would be a comfort to me, to assist me, not only for my sake, but your own that you might understand your affaires, before

[1] The year is not given in the MS. original, but it must be 1698.

it shall please God to take me from you, which if suddenly will leave you in perplexity and losse. I doe not say all this out of parsimony, for what you spend will be out of what will in short time, be your owne, but I would have you be a man of businesse as early as you can bring your thoughts to it. I hope, by your next you will give me account of the reception of our ambassador;[1] of the intrigues at this time between the two nations, of the establishment of the commerce, and of anything that may be innocently talked of without danger, and reflection, that I may perceive whither you look about you or noe and penetrate into what occurres, or whither the world passes like a pleasant dream, or the amusement of fine scenes in a play without considering the plot. If you have in ten weeks spent half your bill of exchange besides your gold, I confesse your money will not hold out, either abroad for yourself or for us at home to supply you, especially if you goe for Italy, which voyage forward and backward will take up more than twenty weekes : thinke well of it, and let me hear more from you, for though I would advise you, I will not discontent you. Mr. Strong hath profered credit by the same merchant he uses for his son, and I will thinke of it, but before I change, you must make up your account with your merchant, and send it to me. My hearty

[1] William, Earl of Portland, whose embassy was of extraordinary splendour. Of intrigues there must have been plenty, for at the very moment that Louis XIV. was for the first- time recognising the Prince of Orange as King of England, King James II. was residing at S. Germains, surrounded by his own Court.

service to young Mr. Strong and tell him I am obliged to him for your sake. I bless God for your health, and pray for the continuance of it through all adventures till it pleases him to restore you to your Sister and friends who wish the same as doth

'Your most affectionate Father,

'CHR. WREN.

'P.S. Poor Billy continues in his indisposition, and I fear is lost to me and the world, to my great discomfort and your future sorrow.'

What answer the younger Christopher sent does not appear; but his father did not 'discontent' him; the young man did make the journey to Italy, then such a formidable undertaking, and was ever after reckoned a very accomplished and travelled gentleman. 'Young Mr. Strong' must have been the son of Sir Christopher's faithful master-mason, Edward Strong, one of a great family of builders and stone-cutters; I suppose the 'poor Billy' of the postscript to have been the writer's youngest son, then nearly nineteen, who however recovered and outlived his father by about fifteen years.

The Royal Society had sustained a severe loss by Charles II.'s death, and if King James took little interest in their discussions, William III. was utterly indifferent. Still it had won a certain position of its own, and was able to keep its steady course. Wren remained one of the members who attended most regularly and contributed to discussions on a variety of subjects, though not perhaps on the 'jessamine-scented gloves,' which figure so often in Pepys' diary, the secret of whose perfumery Wren once undertook to find out. He was again chosen Grand Master of the Freemasons, and continued in that office until 1702.

His friend and fellow-member in the Royal Society, Robert Boyle, had written a book called 'A Free Discourse against Swearing,' which was published after his death. Wren followed this up by an order which he had affixed in many parts of S. Paul's, while the building went on :—

' Whereas, among labourers, &c. that ungodly custom of swearing is too frequently heard, to the dishonour of God and contempt of authority; and to the end, therefore, that such impiety may be utterly banished from these works, intended for the service of God and the honour of religion—it is ordered that customary swearing shall be a sufficient crime to dismiss any labourer that comes to the call, and the clerk of the works, upon sufficient proof, shall dismiss them accordingly, and if any master, working by task, shall not, upon admonition, reform this profanation among his apprentices, servants and labourers, it shall be construed his fault ; and he shall be liable to be censured by the Commissioners.'

Such was Sir Christopher's care for his grand work : it was intended for the service of God, and therefore was to have no blemish which Wren's diligence could avoid. He was constantly there and shrank neither from fatigue nor from risk. The famous Duchess of

Marlborough, in her quarrels with Vanbrugh over the building of Blenheim, complained bitterly that he asked 300*l.* a year for himself and a salary for his clerk, ' when it is well-known that Sir Christopher Wren was content to be dragged up in a basket three or four times a week to the top of S. Paul's, and at great hazard, for 200*l.* a year.' Probably it was because her Grace considered his charges so moderate that, after her last quarrel with Vanbrugh, she engaged Sir Christopher to build Marlborough House, at the corner of Pall Mall. The site presented great difficulties, but the building in red brick and stone was a handsome one, and lately has been much enlarged. Vanbrugh's first start in life was his being engaged by Wren to act as clerk of the works to the buildings at Greenwich. Gibbs and Hawksmoor were also pupils of Wren's, and worked under him at some of the innumerable works on which he was engaged. The building of Greenwich was vigorously continued, and in 1705,[1] ' they began to take in wounded and worn-out seamen, who are exceedingly well provided for.'

At the beginning of 1698, Peter the Great made his extraordinary voyage to England and took possession of Evelyn's house, Sayes Court, at Deptford, in order to be near the dockyard and inspect the ship-building. He was anything but a desirable tenant. ' There is a house full of people and right nasty,' wrote Evelyn's servant. 'The Czar lies next your library, and dines in the parlour next your study. He dines at ten o'clock and six at night, is very seldom at

---

[1] Evelyn's *Diary*, June, no date of day.

home a whole day, very often in the King's yard, or by water, dressed in several dresses. The King is expected here this day, the best parlour is pretty clean for him to be entertained. The King pays for all he has.'[1] The Czar's three months' occupancy of Sayes Court left it a wreck, and Evelyn got Sir Christopher, and the Royal gardener, Mr. Loudon, to go down and estimate the repairs which would be necessary. They allowed 150*l.* in their report to the Treasury, but could not by any money replace the beautiful holly hedge through which Peter the Great had been trundled in a wheel-barrow, or repair the garden he had laid waste.

In 1699, Wren finished the last of those City churches which the Fire had injured or destroyed. S. Dunstan's in the East had suffered severely by the Fire : the walls of the church had not fallen, but the interior had been much damaged and the monument to the famous sailor and discoverer, Sir John Hawkins, who was buried there, perished. The old church had a lofty wooden spire cased with lead, which of course fell and was consumed. When Sir Christopher had repaired the body of the building the parishioners were anxious to have back the spire also, and Dame Dionis Williamson, a Norfolk lady, who had been a great benefactress to S. Mary's, Bow, gave 400*l.* towards this object. It is one of the most curious of all Wren's spires, as it rests on four arches springing from the angles of the tower. Three more such spires exist, two in Scotland and one at Newcastle. Tradition says that the steeple

---

[1] Evelyn's *Diary*, Jan. 30, 1698.

of S. Dunstan's was the design or the suggestion of Wren's daughter Jane. Perhaps, like the leaning tower of Pisa, it is more wonderful than satisfactory to the eye, but Sir Christopher was certainly proud of it and confident in its stability. Great crowds assembled to see the supports taken away, and Wren watched with a telescope, says the story, on London Bridge for the rocket which announced that all was safely done, but it is hardly probable that he was anxious about the result.

Four years later, when the tempest known as the 'great storm' raged in England, destroying twelve ships in the Royal navy, many merchant vessels, and a great number of buildings, some one came with a long face to tell Sir Christopher, that '*all* the steeples in London had suffered;' he replied at once, 'Not S. Dunstan's, I am sure.' He was perfectly right, and the account given of the others was an exaggeration.

On February 1, 1699, the Morning Prayer Chapel of S. Paul's was opened for service. Later in the same month, a fire broke out at the west end of the choir, where 'Father Smith' was still at work. It caused considerable alarm, and was got under with some damage, especially to two of the pillars, and to a decorated arch. The gilding also lost some of its brightness. A nameless poem [1] fixes the date of this fire, which has been much disputed. It may have been in consequence of this alarm that Sir Christopher covered all the woodwork of the upper parts of the Cathedral

[1] *Documents illustrating*, etc., p. 158.

with 'a fibrous concrete' said to resist fire so well that faggots might be kindled below it with impunity.

While S. Paul's was thus advancing towards its full beauty, the care of Westminster Abbey was assigned to Wren. Little or no attention seems to have been spent on it between the time of Charles I.'s reign and that in which it was handed over to Wren.

With the energy which his sixty-seven years had not checked, he examined the grand building where he had worshipped as a schoolboy, and instantly ordered some of the most needful repairs.

In 1713 he sent in a statement to Dr. Atterbury, who was both Bishop of Rochester and Dean of Westminster, having in that year succeeded to Wren's old friend, Bishop Sprat: from this paper, though it is anticipating the date, some extracts are here given.

'When I had the Honour to attend your Lordship, to congratulate your Episcopal Dignity, and pay that Respect which particularly concerned myself as employed in the chief Direction of the Works and Repairs of the Collegiate-Church of S. Peter in Westminster, you was pleased to give me this seasonable admonition, that I should consider my advanced Age; and as I had already made fair steps in the Reparation of that ancient and ruinous Structure, you thought it very requisite for the publick Service, I should leave a Memorial of what I had done, and what my Thoughts were for carrying on the Works for the future.' Then follows the history of the building of the abbey up to the reign of Henry

III., who rebuilt it 'according to the Mode which came into Fashion after the Holy War.

'This we now call the *Gothick* manner of Architecture (so the Italians called what was not after the *Roman* style), tho' the *Goths* were rather Destroyers than Builders; I think it should with more Reason be called the *Saracen* Style; for those People wanted neither Arts nor Learning, and after we in the West had lost both, we borrowed again from them, out of their Arabick Books, what they with great Diligence had translated from the *Greeks*. . . . . . They built their Mosques round, disliking the *Christian* form of a Cross: the old quarries whence the Ancients took their large blocks of marble for whole Columns and Architraves were neglected, for they thought both impertinent. Their carriage was by camels, therefore their Buildings were fitted for small stones, and Columns of their own fancy consisting of many pieces, and their Arches were pointed without key-stones which they thought too heavy. The Reasons were the same in our Northern Climates abounding in free stone, but wanting marble. . . . . The Saracen mode of building seen in the East, soon spread over Europe and particularly in *France*, the Fashions of which nation we affected to imitate in all ages, even when we were at enmity with it.' . . . .
Wren laments over the mixture of oak with the less-enduring chestnut wood in the roof of the Abbey, and the use of Rygate stone which absorbed water, and in a frost scaled off. He says he cut all the ragged ashlar work of Rygate stone out of the east window,

replacing it with durable Burford stone, and secured all the buttresses on the south side. The north side of the Abbey is so choked up by buildings, and so shaken in parts by vaults rashly dug close to its buttresses, that he can do little.

'I have yet said nothing of King Henry VIIth's Chapel, a nice embroidered Work and performed with tender Caen stone, and though lately built in comparison, is so eaten up by our Weather, that it begs for some compassion, which I hope the Sovereign Power will take as it is the Regal Sepulture.' The most necessary outward repairs of stonework, he says, are one-third part done; the north front, and the great Rose Window there are very ruinous; he has prepared a proper design for them. Having summed up the repairs still essential for the security of the building, he proceeds to state what are, in his judgment, the parts of the original design for the Abbey still unfinished.

'The original intention was plainly to have had a Steeple, the Beginnings of which appear on the corners of the Cross, but left off before it rose so high as the Ridge of the Roof, and the Vault of the Quire under it, is only Lath and Plaister, now rotten and must be taken care of.

. . . .

I have made a Design, which will not be very expensive but light, but still in the *Gothick* Form, and of a Style with the rest of the structure, which I would strictly adhere to, throughout the whole intention: to deviate from the old Form would be to run into a disagreeable mixture which no Person of a good Taste could relish. I have varied a little from the usual Form, in giving twelve sides to the Spire instead of eight, for Reasons, to be discerned upon the Model.

'The Angles of Pyramids in the Gothick Architecture were usually enriched with the Flower the Botanists call the Calceolus, which is a proper form to help workmen to ascend on the outside to amend any defects, without raising large scaffolds upon every slight occasion; I have done the same, being of so good Use, as well as agreeable Ornament. . . . . It is evident, as observed before, the two West Towers were left imperfect, and have continued so since the Dissolution of the Monastery, one much higher than the other, though still too low for Bells, which are stifled by the Height of the Roof above them; they ought certainly to be carried to an equal Height, one story above the ridge of the Roof, still continuing the Gothick manner, in the stone-work, and tracery. . . . . It will be most necessary to rebuild the great North Window with Portland stone, to answer the South Rose Window which was well rebuilt about forty years since; the stair-cases at the corners and Pyramids set upon them conformable to the old style to make the whole of a piece. . . . . For all these new Additions I have prepared perfect Draughts and Models, such as I conceive may agree with the original scheme of the old architect, without any modern mixtures to show my own Inventions:

in like manner as I have among the Parochial Churches of *London* given some few Examples (where I was obliged to deviate from a better style), which appear not ungraceful, but ornamental to the East part of the city; and it is to be hoped, by the publick care, the West part also, in good time will be as well adorned: and surely by nothing more properly than a lofty Spire and Western Towers to Westminster Abbey.'

With this, still unfulfilled hope, Wren's interesting paper closes. Nine years afterwards he did, however, finish the north front, commonly known as Solomon's Porch.

Wren is so commonly spoken of as having built— and spoilt—the western towers, that it is well here to mention that his share in them is very small; he only restored with a careful hand the lower portion of the towers then standing.[1] They were continued by Hawksmoor after Wren's death, and by two other architects in succession after the death of Hawksmoor in 1736. No one of these had, as Wren had, the high-minded desire to do justice to 'the original architect without any modern mixtures of my own.'

[1] *Three Cathedrals*, Longman, p. 86-88.

CHAPTER XIII.

1700–1708.

MEMBER FOR WEYMOUTH—RISING OF THE SAP IN TREES—PRINCE GEORGE'S STATUE—JANE WREN'S DEATH—THANKSGIVING AT S. PAUL'S—LETTER TO HIS SON—SON MARRIES MARY MUSARD—DEATH OF MR. EVELYN—QUEEN ANNE'S ACT FOR BUILDING FIFTY CHURCHES—LETTER ON CHURCH BUILDING.

'The old knight turning about his head twice or thrice to take a survey of this great metropolis, bid me observe how thick the City was set with churches, and that there was scarce a single steeple on this side Temple Bar. "A most heathenish sight!" says Sir Roger; "there is no religion at this end of the town. The fifty new churches will very much mend the prospect, but church work is slow, church work is slow."'—*The Spectator*, No. 383.

CHAPTER XIII.

In 1700 Wren was returned by the boroughs of Weymouth and Melcombe Regis to a somewhat stormy Parliament.

He was finishing several of the City churches by the addition of towers to some, where, as at S. Magnus, London Bridge, and S. Andrew's, Holborn, the main parts had been previously built.

He gave a design for All Saints' Church, Isleworth; it was, however, reckoned too costly, and nothing was done until, in 1705, Sir Orlando Gee left a legacy of 500*l.* towards the rebuilding of the church, when Wren's design was partially adopted, and the work done by his faithful master-mason, Edward Strong.[1]

With all this work, Wren yet found time to write a treatise on 'The rising of the sap in trees.' It is a short treatise, evidently copied by a copyist, though a little indian-ink drawing at the side is probably Wren's own. The question in dispute seems to have been whether this natural rising of the sap contradicted the newly discovered law of gravity.

'It is wonderful,' he says, 'to see the rising of the sap in Trees. All will bleed more or less when they are

---

[1] *Environs of London*, vol. iv. p. 458. Lysons.

tapped by boring a hole through the Bark, some very considerably, as Birch, which will afford as much liquor every day almost as the milke of a cow; in a Vine when a bough is cut off it will if not stopped bleed to death. Now by what mechanisme is water raised to such a height, as in Palmitos to 120 foot high? A skillfull Engineer cannot effect this without great force and a complicated engine, which Nature doth without sensible motion; it steals up as freely as the water descends: the reason of this is obscure as yett to naturalists.' After some discussion of various theories, he proceeds to show by the help of the little drawing, 'that the onely Vicissitudes of heat and cold in ye aire is sufficient to raise the sap to the height of the loftiest trees.' Then follows the proof of this by mechanics refuting the notion of 'a secret motion in nature contrary to that of the gravity, by which plants aspire upwards.

'But though I have shown how the sap may be mechanically raised from the Root to the top of the loftiest trees, yett how it comes to be varied according to the particular nature of the Tree by a Fermentation in the Root; how the Raine water entering the Root acquires a spirit that keeps it from freezing, but also gives it such distinguishing tastes and qualities is beyond mechanical Philosophy to describe and may require a great collection of Phenomena with a large history of plants to shew how they expand the leaves and produce the Seed and Fruit from the same Raine water so wonderfully diversified and continued since the first Creation.'

Another paper of the same date was written 'On the surface of the terrestrial Globe,' but this does not appear to have been preserved. Many of Sir Christopher's writings and many also of his inventions were lost by Mr. Oldenburg, the Royal Society's secretary, of whom Wren frequently complained that he not only neglected to enter them on the Society's Register, but conveyed them to France and Germany, where they appeared, attributed as inventions to those who had stolen them.

One cannot but admire the versatility of mind which enabled Wren, in the midst of great architectural works, and endless business details, to write papers such as these, and to digest and decide upon Flamsteed's long letters on the Earth's motion, his quarrels with Mr. Halley, and his measurement of the height of the Welsh hills.

The progress of Greenwich and Chelsea Hospitals, the growth of his beautiful S. Paul's, the repairs of the Abbey, were now the absorbing interests of Wren's life. From the house in Whitehall which he occupied with his daughter he could easily reach the two former by water, or the latter on foot. Two most interesting pictures by Canaletto,[1] giving a general view of the city and of Westminster, enable us to realise what the whole effect must have been in an atmosphere far clearer than at present, before the river was cut by iron bridges, or the city robbed of steeple or tower. The death of King William and the accession of Queen Anne in the spring of 1702 made little difference to

[1] In the possession of H.M. the Queen.

Wren, except to his advantage. He appears to have been on very good terms with her, and with her Danish husband. He is said to have built S. Anne's, Soho,[1] and to have made it externally to resemble a Danish church as much as he could, out of compliment to Prince George. He also gave to the Town Hall of Windsor, a statue of Prince George, to correspond with that of Queen Anne. The Prince is dressed in a Roman costume, and the pedestal has the following inscription:

SERENISSIMO PRINCIPI
GEORGII PRINCIPI DANIAE
HEROI OMNI SAECULO VENERANDO
CHRISTOPHORUS WREN, ARM:
POSUIT MDCCXIII.

One marvels how 'Est-il possible' came to merit such an inscription as this!

In 1702 Sir Christopher suffered a grievous loss by the death of his only daughter, Jane, on the 29th of December. She was laid in the vault of S. Paul's close to the graves of Dr. and Mrs. Holder,[2] and her father wrote the short Latin inscription which records her virtues, her skill in music, and implies how loving and how congenial a companion he had lost in her. She was but twenty-six when she died. The sculptor, Bird,[3] of whose power Wren had a good opinion,

---

[1] I can find no proof of this, and it is not mentioned in any list of his buildings that I have seen.

[2] Dr. Holder died 1694.

[3] Francis Bird, born in London 1667. His masterpiece was the monument to Dr. Busby. He died in London 1731. A stonecutter of the same name at Oxford is mentioned by Plot in connection with an invention for staining marbles and cutting them like a cameo, who I am inclined to think was a relation.

carved a monument in low relief, representing Jane
Wren playing on an organ; a harp and a spinnet are
beside her, and a group of angels in the clouds above,
one of whom holds the music. It is but an ordinary
piece of monumental sculpture, now much obscured by
dust. Jane Wren's death must have left a great blank
in the life of the father whose interests and pursuits
she had shared, and one wishes she could have lived
long enough to see the top stone laid on the dome of S.
Paul's. The Duke of Marlborough's brilliant victory
at Blenheim, on Aug. 13, 1704, brought Queen Anne
and all her court in their utmost splendour to a thanksgiving at S. Paul's on the 7th of September. 'The
> streets were scaffolded from Temple Bar, where the
> Lord Mayor presented her Majesty with the Sword,
> which she returned. Every Company was ranged
> under its banners, the Citty Militia without the
> rails, which were all hung with cloth suitable to the
> colour of the banner. The Lord Mayor, Sheriffs
> and Aldermen were in their scarlet robes, with
> caparisoned horses; the Knight Marshall on horse-
> back, the Foot Guards; the Queen in a rich coach
> with eight horses, none with her but the Duchess of
> Marlborough in a very plain garment, the Queene
> full of jewells. Music and trumpets at every Citty
> Company. The great Officers of the Crown, Nobility
> and Bishops, all in coaches with six horses, besides
> innumerable servants, went to S. Paul's where the
> Deane preached. After this the Queen went back
> in the same order to S. James's. The Citty Com-
> panies feasted all the nobility and Bishops, and

illuminated at night. Music for the Church and anthems by the best masters. The day before wet and stormy, but this was one of the most serene and calm days that had been all the year.'[1]

No doubt it was a splendid pageant, the grandest that had been seen since those which celebrated the Restoration, and S. Paul's, despite the scaffolding still round the dome, must have looked magnificent. In 1705, Sir Christopher's eldest son went abroad again, travelling this time to Holland, where in the excitement of Marlborough's brilliant campaign he very nearly joined the army as a volunteer.

A letter[2] to him from Sir Christopher is extant; the handwriting is not quite so steady as in the former letter, but still clear.

'Whitehall, Oct. 11, 1705.

'Dear Son,—I received at once three of y^r le^{trs} : one from Harlem, Sep. 26, another from Amsterdam of Sep. 28, O.S., a third of Oct. 13, N.S., by all which I rejoyced in your good Health & your recovery from your cold. I am very well satisfied you have layd aside your designe for the Army ; which I think had not been safe or pertinent, at least not soe much as Bookes & Conversation with ye learned. Your Traffic for good Bookes I cannot disapprove. You tell me Gronovius[3] is 25 volumes, I am told they are 26, and that the last is the best & comonly

---

[1] Evelyn's *Diary*, September 7, 1704.
[2] Hitherto unpublished.
[3] G. F. Gronovius, 1613-1672. He was the author of many works, chiefly annotations of the classics, and succeeded Heinsius in the Greek chair at Leyden.

sold by its selfe, you will have a care [a word seems to be omitted] being imposed upon. Mr. Bateman in his (?) will give you advice how you may get them into the Secretary's packets. You remember how much trouble Mr. Strong was put to at Dover by the impertinence of the Customer there. I hope this may bee prevented. Wee have not yet rejoyced for Barcelona[1] though you have; though wee doe not doubt it and wagers are layd 6 to one: last night the seales were given to Mr. Cowper & changes are made of Lord Lieutenants. Give my Service to Mr. Roman & thanks for his Civilities to you. I am importuned to take a little journy to my cosin Munson's to christen her 8th son. Wee are told here that my Ld D. of Marlborough goeth certainly to Vienna, & you resolve well to wait on him before he goes, & then I thinke you have little else to doe but to take the best opportunity to returne, which I am told may happen if you come with my Ld Woodstock[2] who will have convoy. Wee are all in good health at both Houses and wish you happinesse wch wee also contrive for you.

'I am, dear Son, your affectionate Father,

'CHR. WREN.'

I suppose the mention of 'both houses,' and the hint of happiness being contrived, refer to young Christopher's marriage, which took place in the following

---

[1] Barcelona was taken by Lord Peterborough and Sir Cloudesley Shovel, October 4, 1705, in the war of the Spanish Succession.

[2] The eldest son of the Earl of Portland, afterwards created Duke of Portland.

year. He married Mary,[1] daughter of Mr. Philip Musard, jeweller to Queen Anne, by whom he had a son, a fourth Christopher Wren.

Wren lost a faithful and valued friend in Mr. Evelyn, who died in the February of 1706, at the age of eighty-five. If Evelyn's diary, of which such frequent use has been made in these pages, is not the same entire revelation of the man himself as is the diary of his friend Pepys, it yet possesses a singular charm in its refinement of thought, and, when the veil is raised, shows us a gentleman and a Christian to be respected as well as loved. He had kept up a steady friendship with Sir Christopher since the day when they first met at Oxford, and had the highest opinion of his powers : 'an excellent genius had this incomparable person,' is his remark after a conversation with Wren. Evelyn was on the S. Paul's Commission from the first, and Wren was destined, a few years later, sorely to miss the support of this constant friend.

The needful sum for covering in the dome of S. Paul's was voted by Parliament in 1708. The question of using copper or lead was greatly discussed ; lead was finally chosen ; it does not clearly appear which way Sir Christopher's judgment inclined. Probably to the lead, as he considered it susceptible of much ornament, and the lead covering of S. Paul's dome is peculiarly beautiful. Bird in this year finished the statue of Queen Anne, which is in the fore court of the Cathedral, and is not without merit. He also carved the relief of

---

[1] A portrait of this lady in full profile, with a pale face and black hair, painted somewhat in the style of Sir Peter Lely, is in the possession of Mrs. Pigott.

the Conversion of S. Paul above the western portico : the height is too great for it to be possible to judge of the goodness of the sculpture.

The Act known as 'Queen Anne's Act for building Fifty New Churches' was passed in this year, and Wren was of course one of the commissioners. At the age of seventy-six he could not undertake the designing of these new churches. They were principally built by Gibbs, Hawksmoor, Vanbrugh and others. S. George's, Hanover Square, S. Anne's, Limehouse, S. George's, Bloomsbury, S. Leonard's, Shoreditch, are some of those built under this Act. Perhaps the best specimen is the beautiful S. Mary-le-Strand, built by Gibbs, on an old site stolen from the Church by the Duke of Somerset in the reign of Henry VIII. Recent careful painting and gilding and the removal of pews have made S. Mary's a charming example of the amount of decoration which can be advantageously bestowed on a Paladian church.

Wren wrote on this occasion a letter to a friend on the Church-building Commission in which he gives the result of his great experience in building town churches. The letter is given with a few omissions. I fear that few of the Queen Anne churches were built strictly on the principles he here lays down ; certainly the hint as to pews was disregarded, and grievous indeed have been the results of such disregard. It has been a common fallacy that all Wren's churches were built for pews, and that anything but high pews would ruin the architectural effect. What was Wren's own opinion is manifest from the letter; the actual effect can be

x

seen, for instance, in a print of S. Stephen's, Walbrook, where this gem of all his churches is represented, just after its completion, with the area clear; or in S. Mary's, Bow, where the pews have lately been diminished into just such 'benches' as the great architect desired.

'Since Providence,' he writes, 'in great mercy has protracted my age, to the finishing the Cathedral Church of S. Paul, and the parochial churches of London, in lieu of those demolished by the fire, (all which were executed during the fatigues of my employment in the service of the Crown from that time to the present happy reign); and being now constituted one of the Commissioners for building, pursuant to the late Act, fifty more Churches in London and Westminster; I shall presume to communicate briefly my sentiments, after long experience, and without further ceremony exhibit to better judgement, what at present occurs to me, in a transient view of this whole affair; not doubting but that the debates of the worthy Commissioners may hereafter give me occasion to change, or add to these speculations.

'1. I conceive the Churches should be built, not where vacant ground may be cheapest purchased in the extremities of the suburbs, but among the thicker inhabitants, for the convenience of the better sort, although the site of them should cost more; the better inhabitants contributing most to the future repairs, and the ministers and officers of the church, and charges of the parish.

'2. I could wish that all burials in churches might be disallowed, which is not only unwholesome, but the pavements can never be kept even, nor pews upright; and if the churchyard be close about the church, this also is inconvenient, because the ground being continually raised by the graves, occasions, in time, a descent by steps in the church, which renders it damp, and the walls green, as appears evidently in all old churches.

'3. It will be enquired, where then shall be the burials? I answer, in cemeteries seated in the outskirts of the town. . . . .

' A piece of ground of two acres in the fields will be purchased for much less than two roods among the buildings; this being enclosed with a strong brick wall, and having a walk round, and two cross walks decently planted with yew trees, the four quarters may serve four parishes, where the dead need not be disturbed at the pleasure of the sexton or piled four or five upon one another, or bones thrown out to gain room. . . . . It may be considered further, that if the cemeteries be thus thrown into the fields, they will bound the excessive growth of the city with a graceful border, which is now encircled with scavengers' dung-stalls.

'4. As to the situation of the churches, I should propose they be brought as forward as possible into the larger and more open streets; not in obscure lanes, nor where coaches will be much obstructed in the passage: nor are we, I think, too nicely to observe east or west in the position, unless it falls out properly; such fronts as shall happen to lie most open to view should be adorned with porticoes, both for beauty and convenience; which together with handsome spires or lanterns, rising in good proportion above the neighbouring houses (of which I have given several examples in the City of different forms), may be of sufficient ornament to the town, without a great expense for enriching the outward walls of the Churches, in which plainness and duration ought principally, if not wholly, to be studied. . . . .

'5. I shall mention something of the materials for public fabrics. It is true, the mighty demand for the hasty works of thousands of houses at once after the Fire of London, and the frauds of those who built by the great, (?) have so debased the value of materials, that good bricks are not to be now had without greater prices than formerly, and indeed, if rightly made, will deserve them; but brickmakers spoil the earth in the mixing and hasty burning, till the bricks will hardly bear weight; though the earth about London, rightly managed, will yield as good bricks as were the Roman bricks (which I have often found in the old ruins of the City), and will endure, in our air, beyond any stone our island affords; which, unless the quarries lie near the sea, are too dear for general use. The best is Portland or Roch-Abbey stone; but these are not without their faults. The next material is the lime: chalk-lime is the constant practice, which, well mixed with good sand, is not amiss, though much worse than hard stone-lime. The vaulting of S. Paul's is a rendering as hard as stone : it is composed of cockle-shell lime well beaten with sand : the more labour in the beating, the better and stronger the mortar. I shall say nothing of marble (though England, Scotland, and Ireland afford good, and of beautiful colours); but this will prove too costly for our purpose, unless for Altar-pieces. In windows and doors Portland stone may be used, with good bricks and stone quoins. As to roofs, good oak is certainly the best, because it will bear some negligence. The churchwardens' care may be defective in speedy mending drips ; they usually whitewash the church, and set up their names, but neglect to preserve the roof over their heads. It must be allowed, that the roof being more out of sight, is still more unminded. Next to oak, is good yellow deal, which is a timber of length, and light, and makes excellent work at first; but, if neglected, will speedily perish ; especially if gutters (which is a general fault in builders) be made to run upon the principal rafters, the ruin may be sudden. Our sea-service for oak, and the wars in the North Sea, make timber at present of excessive price. I suppose, ere long, we must have recourse to the West Indies, where most excellent timber may be had for cutting and fetching. Our tiles are ill made, and our slates not good : lead is certainly the best and lightest covering, and being of our own growth and manufacture, and lasting, if properly laid, for many hundred years, is, without question, the most preferable ; though I will not deny but an excellent tile may be made to be very durable : our artisans are not yet instructed in it, and it is not soon done to inform them. .... Now, if the churches could hold each 2,000, it would yet be very short of the necessary supply. The churches, therefore, must be large; but still, in our reformed religion it should seem vain to make a parish church larger than that all who are present can both hear and see. The Romanists, indeed, may build larger churches; it is enough if they hear the murmur of the Mass, and see the elevation of the Host; but ours are to be fitted for auditories. I can hardly think it practicable to make a single room so capacious, with pews and galleries, as to hold above 2,000 persons, and all to hear the service, and both to hear distinctly, and see the preacher. I endeavoured to effect this in building the parish Church of S. James, Westminster, which, I presume, is the most capacious, with these qualifications, that hath yet been built; and yet, at a solemn time, when the church was much crowded, I could not discern from a gallery that 2,000 were present. In this church I mention, though very broad, and the middle nave arched up, yet as there are no walls of a second order, nor lanterns, nor buttresses, but the whole roof rests upon the pillars, as do also the galleries, I think it may be found beautiful and convenient, and, as such, the cheapest of any form I could invent.

'7. Concerning the placing of the pulpit, I shall observe a moderate voice may be heard fifty feet distant before the preacher, thirty feet on each side, and twenty behind the pulpit; and not this unless the pronunciation be distinct and equal, without losing the voice at the last word of the sentence, which is commonly emphatical, and, if obscured, spoils the whole sense. A Frenchman is heard further than an English preacher, because he raises his voice, and sinks not his last words: I mention this as an insufferable fault in the pronunciation of some of our otherwise excellent preachers, which schoolmasters might correct in the young as a vicious pronunciation, and not as the Roman orators spoke: for the principal verb is, in Latin, usually the last word; and if that be lost, what becomes of the sentence?

'8. By what I have said, it may be thought reasonable, that the new church should be at least sixty feet broad, and ninety feet long, besides a chancel at one end, and the belfry and portico at the other.

' These proportions may be varied; but to build more than that every person may conveniently hear and see is to create noise and confusion. A church should not be so filled with pews, but that the poor may have room enough to stand and sit in the alleys; for to them equally is the Gospel preached. It were to be wished there were to be no pews, but benches; but there is no stemming the tide of profit, and the advantage of pew-keepers; especially since by pews, in the chapel of ease, the minister is chiefly supported. It is evident these fifty churches are enough for the present inhabitants, and the town will continually grow: but it is to be hoped, that hereafter more may be added, as the wisdom of the Government shall think fit; and, therefore, the parishes should be so divided as to leave room for subdivisions, or at least for chapels of ease.

'I cannot pass over mentioning the difficulties that may be found in obtaining the ground proper for the sites of the churches among the buildings, and the cemeteries in the borders without the town; and, therefore, I shall recite the method that was taken for purchasing in ground at the north side of S. Paul's Cathedral, where, in some places, houses were but eleven feet distant from the fabric, exposing it to the continual dangers of fires. The houses were seventeen, and contiguous, all in leasehold of the Bishop, or Dean alone, or the Dean and Chapter, or the petty-Canons, with divers under-tenants. The first we recompensed in kind, with rents of like value for them and their successors; but the tenants in possession for a valuable consideration; which to find what it amounted to, we learned by diligent inquiry, what the inheritance of houses in that quarter were usually held at; this we found was fifteen years' purchase at the most, and, proportionably to this, the value of each lease was easily determined in a scheme, referring to a map. These rates, which we resolved not to stir from, were offered to each; and, to cut off much debate, which it may be imagined everyone would abound in, they were assured that we went by one uniform method, which could not be receded. We found two or three reasonable men, who agreed to these terms; immediately we paid them, and took down their houses; others, who stood out at first, finding themselves in dust and rubbish, and that ready money was better, as the case stood, than to continue paying rent, repairs, and parish duties, easily came in. The whole ground at last was cleared, and all concerned were satisfied, and their writings given in. . . . . This was happily finished without a judicatory or jury; although, in our present case, we may find it perhaps, sometimes necessary to have recourse to Parliament.'

CHAPTER XIV.

1709—1723.

PRIVATE HOUSES BUILT—QUEEN ANNE'S GIFTS—LAST STONE OF S. PAUL'S—WREN DEPRIVED OF HIS SALARY—HIS PETITION—'FRAUDS AND ABUSES'—INTERIOR WORK OF S. PAUL'S—WREN SUPERSEDED—PURCHASE OF WROXHALL ABBEY—WREN'S THOUGHTS ON THE LONGITUDE—HIS DEATH—BURIAL IN S. PAUL'S—THE END.

Heroick souls a nobler lustre find,
E'en from those griefs which break a vulgar mind.
That frost which cracks the brittle, common glass,
Makes Crystal into stronger brightness pass.
      Bp. Thos. Sprat, quoted in *Parentalia*.

CHAPTER XIV.

THE year 1709 passed in steady work, and has little but finishing touches to the churches to be recorded, unless some of the various private houses built by Wren belong to this period. A house for Lord Oxford, and one for the Duchess of Buckingham, both in S. James's Court; two built near the Thames for Lord Sunderland and Lord Allaston; one for Lord Newcastle in Queen's Square, Bloomsbury; and a house, so large and magnificent that it has been divided in late years into four, in Great Russell Street. This house was afterwards occupied by Wren's eldest son, and in turn by his second son Stephen.

Sir Christopher himself, while keeping the house in Whitehall from which his letters are dated, had received from Queen Anne the fifty years' lease of a house at Hampton Green at a nominal rent of 10*l.* a year;[1] he must have found great refreshment in going there occasionally by the then undefiled Thames, to country rest and quiet. Queen Anne was uniformly gracious and friendly to her Surveyor, and presented him with a buhl cabinet inlaid with red tortoiseshell of remarkably handsome work and design.[2]

[1] This lease was renewed to his eldest son in 1737 for 28½ years, running on from 1758.
[2] Now in the possession of Mrs. Pigott.

The following year saw the crown put to the labour of thirty-five years. Mr. Christopher Wren, who had been a year old when the first stone was laid, now laid the last stone of the lantern above the Dome of S. Paul's in the presence of his father, Mr. Strong the master-builder, his son, and other free and accepted masons, most of whom had worked at the building. The scene could hardly be better painted than in the words of Dean Milman : [1]

> 'All London had poured forth for the spectacle, which had been publicly announced, and were looking up in wonder to the old man . . . who was on that wondrous height setting the seal, as it were, to his august labours. If in that wide circle which his eye might embrace there were various objects for regret and disappointment; if, instead of beholding the various streets of the city, each converging to its centre, London had sprung up and spread in irregular labyrinths of close, dark, intricate lanes ; if even his own Cathedral was crowded upon and jostled by mean and unworthy buildings ; yet, on the other hand, he might survey, not the Cathedral only, but a number of stately churches which had risen at his command and taken form and dignity from his genius and skill. On one side the picturesque steeple of S. Mary-le-Bow ; on the other the exquisite tower of S. Bride's, with all its graceful, gradually diminishing circles, not yet shorn of its full and finely-proportioned height. Beyond, and on

[1] *Annals of S. Paul's*, p. 432.

all sides, if more dimly seen, yet discernible by his partial eyesight (he might even penetrate to the inimitable interior of S. Stephen's, Walbrook), church after church, as far as S. Dunstan's-in-the-East, perhaps Greenwich, may have been vaguely made out in the remote distance; and all this one man had been permitted to conceive and execute;—a man not originally destined or educated for an architect, but compelled as it were by the public necessities to assume the office, and so to fulfil it, as to stand on a level with the most consummate masters of the art in Europe, and to take his stand on an eminence which his English successors almost despair of attaining.'

There then the Cathedral stood, complete externally in its stately beauty, the work of one man, who, it has been truly said, 'had the conception of a painter as well as an architect.' View the Cathedral when and where we will, with every disadvantage of smoky atmosphere and lack of space, it yet fascinates the eye by the perfection of its lines and the majesty of the whole effect, so as to leave no power of criticising petty defects. Such was the triumphant success achieved by Wren's patient genius, but

> Envy will merit as its shade pursue;

and a series of troubles fell upon him.

There will always be a number of people who imagine that anything can be procured by money, and that for the sake of money anything and everything will be done. People of this mind considered that

Sir Christopher Wren prolonged the process of building S. Paul's in order to prolong his own enjoyment of the 200*l.* a year which was the salary he had himself chosen, though it was considered utterly inadequate by the Commissioners when first the work began.

Accordingly in 1696–7, a clause was inserted in the Act 'for the completing and adorning S. Paul's' 'to suspend a moiety of the Surveyor's salary until the said Church should be finished ; thereby the better to encourage him to finish the same work with the utmost diligence and expedition.'[1]

No doubt they considered that the Cathedral could be finished off regardless of details, and so left like the shell of an ordinary house to be adorned by any chance person ; and to this end they offered their grim 'encouragement'!

It was an insult to a man like Wren, who had again and again—as in the case of Greenwich—given his skill for nothing, and it was doubly unjust because, what delays there were, sprang from the conceit and ignorance of the S. Paul's Commission. Wren protested, but took no active step until he had seen the Dome of his beloved Cathedral completed.

Then he sent in a petition to Queen Anne as follows :—

'The most humble petition of Sir Christopher Wren
'Sheweth,

'That there being a Clause in an Act of Parliament which suspends a moiety of your Petitioner's salary

---

[1] It must be to this that Wren refers in his letter to his son, p. 282.

at S. Paul's, till the building be finished, and being obstructed in his measures for completing the same, by the arbitrary proceedings of some of the Commissioners for that fabric,—

'Your Petitioner most humbly beseeches your Majesty graciously to interpose your Royal Authority so as that he may be suffered to finish the said building in such manner and after such designs as shall be approved by your Majesty or such persons as your Majesty shall think fit to appoint for that purpose ; and your Petitioner, etc.,

'CHRISTOPHER WREN.'

This petition was sent to the Commissioners, whose reply was, that when Sir Christopher had acted without their approbation his performances had proved very faulty;(!) they then digressed into remarks on their own devotion to the Queen's service, and into a series of petty charges against some of the workmen employed in the Cathedral, especially the bell-founder, Richard Phelp, and Richard Jennings the master-carpenter, whom they charged with a variety of frauds and abuses, and begged should be at once dismissed ; they also venture to assert that 'Sir Christopher, or some employed by him, may be supposed to have found their advantage in this delay.' There is little attempt at proof in this reply of the Commissioners, but much supposition and conjecture. A pamphlet, 'Frauds and Abuses at S. Paul's,' published anonymously at this time, sets out all their suspicions in detail. Sir Christopher replied in a pamphlet entitled 'An Answer to

Frauds and Abuses in S. Paul's,' and laid a petition before the Archbishop of Canterbury and the Bishop of London, in which he sets out his grievances, how little power had been really given to him and how far he had ' been limited and restrained.'

'However,' he says, ' it has pleased God so far to bless my sincere endeavours, as that I have brought the building to a conclusion so far as is in my power, and I think nothing can be said now to remain unperfected, but the iron fence round the Church, and painting the Cupola, the directing whereof is taken out of my hands, and therefore I hope I am not answerable for them, nor that the said suspending clause can, or ought, to affect me any further on that account. As for painting the Cupola, your Lordships know that it has been long under consideration ; that I have no power left me concerning it ; and that it is not yet resolved in what manner to do it, or whether at all. And as for the iron fence, it is so remarkable and so fresh in memory, by whose influence and importunity it was wrested from me, and the doing of it carried in a way which I venture to say will ever be condemned. I have just this to observe further, that your Lordships had no hand in it ; and consequently ought not share in the blame that may attend it.'

He then asks them for their warrant for the payment of the arrears, amounting to more than 1,300*l.*, which were due to him, and says he will ever be ready in the future, to give his advice and assistance in anything about the said Cathedral. Archbishop Tenison and Bishop Compton laid Wren's petition before the Attorney-General, Sir Edward Northey, who pronounced 'that Sir Christopher Wren's case was very hard, but that the terms of the Act were so positive that it could not be overridden, but the Commissioners ought in justice to find some remedy.'

Wren then addressed the House of Commons in a petition in which he repeats that his 'measures for completing the Cathedral are wholly over-ruled and frustrated.'

The House considered the matter, and cut the knot by declaring the Cathedral to be finished, and directing the payment of all the arrears of the architect's salary.

Their prompt decision gratified Sir Christopher, who contrasts it with the conduct of the Commission, 'which was such as gave him reason enough to think that they intended him none of the suspended salary if it had been left in their power to defeat him of it.'

The attacks on Jennings, whom Wren firmly defended, fell to the ground: they probably had as little foundation as the 'Screw Plot,' by which at a Thanksgiving, by one man's moving a few of the bolts and screws, the whole dome was to fall in.[1] The bell-founder Phelps, who had removed the faulty bell put up by Wightman under the direction of the Commissioners, also triumphed: he offered to give a bond to the Dean and Chapter to recast the bell at his own expense if, after a year's trial, they were dissatisfied with it: as this offer was never claimed, Wren justly says that they were either content with the bell or else

[1] *Documents illustrating, &c.*, p. 62.

showed great neglect. Until the last few years it was the only bell possessed by the Cathedral.

To perfect S. Paul's some things had still to be done, and, rather than these should suffer, Wren was willing still to undergo the slights and annoyances of the other S. Paul's Commissioners, amongst whose names one wishes that of Sir Isaac Newton did *not* appear, without clear evidence that he stood by his early patron and friend. One hopes it may have been so, certainly he was not a frequent attendant at the meetings.

Within the Cathedral there was some important work to do. Gibbons' carving had to be completed, and the beautiful iron-work gates on either side of the choir had yet to be set up. For this work Wren employed a M. Tijou, at that time a famous worker in iron, though no account of him is to be obtained at the present day. Possibly he was one of the French refugees. Wren saw both the carving and the gates successfully finished. But for the east end of the Cathedral he had a magnificent design which is unfulfilled to this day. He intended to inlay the columns of the apse with rich marble, to use a considerable amount of colour and gilding, and to place over the Altar a hemispherical canopy supported on four writhed pillars of the richest Greek marbles, with proper decorations of architecture and sculpture : he had prepared his model and the needful drawings, Bishop Compton had even received some specimens of marble from a Levant merchant in Holland, but unluckily the colours and the class of marble were not what Wren desired, and the plan waited for a better opportunity, which, in Wren's lifetime, never came. Thus, of all this grand design, the only trace is the painting of the apsidal pillars, in imitation of lapis lazuli, which was meant as a temporary experiment, and the model of the canopy in the possession of the Dean and Chapter. Hardly anything could be done which would more enhance the interior beauty of S. Paul's than the erection of this canopy.

Besides the adornment of the east end of the Cathedral there was also that of the dome to be accomplished. The decoration of S. Paul's is so vexed a question that one almost fears to touch upon it, but the statement in the 'Parentalia' is explicit.

'The judgement of the Surveyor was originally, instead of painting in the manner it is now performed, to have beautified the inside of the Cupola with the more durable ornament of mosaic work, as it is nobly executed in the Cupola of S. Peter's in Rome, which strikes the eye of the beholder with a most magnificent and splendid appearance; and which, without the least decay of colour, is as lasting as marble, or the building itself. For this purpose he had projected to have procured from Italy four of the most eminent artists in that profession; but as this art was a great novelty in England, and not generally apprehended, it did not receive the encouragement it deserved; it was imagined also that the expense would prove too great, and the time very long in execution; but though these, and all objections were fully answered, yet this excellent design was no further pursued.'

In weighing the value of this evidence as to Sir Christopher's views, it is important to remember that the 'Parentalia' was, though edited by Stephen the grandson, actually written by Christopher, the son who was constantly with his father and shared in his interests, and had himself seen, and no doubt described to Sir Christopher that very cupola of S. Peter's, of which he speaks.

The question of the iron fence round the Cathedral, of which Wren made mention in his petition, was much in his thoughts; he wished it to be low, and made of hammered iron, the Commissioners were determined that it should be high, and made of cast iron.

Wren, who doubtless intended to employ Tijou, and have a low, graceful railing which would throw up the height and solid grandeur of the Cathedral, repeatedly expressed his opinion; but the majority overruled him, and the Cathedral was imprisoned by a high, heavy, clumsy fence, the gates of which were sedulously closed, and were but too apt an emblem of the manner in which the Cathedral was soon shut off from its true uses. A century later, and Bishop Blomfield could say, 'I never pass S. Paul's without thinking how little it has done for Christianity.' Now the iron fence has departed,[1] and with it all possibility of such a reproach.

During all this time Wren was engaged on the Abbey repairs and the affairs of Chelsea College.

---

[1] The Dean and Chapter of S. Paul's removed the fence in 1874, and substituted the present open, low one, thus removing a blemish from the exterior of the Cathedral.

The Duke of Ormonde sends him a summons in November, 1713, the more pressing, as several Commissioners are out of town, to meet him 'at twelve of the clock at his Grace's house at the Cockpitt, in order to give directions for the cloathing of the Invalide Companys who are in a perishing condition for want thereof, not having been cloathed for near these three years past.' The death of Evelyn and that of Sir Stephen Fox had lost to Chelsea Hospital its two best friends, but doubtless the Duke and Sir Christopher were able to provide for this emergency.

We hear of Wren at this time busied as of old for the Royal Society, going, with his son and Sir Isaac Newton, to inspect a house in Crane Court,[1] and finally buying it as a residence for the Society.

Again he appears with Newton, and the son who seems to have been his constant companion, going down to Greenwich as visitors of the Royal Observatory there and making their report upon it. As Flamsteed hated Newton, and greatly resented any formal visitation, the expedition must have taxed even Wren's peace-making powers, but Flamsteed never seems to have quarrelled with him.

In the summer of the following year 'good Queen Anne' died, and with her all real chance of the return of the Stuart family, despite the gallant and devoted attempts made for 'Prince Charlie' in 'the '15' and 'the '45.' The sixth and last English reign which

[1] The Royal Society occupied this house, till 1847, when it was pulled down to make room for the new Record Office.—*Hist. R. S.*, p. 399. Weld.

Wren was destined to see began in 1714 with the accession of George I.

The S. Paul's Commission was renewed, with, of course, Wren's name upon it, but the annoyances of his position increased.

In his design, S. Paul's stood complete with a plinth over the entablature, and with statues on the four pediments only. The Commissioners took it into their heads that a balustrade with vases was greatly needed, and that it should be put up, unless Wren could 'set forth in writing, under his hand, that it is contrary to the principles of architecture and give his opinion in a fortnight's time.' This looks very like a device for tormenting the old man of eighty-five, and revenging themselves for their previous defeat. Exactly within the fortnight Wren sent an answer which certainly shows no trace of failing powers.

> 'I take leave, first, to declare that I never designed a balustrade. Persons of little skill in architecture did expect, I believe, to see something they had been used to in Gothick structures; and ladies think nothing well without an edging. I should gladly have complied with the vulgar taste but I suspended for the reasons following.'

The technical reasons are given, and he adds:
> 'that as no provision was originally made in my plan for a balustrade, the setting up one in such a confused manner over the plinth must apparently break into the harmony of the whole machine, and, in this

particular case, be *contrary to the principles of architecture.*'

Nothing daunted, either by Wren's reasons or his sarcasm, and regardless of their implied promise, the wise Commissioners of the Cathedral set to work on their balustrade.

This transaction belongs to the autumn of 1717. In the April of the ensuing year, George I., who cared nothing about art or architecture, and who only wished to gratify his German favourites, was easily prevailed upon to dismiss Sir Christopher Wren from that post of Surveyor-General which he had held for forty-eight years, and to bestow it upon William Benson, a favourite's favourite, as ignorant and incapable as he was grasping and unscrupulous. There was probably but little outcry, for, as Steele[1] had truly said, ' Nestor,' under which name he described Wren, ' was not only

> in his profession the greatest man of that age, but had given more proofs of it than any man ever did ; yet for want of that natural freedom and audacity which is necessary in commerce with men, his personal modesty overthrew all his public actions.'

The person least disposed to make a complaint was Wren himself. Finding his patent superseded, he quietly retired to his house at Hampton Court, saying, ' Nunc me jubet Fortuna expeditius philosophari.'[2] One other comment he made, as a note to the date

---

[1] *The Tatler*, No. 52, 1709. Both the paper and its note contain eloquent tributes to Wren. It is remarkable that Steele wrote this at the very time Wren's salary was first ' suspended.'

[2] 'Now Fortune commands me to apply myself more closely to Philosophy.'

(April 26, 1718) of this dismissal: Ὅτι ἀνέστη Βασιλεὺς ἕτερος ὃς οὐκ ᾔδει τὸν Ἰωσήφ : καὶ οὐδὲν τούτων τῷ Γαλλίωνι ἔμελεν. ✠ '[1]

It is some satisfaction to know that Benson so disgraced himself as in five years' time to be dismissed, and narrowly escaped a prosecution by the House of Lords. Pope held him up to deserved scorn in the 'Dunciad,' where he also says :

> While Wren with sorrow to the grave descends,

but this, one is glad to think, tells rather what might have been Sir Christopher's state of mind than what it really was.

Wren had had the interest of watching his eldest son's career in Parliament as member for that borough of Windsor which he had himself represented.

This son's wife had died, and in 1715 he married again. His second wife was Constance, daughter of Sir Thomas Middleton, and widow of Sir Roger Burgoyne ; by this marriage he had another son, named Stephen. On this occasion Sir Christopher bought the estate of Wroxhall Abbey[2] in Warwickshire,

---

[1] 'Then another king arose which knew not Joseph.'—*Acts* vii. 18. 'And Gallio cared for none of these things.'—*Acts* xviii. 17.

[2] Now spelt Wroxall. This property remained in the hands of Sir Christopher's direct lineal descendants (five Christophers held it in succession) until 1861. Wren's son and heir died in 1747, and is buried in Wroxhall Abbey ; his son Christopher displeasing him, he left away much of the estate to his stepson, Sir Roger Burgoyne. At the death of the elder Christopher many of the great architect's plans and drawings were bought by Mr. Justice Blackburn, who presented them to All Souls' College. The *Parentalia* was principally written at Wroxhall by Sir Christopher's son Christopher, and was published by his second son Stephen Wren, M.D., in 1750. See *Worthies of Warwickshire*, p. 852, and *Biog. Hist. of England*, vol. iii. p. 329. Noble.

which had belonged to the Burgoynes and was heavily encumbered. Sir Christopher is said to have stayed at the Abbey occasionally, and to have designed the kitchen garden wall which is built in semicircles. It was probably when he thus became a Warwickshire Squire that he gave the designs for S. Mary's Church at Warwick, designs entirely different from those adopted in the present building, which is said to have been designed and built by one Francis Smith, a mason in the town.

But the greater part of Wren's declining years was spent at Hampton Court, from which he went up to London to watch the progress of the works at Westminster Abbey, the surveyorship of which he still kept. A report was spread that the ceiling of the Sheldonian Theatre, in which, as a piece of mechanical construction, Sir Christopher took great pride, was giving way. Careful examination proved this to be a perfectly groundless rumour, and no further annoyance arose to disturb the calm evening of the old man's life. To be 'beneficus humano generi,' as he said, had ever been his aim and wish. He now employed his leisure in looking over old papers on astronomy and mathematics and the method of finding out the longitude at sea. It had been long considered by the general world as impossible to find out as was the secret of perpetual motion, and the attempt at either discovery was treated with equal ridicule. The merchants, and captains of merchant ships were, however, from bitter experience of vessels and crews wrecked or lost, aware of the immense importance of the discovery of the longitude, if it could be made. They presented, in 1714, a petition to Parliament, begging that a reward might be offered 'for such as shall discover the same.' This, after due consideration, was done by a Bill, passed rapidly through both Houses, offering a reward of 20,000*l.* for the discovery.[1]

The subject was one which greatly occupied Wren, who all his life had been interested in sailors and sea matters. He amused himself by throwing his latest thoughts on the longitude into the form of three cryptographs :[2]

1. OZVCVAYINIXDNCVOCWEDCNMALNABECIRTEWNG-RAMHHCCAW.
2. ZEIYEINOIEBIVTXESCIOCPSDEDMNANHSEFPRPIW-HDRAEHHXCIF.
3. EZKAVEBIMOXRFCSLCEEDHWMGNNIVEOMREWWE-RRCSHEPCIP.

[1] The reward was adjudged in two portions of 10,000*l.*, to Mr. J. Harrison in 1726 and 1775, for making two chronometers, which gave the longitude within 10′ 45″ of the truth. Rewards were offered for further discoveries. The Board of Longitude was abolished in 1828.—*Life of Sir Isaac Newton*, vol. ii. p. 258-267. Sir David Brewster.

[2] These cryptographs were first published by Sir David Brewster in his *Life of Sir Isaac Newton*, vol. ii. p. 263, ed. 1855. No key was found until Mr. Francis Williams, of Grange Court, Chigwell, sent the following :

1. WAcCHhMArGNwETrICeBAnLAmNCdEWcOUcNDxINi-
Wach magnetic balance wound in VAvCUzO.
vacuo. (One letter a misprint).

Omitted letters make CHR. WREN, MDCCXIV.

2. FIcXHhEArDHwIPrPEeSHnANmDEdSPcOIcSExTUiBEi-
Fix head hippes handes poise tube ONiEYieZ.
on eye. (One letter a misprint).

Omitted letters make CHR. WREN, MDCCXIIII.

A copy, signed by Halley as a true one, of this cipher was sent to the Royal Society in 1714 by Wren's son. Probably Sir Christopher had not perfected his instruments sufficiently to proclaim his discovery, and did not wish either to lose his idea, or, when later on he disclosed it, to appear as a plagiarist in case a similar method had suggested itself to anyone else. Old age had weakened Wren's limbs, but had had little effect on his clear understanding; his scientific pursuits interested him still, and were among the employments of those few leisure years which closed a life of incessant work. He gave, however, the greater part of his time and care to the diligent study of the Holy Scriptures, which all his life he had loved; and thus, serene and gentle as ever, waited for his summons.

Once a year it was his habit to be driven to London, and to sit for a while under the dome of his own Cathedral. On one of these journeys he caught a cold, and soon afterwards, on February 25, 1723, his servant, thinking Sir Christopher slept longer after dinner than was his wont, came into the room and found his master dead in his chair, with an expression of perfect peace on the calm features.

   3. PIcPEhSCrReŵWErMOeVInNGmWHdEEcLScFRxOMi-
      Pipe   screwe   moving   wheels   from
      BEvAKzE.
      beake.

Omitted letters make CHR. WREN, MDCCXIV.

   The three last omitted Z,s occurring in the first part of each cipher to show that that part must be taken *last.—Report of the British Association for* 1859.

They buried him near his daughter in the south-east crypt of S. Paul's, by one of the windows, under a plain marble slab with this inscription: 'Here lieth Sir Christopher Wren, the builder of this Cathedral Church of S. Paul, &c., who died in the year of our Lord MDCCXXIII., and of his age XCI.'

The spite of those who had hampered his genius in life showed itself again after his death. The famous inscription, written by his son:—'Subtus conditur hujus Ecclesiae et Urbis Conditor Christophorus Wren, qui vixit annos ultra nonaginta, non sibi, sed bono publico. Lector, si Monumentum requiris circumspice.'[1]—was placed in the crypt, and in the Cathedral itself there was nothing to preserve the memory of its architect.

This has in later years been remedied and the inscription is now in gold letters over the door of the north transept. Some of Sir Christopher's plans have, as has been shown, been executed; and further, the Cathedral has been set in green turf, and all around it is cared for instead of neglected, the once empty campanile is filled by twelve bells, whose music floats down over the roar of London, as if out of the sky itself, and the Dome is filled by vast congregations in the way which Sir Christopher almost foresaw.

In the Cathedral his memory is cherished; but in

---

[1] 'Beneath is laid the builder of this church and city, Christopher Wren, who lived more than ninety years, not for himself, but for the good of the State. Reader, if thou ask for a monument, look around thee.'

the city of London, which he rebuilt from its ashes, no statue has been erected to him, no great street has been honoured by taking as its own the name of Christopher Wren, though a name

On fame's eternall beadroll worthie to be fyled.

APPENDICES.

APPENDIX I.

REVERENDO PATRI DOMINO CHRISTOPHORO WREN, S.T.D. ET D.W. CHRISTOPHORUS FILIUS HOC SUUM PANORGANUM ASTRONOMICUM D. D. XIII. CALEND. NOVEM. ANNO 1645, p. 73.

> Si licet, et cessent rerum (Pater alme) tuarum
>   Pondera, devotae respice prolis opus.
> Hic ego sidereos tentavi pingere motus,
>   Coelicaque in modulos conciliare breves.
> Quo (prolapsa diù) renoventur tempora gyro,
>   Seculaque, et menses, et imparilesque dies.
> Quomodo Sol abeat, redeatque, et temperet annum,
>   Et (raptum contra) grande perennet iter;
> Cur nascens gracili, pleno orbe refulget adulta,
>   Cur gerat extinctas menstrua luna faces.
> His ego numinibus dum cito, atque ardua mundi,
>   Scrutor, et arcanas conor inire vias,
> Adsis, O! faveasque, pater, succurre volanti
>   Suspensum implumis dirige prolis iter,
> Ne male, praecipiti, nimium prae viribus audax
>   (Sorte sub Icarea) lapsus ab axe ruam:
> Te duce, fert animus, studiis sublimibus hisce
>   Pasci, dum superas detur adire domos.

APPENDIX II.

CHURCHES, HALLS, COLLEGES, PALACES, OTHER PUBLIC BUILDINGS, AND PRIVATE HOUSES, BUILT AND REPAIRED BY SIR CHRISTOPHER WREN.

Churches.

S. Alban, Wood Street.
* All Hallows, Bread Street.
    „   Lombard Street.
    „   Upper Thames St.
All Saints, Isleworth.
S. Andrew, Holborn.
    „   by the Wardrobe.
SS. Anne & Agnes.
S. Anne, Soho (?).
* S. Antholin, Watling St.
S. Augustine.
* S. Bartholomew, Bartholomew Lane.
* S. Benedict, Gracechurch Street.
*   „   Fink, Threadneedle Street.
S. Benedict, Paul's Wharf.
S. Bride, Fleet Street.
Chichester Cathedral.
Christ Church, Newgate.
* S. Christopher, Threadneedle Street.
S. Clement Danes, Strand.
    „   Eastcheap.
Dartmouth Chapel, Blackheath.
* S. Dionysius, Back Church.
S. Dunstan in the East.
S. Edmund the King, Lombard Street.
S. Faith (Crypt of S. Paul's).
S. George, Botolph Lane.
S. James, Garlickhithe.
    „   Westminster.

S. Lawrence, Jewry.
S. Magnus, London Bridge.
S. Margaret Lothbury, Pattens, Rood Lane.
S. Martin, Ludgate Hill.
S. Mary, Abchurch.
    „   Aldermanbury.
    „   Aldermary.
    „   at Hill.
    „   le Bow.
*   „   Somerset.
    „   Woolnoth.
S. Mary Magdalen, Old Fish St.
S. Matthew, Friday Street.
S. Michael, Bassishaw.
    „   Cheapside.
    „   Cornhill.
*   „   Crooked Lane.
*   „   Queenhithe.
    „   Royal, College Hill.
S. Mildred, Bread Street.
*   „   Poultry.
S. Nicholas, Cole Abbey.
S. Olave, Jewry.
S. Paul's Cathedral.
S. Peter's Abbey, Westminster.
    „   Cornhill.
Salisbury Cathedral.
S. Stephen, Coleman Street.
    „   Walbrook.
S. Swithin, Cannon Street.
S. Vedast, Foster Lane.

* Signifies that the church has been destroyed.

Halls.

Mercers Company.	Saddlers Company
* Grocers ,,	Cordwainers ,,
Drapers ,,	Paper Stainers ,,
* Fishmongers ,,	Curriers ,,
* Goldsmiths ,,	Masons ,,
Skinners ,,	* Plumbers ,,
Merchant Taylors ,,	Innholders ,,
Haberdashers ,,	Founders ,,
* Salters ,,	Coopers ,,
Ironmongers ,,	Tilers and Bricklayers ,,
Vintners ,,	Joiners ,,
* Dyers ,,	Weavers ,,
Brewers ,,	Plasterers ,,
* Leathersellers ,,	Stationers ,,
Cutlers ,,	Apothecaries ,,
Bakers ,,	Pinmakers ,,
Tallow Chandlers ,,	Coachmakers ,,
Girdlers ,,	

Many of these buildings have been considerably altered since Wren's time, and many are now let as warehouses, or turned to other uses. *Some*

Colleges.

Christ Church, Oxford.	Pembroke, Cambridge.
Emmanuel, Cambridge.	* Physicians, Warwick Lane, London.
Holy Trinity ,,	
,, Oxford.	Queen's (?) Oxford.
Morden, Blackheath.	Sion, London.

Palaces.

Hampton Court.   Kensington.   * Newmarket.   Winchester.

Other Public Buildings.

Alderman's Court, Guildhall.	Bohun's Almshouses, Lee.
Archbishop Tenison's Library.	Bushey Park, { Pavilion.
Ashmolean Museum.	{ Ranger's house at.

* Signifies that the building has been destroyed.

Chapter House, S. Paul's.
* Custom House, Port of London.
Deanery, St. Paul's, London.
Hospitals, { Chelsea College.
{ Greenwich.
London, City of.
Merchant Taylors' Almhouses, London.
Middle Temple, front of.
Monument, the.

Monument { to Edward V. & Richard, Duke of York
Observatory, Greenwich.
* Royal Exchange, London.
Sheldonian Theatre, Oxford.
* Temple Bar.
* Theatre Royal, Drury Lane.
* Theatre in Salisbury Court.
Tower of London.
Windsor, Town Hall.

Private Houses.

Allaston's, Lord, London.
Bloomsbury, two in.
Buckingham's, Duchess of, London.
Chichester, two at.
Cooper's, Madam, London.

Fawley Court, Oxon.
Marlborough's, Duchess of, London.
Oxford's, Earl of, London.
Sunderland's, Lord, London.
Windsor, two at.

This list, which is, I fear, imperfect, only professes to give such buildings as were actually built or repaired; there are, besides, a large number of unexecuted designs.

APPENDIX III.

Sir Christopher Wren left the rough drafts of four tracts on architecture, which are printed in the ' Parentalia,' and a few notes on Roman and Greek buildings, some of which Mr. Elmes transcribed in his ' Life; ' they are for the most part very technical and are incomplete. The copy of the ' Parentalia ' now in my hands contains the autograph draft of a Discourse on Architecture, which, as I think, has never been printed; it appears to me to be of great interest. It is therefore given entire, though I regret I cannot give the quaint prints of Noah's Ark, the Tower of Babel, Babylon, &c., with which the original is illustrated. The two former prints tally so exactly with the descriptions in the ' Discourse '—the print of the ark containing a small section, an elevation, and a vignette of a man feeding one of the creatures, besides a large drawing of the floating Ark—that I incline to think they were engraved, either by Wren himself, or from his drawings. Engraving was an art he well understood. He divides with Prince Rupert the honour of the invention of mezzo-tint. The prints are numbered Pl. IV. and V. respectively, and have no signature.

Discourse on Architecture.

WHATEVER a man's sentiments are upon mature deliberation, it will be still necessary for him in a conspicuous Work to preserve his Undertaking from general censure, and so for him to accomodate his Designs to the gust of the Age he lives in, thô it appears to him less rational. I have found no little difficulty to bring Persons, of otherwise a good genius, to think anything in Architecture would be better then what they had heard commended by others, and what they had view'd themselves. Many good Gothick forms of Cathedrals were to be seen in our Country, and many had been seen abroad, which they liked the better for being not much differing from ours in England: this humour with many is not yet eradicated, and therefore I judge it not improper to endeavour to reform the Generality to a truer taste in Architecture by giving a larger Idea of the whole Art, beginning with the reasons and progress of it from the most remote Antiquity; and that in short touching chiefly on some things, which have not been remarked by others.

The Project of Building is as natural to Mankind as to Birds, and was practised before the Floud. By Josephus we learn that Cain built the first City, *Enos*, and enclosed it with Wall and Rampires; and that the Sons of Seth, the other son of Adam, erected two Columns of Brick and Stone to preserve their Mathematical Science to Posterity, so well built that thô ye one of Brick was destroy'd by the Deluge, ye other of Stone was standing in ye time of Josephus. The first Peece of Naval Architecture we read of in Sacred History was the *Arke* of *Noah*, a work very exactly fitted and built for the Purpose intended.

It was by measure just 6 times as Long as Broad, and the Heighth was ⅗ of the Breadth. This was the Proportion of the Triremes afterwards. The Dimensions, and that It was 3 Stories high, and that It had a Window of a Cubit Square is only mention'd; but many things sure were of necessity to be contrived for Use in this Model of the Whole Earth.

First, One small Window was not sufficient to emit the Breath of all the Animals; It had certainly many other Windows as well for Light as Air. It must have Scupper-Holes and a large Sink and an Engin to Pump It; for It drew, as I compute, with all its Cargo and Ballast, at least 12 foot Water. There must be places for Insects the only Food of some Birds and Animals. Great Cisterns for Fresh Water not only for Land Animals, but for some Water fowl and Insects. Some Greens to grow in Tubs, the only food of Tortoises and some Birds and Insects; since we certainly have learnt that nothing is produced by Spontaneous Generation, and we firmly believe there was no new Creation. I need not mention stairs to the several Stories, with many other things absolutely necessary for a year's Voyage for Men and Animals, thô not mention'd in the Story, and Providence was the Pilot of this Little World, the Embrio of the next.

Most certainly Noah was divinely qualified not only as a Preacher of Righteousness but the greatest Philosopher in the 'Historia Animalium' that ever was; and it was Work enough for his whole Family to feed them, and take care of the young Brood; for in a year's time there must be a great increase in the Ark, wch was food for the Family, and the Beasts of Prey.

The first Peece of Civil Architecture we meet with in Holy Writ is the Tower of Babel. Providence scatter'd the first Builders, so the Work was left off, but the Successors of Belus the son of Nimrod probably finished It and made it His Sepulchre, upon his Deification.

It was built of Burnt Brick Cemented with Bitumen.

Herodotus gives us a surprizing Relation of it wch being set down by measure is not beside our subject to observe. It consisted of Eight several Stories; the First was one Stade, or 625 foot square, and of the same measure in Height upon which were rais'd seven more,' wch if they were all equal with the First would amount to 2,500 foot, which is not credible: the Form must be therefore Pyramidal and being adorn'd on the outside with Rows of Galleries in divers stories diminished in Height in Geometrical Proportion; so the whole Mass would have the Aspect of Half an Octaedron, which is that of all the Egyptian Pyramids.

These Corridors being Brick wasted in more than 1600 years: and it was these which Alexander actually began to Repair, not the whole Bulk, as I suppose.

How Herodotus had his measures I question, for He flourish'd but 100 years before Alexander's Conquests of Babylon, so it was then 1500 years Old.

I proceed next to those mighty Works of Antiquity the Wonderful *Pyramids* of Egypt yet remaining without considerable decay after almost 4000 years: for 2000 years. agoe, they were reckon'd by Historians of Uncertain Original.

I cannot think any Monarch however Despotick could effect such things meerly for Glory; I guess there were reasons of State for it.

Egypt was certainly very early Populous, because so Productive of Corn by the help of Nile, in a manner without labour. They deriv'd the River when it rose, all over the Flat of the Delta; and as the People increas'd, over a great deal of Land that lay higher. The Nile did not always Flow high enough for a great Part of the then inhabited Country, and without the Nile, They must either Starve or prey upon those who had Corn; This must needs create Mutiny and Bloodshed, to prevent which it was the Wisdom of their ancient Kings and Priests to Exact a certain Proportion of Corn, and lay it up for those who wanted the benefit of the Rivers when it disappointed their sowing.

Thus Joseph lay'd up for seven years, and sur'ly He was not first: this Provision being ever so essentially necessary to support the Popularity and consequently the Grandure of the Kingdom; and continued so in all Ages, till the Turks neglected all the upper Canales except one which still suppli'd Alexandria. Now what was the consequence? It was not for the Health of the Common People nor Policy of the Government for them to be fed in Idleness: great Multitudes were therefore imploy'd in that which requir'd no great Skill, the Sawing of Stone Square to a few different scantlings, nor was there any need of Scaffolding or Engines, for hands only would raise them from step to step: a little teaching serv'd to make them set Line: and thus these great Works in which some Thousands of hands might be imploy'd at once, rose with Expedition: the difficulty was in mustering the men to move in order under proper Officers, and probably with Musick, as Amphion is said much about the same Age to have built the walls of Thebes with his Harp; that is Musick made the Workmen move exactly together without which no great weight can be moved, as Seamen know, for the Sheet Anchor will by no means be moved without a fiddle to make men exert their United force in equal time: otherwise they pull one against another and lose great part of their force.

The next observable Monument of great Antiquity which yet remain is the Pillar of Absolom.

By the description given of it, and what I have learnt from Travellers who have seen it, we must allow it to be very Remarkable though not great.

It is compos'd of seven Pillars six about in a Hexagon, and one in the middle and the Tholus solid, a large Architrave, Frize and Cornice lie upon the Pillars which are larger in proportion to their height then what we now allow to the Tuscan order, so likewise is the Entablature larger.

This whole composition though at least 30 foot high, is all of the one Stone, both Basis, Pillars and Tholus cut as it stood out of the adjacent Cliff of white Marble.

I could wish some skilful Artist would give us the exact dimensions to inches, by which we might have an idea of the

Antient Tyrian manner; for it was probable Solomon by his correspondence with King Hiram employ'd the Tyrian Artists, in his Temple; and from the Phœnicians I derive as well the Arts as the Letters, of the Graecians, thô it may be, the Tyrians were Imitators of the Babylonians, and they of the Egyptians. Great Monarchs are ambitious to leave great Monuments behind them, and this occasions great Inventions and Mechanick Arts.

What the Architecture was that Solomon used we know little of, though Holy Writ hath given us the general dimensions of the Temple, by which we may in some manner collect the Plan but not of all the Courts.

Villapandus hath made a fine Romantick Piece after the Corinthian Order, which in that age was not used by any Nation: for the First Ages used grosser Pillars then Dorick. In after Times they began to refine from the Dorick, as in the Temple of Ephesus (the United Work of all Asia) and afterwards improved into a Slenderer Pillar, and Leavy Capital of various inventions which they called Corinthian. So that if we run back to the Age of Solomon, we may with reason believe they used the Tyrian manner, as gross at least as the Dorick, and that the Corinthian manner of Villapandus is meer fancy: Nay when long after Herod built the *Atrium Gentium*, he that carefully considers the description in Josephus will find it to be a Tripple Portico, and thick Pillars of the grosser Proportions which being whole stones of an incredible Bulk—our Saviour's Disciples admired them: *Master*, said they, *see what stones are here!* Titus would have sav'd this noble structure, but a soldier throwing a torch upon the Roof which was Cedar planks covered with Bitumen, it easily took Fire and consumed the whole Building. All the City was thus covered flat with Bitumen (easily gathered from the Lake of Sodom) and upon the flat roofs the Jews celebrated under Palm-boughs the Feast of Tabernacles.

The Body of the First Temple was gilt upon Bitumen, which is good Size for gilding and will preserve the timber. The Roof and Cedar Wainscot within being carved with

Knotts was gilded all over with a thick Leaf, so I understand the word *Overlay'd* ; for if it was cover'd with plate apply'd over the knots and Imbossments the gold nails to fix it on would have increased the Weight of the plate, whereas the quantity of the Nails is reckoned but small in Proportion. The Doors might be plated over and nail'd, and the Hinges and Bars, called Chains, might be solid ; for these were afterwards stripp'd when the Egyptians pillaged the Temple in the Reign of Rehoboam.

That Herod did more than the Upper Portico doth not appear, for the substruction under the Portico was certainly Solomon's Work. The whole Hill Moriah was wall'd upright by him from the bottom of the Valley which render'd a broad Area above for all the Buildings of the Courts. This is the work in which were us'd stone of 10 and 12 Cubits, call'd as well they might *Costly Stones.*

Now it may well be inquired how in an uneven craggy Country, as it is about Jerusalem, such mighty Loads of Stone could be brought. I shall give my thoughts.

Solomon had an Army of Labourers in his Works ; now suppose 12 Cubits long and 2 broad, and 1 thick, this would amount to 648 of our solid feet, which in marble would be 64 Tuns and more. Eight men can draw a Tun, but the ground being hilly, we will allow 10 men to a Tun which would be 640 men. Now how all these men can be brought to draw together I show as follows. First, 10 men draw in a Rope (as bargemen with us) at the end of this Rope is a Spring-tree (as our Coachmen use for ye two fore Horses) to each end of which is a rope so 20 men can draw in the second rank ; each rope hath again its Spring-tree, and so on to a sixth rank each rank doubling the number and supposing 10 men to govern the rest (possibly with Musick) makes the number 640 men ; and this will be found readier than capsterns, and by this means much vaster stones may be mov'd and even by Barbarous People without Engins. I cannot otherwise see what need Solomon had of such great multitudes of Labourers as *Threescore and ten Thousand Bearers of Burdens,* and *Fourscore Thousand Hewers of stone in the Mountains,* &c. Probably too they were employ'd by Months, and the rest were by turns to till the ground and bring food for the Labourers that the Country Work might proceed.

The Walls of Babylon were most stupendious Works, built with Brick and Cement with Bitumen; the Height of them, according to Herodotus, was Two Hundred Royal Cubits, and the Breadth Fifty; which in our measure (reckoning every Royal Cubit with Herodotus 1 foot 9 inches which is 3 inches above the common cubit measure) makes the Height 375 foot and the Breadth 93 ft. 9 in.

In these Walls were one hundred gates of Brass with Ornaments in Architecture of the same metal. Besides the first Wall, (which was encompassed with a wide and deep Foss always supply'd with water the sides of which were Lin'd with Brick) was an inner Wall built of near the same strength, thô not altogether of the same Breadth.

The extent of the City must add to the Surprise which being a Square contained a Front on every Side of one hundred and Twenty Stadia, that is Fifteen of our miles, and makes up in the whole Threescore miles.

Another stupendious Fabrick of I think also Tyrian architecture, was the monument of Porsenna, King of Etruria. This Sepulchre we have describ'd by Pliny, with the particular Dimensions in Feet which I have accordingly Delineated.

First, a Basis of squar'd stone fifty foot high rais'd the Pile above any vulgar contiguous Buildings which being solid only in those Parts that bore weight was so contriv'd withinside as to form a very intricate Labyrinth, into which whoever enter'd without a clew of thread would not be able to find the way out. Upon this Basis stood five Pyramids of 150 foot high; Four in the Angles, and one in the Centre; Bodies call'd Pyramids thô it is manifest they must have been so cut off as to have a large space on the Top to carry a Second Story of Four more lofty Pyramids of 100 foot high; and over them a third Order of Five more. Now how these could be borne is worth the consideration of an architect. I conceive it might be thus perform'd securely.

Set half Hemispherical Arches, such as we make the heads of Niches, but lay'd back to back, so that each of these have its Bearing upon three Pyramids of the Lower Order, that is two angular ones and the middle Pyramids; and these cutting one another upon the Diagonals will have a firm bearing for all the Works above.

Pliny mentions a Brass Circle and Cupola, lay'd upon the Five Lower Pyramids, not I suppose to bear anything, but chiefly for Ornament, and to cover the stone work of the Arches upon the strong Spandrells of which if another Platform were rais'd upon that might the upper structure be built and the whole have a stupendious effect, and seemingly very open. Pliny took his Description of this extraordinary Pile from the Measures set down by Varro, a diligent and therefore credible author, who probably might have taken his Dimensions when it was standing before the absolute conquest of Etruria by the Romans; the summary then of this prodigious Edifice (erected to show the Vanity of the Eastern Monarchy could be exceeded by the Italians) may be thus compriz'd.

The Basis of the whole was 300 ft. square, and 50 ft. high; upon which stood Five Pyramids each of 75 ft. square at 150 ft. high; upon which rested the Brazen Circle and Cupola, stil'd by Pliny *Petasus*, (which I take to be a Brass Covering securing the Arches) from which hung little Bells by Chains, which sounded as they mov'd by the Winds.

The Four Pyramids of the Second Order of 100 ft. high standing upon the Circle or Brim of the *Petasus* as upon an Entablature, were evidently the Four First Angular Pyramids continu'd to an Apex, or near to a Point, so each will be in all from the Basis 450 ft. high, and rise as high as the *Petasus*; above which was again a Platform containing the Third Order of Five more Pyramids, of which the four angular Pyramids rested firmly upon the keys of the Diagonal Sections of the half Hemispherical Vaultings, which were called by the Ancients *Conchae* resembling the heads of Niches joyn'd back to back. This Platform I take to have been round as being the Horizontal Section of the *Petasus*; and the Bases of the

Five Upper Pyramids would be contiguous, and thus would be of the same shape and as high as the same below, as Varro asserts with some suspicion, fearing how they would stand, but I with confidence, the Proportions persuading, which indeed are very fine.

The Heighth to the Breadth of the Basis is 6 to 1. The Heighth of the Pyramids to the Brass *Petasus* is 2 to 1, but taking in their whole heighth it would have 4 to 1, but allowing the Point of the Pyramid to be taken off (as it ought) and allowing for the Brasen Brim and Bells it will be 250 foot, above which was the Floor that bore the Five upper Pyramids of 4 to 1, so the Heighth is 550 foot as 6 to 11.

I have ventured to put some Ornaments, at ye Top belonging to the Tuscan superstition, (They then us'd not Statues) They are Golden Thunderbolts, so the whole will be 600 foot high, that is double to the Basis and the Heighth to the Brass circle will appear half the Face, or like the Façade of a Tuscan Temple, to which the Breadth of the Brim of the *Petasus* and the Bells supply the Place of an Entablature:

I have been the longer in this Description because the Fabrick was in the Age of Pythagoras and his School, when the World began to be fond of Geometry and Arithmetick.

N.B. In all the Editions of Pliny for *Tricenum* read Tricentinûm as the sense requires.

> At the end of the Discourse on Architecture is an elevation, drawn in pen and sepia, of the tomb of Mausolus, as Sir Christopher supposed from Pliny's account that it must have been constructed. It is drawn to a scale, with indications of statues, of which he supposed there to have been forty-eight. It is remarkable how closely Sir Christopher's conjectural elevation tallies with what recent excavations have brought to light.

INDEX.

ABBOT, Bishop of London, 11, 14; Archbishop of Canterbury, 24

Académie Royale des Sciences, 148

Addison, 74, 179

All Hallows, Bread Street, rebuilt by Wren, 232; destruction of, 232, 234

—— Lombard Street, rebuilt by Wren, 271, 272

—— Thames Street, 240

All Saints, Isleworth, 298

Andrewes, Lancelot, Dean of Westminster, Bishop of Chichester, of Ely, of Winchester, kindness of, to Matthew Wren, 6, 7; his prophecy, 10 13; his death, 14; funeral of, at St. Saviour's, Southwark, 15; care of, in giving church preferment, 31; chaplain sent to the New Forest by, 40; appointment of Mr. Bois by, 46; quoted by Bishop Wren, 62; church views of, 120; legacy of, to Pembroke College library, 134

'Annals of England,' 20, 58, 77, 122

Anne, Queen, 300, 301, 305, 317, 320, 327

Annual Register,' the (1765), 174

Arches Court, The, origin of the name, 184

Architecture, 119, 148, 150, 171, 184, 197, 240, 268, 290, 329; Discourse on, by Sir C. Wren. *See* Appendix III., 340

Artillery Company, the, 185

Ashburnham, Mr., 75

Ashmole, Mr. Elias, founder of the Ashmolean Museum, 217

Atterbury, Dean of Westminster, and Bishop of Rochester, 203, 209

Aubrey, the Wiltshire Antiquary, 91

Ayliffe's 'Oxford,' 125, 141

BANCROFT, Archbishop, 14
Barrow, Dr. Isaac, eulogy of, on Christopher Wren, 128, 129

Barwick, Dr., Dean of Durham, of S. Paul's, 'Life of,' 72, 76, 85, 110, 112, 115, 120, 140

Bathurst, Dr., 144, 145, 270, 271

'Beauties of England and Wales,' 16

Bedloe, witness in the Popish plot, 227

Benson, William, appointed by George I. to supersede Wren, 329, 330

Bernini, Giov., 145, 149

Billing, A., 'Restoration of the Church of S. Sepulchre,' 183

BIR

Bird, Francis, sculptor, 300, 304
'Black Book of the Garter,' the, 4, 68
Blenheim Palace, building of, by Vanbrugh, 286
Blenheim, victory of (1704), 301
'Blue Book of the Garter,' the, 68
Blunt, 'Key to the Holy Bible,' 46
Bois, Mr. John, 46
Bow Church. *See* S. Mary-le-Bow
Boyle, Robert, 283
Brewster, Sir David, 'Life of Newton,' 330
British Association, the, report of, for 1859, 333
Brouncker, Lord, 124, 126, 143
Burnet, Bishop of Salisbury, 279
Burton, Henry, 251
Busby, Dr., head-master of Westminster, 41, 300
Bushnell, John, 179
Butler, Bishop of Bristol, 65
Butler, Samuel, 130

CAMBRIDGE, 6, 15, 45, 216
Canova, Antonio, 192
Catechism, the, clergy compelled to use, 22, 50
Cave, Dr. William, 240
Cemeteries, Wren's plan for placing outside London, 307
Chardin, Sir John, 230, 231
Charles I., his journey to Spain as Prince of Wales, 7-9; his coronation in Scotland, 16; sets up his standard at Nottingham (1642), 60; sends a pardon to Laud, 70; his flight from Oxford, 75; his death, 86; his bust by Bernini, 149; proposed monument to, 209, 210
Charles II., escape of, after the battle of Worcester, 91; letter of, to Monk from Breda, 112; entry of, into London, 117; encourage-

COR

ment given by, to the founding of the Royal Society, 124, 130; spirited behaviour of, at the Fire of London, 156; first stone of the Royal Exchange laid by, 178; portion of the tax on coal given to building of S. Paul's by, 198; palace at Newmarket built for, 225; death of, 246
Chelsea College, building of the hospital at, 239, 240, 300, 326, 327
Chichester, sack of, by the Parliamentary troops, 79, 123
— cathedral of, spire repaired by Wren, 243
Christ Church, Newgate, repaired by Wren, 260
Christ Church, Oxford, gateway at, built by Wren, 232
'Church Quarterly Review,' the, 65, 123
Cibber, Caius, 207
City churches, the. *See* Names of Churches. For complete list of, see Appendix II., 338
City Church and Churchyard Protection Society, 191; Report of, 205
City companies' halls rebuilt by Wren, 266. For list of, see Appendix II., 339
Clarendon, Lord, 19, 20, 23, 47, 110, 121, 160
Claypole, Richard, 99
Coal, portion of tax on, granted for the rebuilding of S. Paul's, 198
Coghill, Faith, 91, 176, 177
Collier, 'Ecclesiastical History,' 20
Common Prayer. *See* Prayer Book
Compton, Bishop of London, 220, 279, 323, 324
Convocation, meeting of, in S. Paul's (1661), 119, 120
Corbet, Bishop of Norwich, of Oxford, 22, 24, 27, 215

INDEX.

COS

Cosin, Dean of Peterborough, Bishop of Durham, 153
Coverdale, Bishop Miles, 219
Cowley, Abraham, 124, 147
Cromwell, Oliver, 9, 91, 99, 102
Cromwell, Richard, 103
Custom-house, the, rebuilt by Wren, 176

DALE, Rev. T. P., rector of S. Vedast's, Foster Lane, imprisonment of, 273
Davenport, 'Oxfordshire Annals,' 25
'Decoy Duck,' the, a pamphlet against Archbishop Williams, 59
Denham, Sir John, 127, 139
De Ros, Lord, 'The Tower of London,' 211
Dore, Abbey of, 19
Doyley, 'Life of Sancroft,' 165, 166
Dunton, John, leader of the expedition against the Sallee pirates, 20
Duppa, Dr. Brian, Bishop of Salisbury, appointed executor of Archbishop Laud's will, 71; Archbishop Tenison secretly ordained by, 123

EAST Knoyle, living of, held by Dr. Wren, 31, 32, 33
Elmes, 'Life of Sir C. Wren,' 90, 97, 200, 230
Ely, 44, 45
Ely House, 118, 119
Ely, Bishop of. *See* Wren; Turner
Emmanuel College, Chapel of, built by Wren, 215, 216
Evelyn, John, 'Diary' of, 15, 49, 50, 51, 89, 93, 94, 95, 99, 114, 117, 118, 127, 145, 146, 154, 155, 181, 206, 209, 215, 217, 226, 228, 229, 230, 242, 244, 260, 286, 287, 302
—— death of, 304
Exchange. *See* Royal Exchange

GOD

FAWLEY Court built by Wren, 245
Fell, Bishop of Oxford, 220
Fergusson 'Hist. of Architecture,' 15, 184, 192
—— 'Illustrated Handbook of Architecture,' 139
Fifty new churches, Act for building the, 305
Fire of London, the, 155, 159, 175, 184, 185, 187, 191, 192, 204, 219, 243, 288
Flamsteed, Astronomer Royal, 216, 299, 327
Fogg, Captain, pillage of S. George's Chapel by, 67
Fox, Sir Stephen, 239, 269, 327
'Fragmentary Illustrations of the History of the Book of Common Prayer,' 120
Freemasons, the Order of, 147, 200, 285
Frogley, Richard, Wren's carpenter, 142
Fuller, Dr. Thomas, 6, 10

GARTER, the Order of the, 4, 5, 16, 34-36, 67, 68, 80, 81, 123, 217
Garth, Samuel, physician and poet, 265
George I., 329
George, Prince, 235, 300
Gibbons, Grinling, 194, 195, 242, 252, 253, 324
Gibbs, James, pupil of Wren's, builder of S. Mary-le-Strand and S. Martin's-in-the-Fields, 233, 286, 305
Goddard, Dr., Warden of Merton College, 77, 78, 103, 104, 105, 124, 125
Godwin, 'De Præsulibus Angliæ Commentarius,' 57, 94

GRA

Grainger, 'Biographical History of England,' 59, 149, 231
Great Haseley, detection of a murder at, 38
Greenwich Hospital, 269, 299
— Observatory, 216, 327
— Palace, 127
Gresham College, London, 98, 103, 105, 123, 240
Gresham Professors. *See* Ward's 'Lives of'
Grey, 'Examination of Neale's Hist. of the Puritans,' 62, 86, 122
Griffiths, Matthew, Rector of S. Mary Magdalene's, Fish St. 248
Gustavus Adolphus, his George and Garter, 37, 67

HACKETT, Dr., 18
Hawksmore, Nicholas, a pupil of Wren's, 206, 286, 293, 305
Hall, Bishop of Norwich, 58
Halley, Dr., 247, 299, 333
Hampton Court Palace, Wren's alterations at, 267, 268.
Hare, A. C., 'Walks in London,' 119, 252
Harris, Renatus, builder of the organ at S. James', Westminster, 243; at S. Paul's, 274, 275
Hatton, E. 'New View of London,' 219, 262, 271, 272
Hawkins, Sir John, monument of, at S. Dunstan's-in-the-East 287.
Henchman, Bishop of London, 154, 222
Henley-on-Thames, 38, 75, 159
Henry VI., 4
Hewet, Dr., 99
Heylin, 'Cyprianus Anglicus,' 15, 22, 44
Hoare, Sir R., 'History of Wiltshire,' 33

KEN

Holder, Dr. 42, 177, 222, 223, 261, 300
Holder, Mrs., 42, 176, 223, 224, 225, 261, 300
Hooke, Robert, 159, 246, 247
Hope, Right Honourable, A. J. B. B. 'Worship in the Church of England,' 65
Hoskyns, C. Wren, 3, 231
Hoskyns, Sir John, 231
Hudson, Dr., chaplain to Charles I., 75
Hume, 'History of England,' 102
Hyde, Mr., 110, 111, 112, 113, 115. *See* Clarendon.

INIGO JONES, 42, 93, 127, 166, 243, 269
Ipswich, Disturbances at, stirred up by Prynne, 44, 45; Tower church at, 65.

JAMES I., visit of, to Cambridge, 6; plans the Spanish match, 7; his opinion of Bishop King, 222
James II., Inscription on Monument effaced by, 208; continues Wren on S. Paul's commission, 248; Declaration by, of liberty of conscience, 260; Abdication of, 263; Residence of, at S. Germain's, 283
Jarman, the city architect, 266
Jeffreys, Judge, his letter to Pepys, 161, 162
Jennings, Richard, Wren's master carpenter, 159, 200, 321, 323
Juxon, Bishop of London, 17, 49, 86, 109; Archbishop of Canterbury, 118

KEN, Prebendary of Winchester, Bishop of Bath and Wells, 220, 234, 260

Kennet, Bishop, 122
Kensington Palace, additions to, made by Wren, 268
King, Bishop of London, his gravestone, 222
Knolles, 'Historie of the Turks,' 19

LAKE, Bishop of Chichester, 260.
Lalanne, L., 'Dictionnaire Historique de la France,' 149
Lambeth Palace, 41, 47, 48, 239
Lane, Mr. Peter, Rector of S. Bennet's, Paul's wharf, 243
Lathbury, 'History of Book of Common Prayer,' 123
Laud, Bishop of S. David's, of London, Archbishop of Canterbury, advice of, respecting chaplains for the Prince of Wales, 7; form of penance, and reconciliation for a renegado prepared with Bishop Wren by, 20; measures taken by, against the lecturers, 22; his treatment of the foreign congregations, 23, 24; works at S. Paul's carried on by order of, 41, 42; yearly report of, to the King, 45; impeachment and imprisonment of, in the Tower, 48, 50; his refusal to escape, 61; Trial of, 69, 70; his execution on Tower Hill, 70; order of, respecting altar-rails, 249
Lecturers, measures taken against, 22, 27
Lenthall, William, Speaker of the House of Commons, 38, 79
Le Sœur, Hubert, his statue of King Charles, 195
Littleton, Lord Keeper, 57
Lloyd, Bishop of S. Asaph, 217, 226, 260, 281
Longitude, the, attempts to discover accurately, 215, 331, 332

London, city of, 25, 41, 98, 142, 154, 155, 179, 186, 188, 335. See Fire; Plague; Tower.
London Bridge, 204, 262, 288
— Stone, 219
Long Parliament, the, 56, 68, 103
Longman, ' Three Cathedrals dedicated to S. Paul's in London,' 198, 222, 273, 293
Louvre, the, 148, 149
Lysons, ' Environs of London,' 298

MACAULAY, 'History of England' 261, 281
Marah, 'Life of Archbishop Juxon,' 18
Marlborough, Duchess of, 285, 286
— Duke of, 301, 302
Mary, Princess, her marriage, 49
— Queen, her arrival in England 263; employs Wren to rebuild Hampton Court, 267; her death, 268
Maw, Bishop of Bath and Wells, 7
' Memorials of the See of Chichester,' 79, 123, 245
Merchant Taylors' School, 6
Milford, Rev. R.N., 33
Milman, 'Annals of S. Paul's Cathedral,' 197, 203, 318
Milton, 122, 232
Monk, George, afterwards General, 71, 72, 103, 112, 114
Monument, the, built by Wren, 207; inscriptions on, 207, 208
Morley, Bishop of Winchester, 220
Morton, Bishop of Durham, 112
Motley ' Life of Barnevelde,' 61

NEALE, 'History of the Puritans,' 58
Neile, Bishop of Rochester, of Lichfield, of Lincoln, of Durham,

NEW

of Winchester, and Archbishop of York, 10, 11, 13, 57, 70
Newcourt, 'Repertorium,' 118, 183, 218, 222, 241, 243, 249, 250, 273
Newmarket, hunting palace built for Charles II. at, 225
Newport, Lord, 218
Newton, Sir Isaac, 154, 193, 232, 246, 247, 324, 327
Noble, 'Biographical History of England,' 225, 330
Non-jurors, the, 264, 281
Norris, Lord, 38, 39
Norwich, diocese of, overrun with lecturers, 22; weavers at, Bishop Wren's treatment of, 23, 25
Notes and queries, 90

OATES, Titus, 226
Oldenburg, Mr., Secretary of the Royal Society, 299
Oughtred, the Rev. W., 78; his death from joy at the Restoration, 79
Oxford, 25, 31, 74, 75, 90, 93, 140, 144, 192, 217, 232

PAPIN, DENYS, inventor of Papin's Digestor, 229, 230
Parentalia, the, 26, 32, 34, 66, 74, 82, 87, 90, 98, 153, 154, 155, 177, 200, 201, 203, 223, 235, 247, 281, 325, 326, 330
Pascal, 101, 102, 148
Pearson, Dr., His sermon at Bishop Wren's funeral, 160
Peck, 'Desiderata Curiosa,' 46, 75, 160
Pembroke Hall, Cambridge, 6, 134; Consecration of chapel of, 162; Bishop Wren buried at, 160; Matthew Wren buried at, 161; Sir C. Wren's son educated at, 265

RED

Pepys' Diary, 118, 142, 143, 144, 156, 158, 161, 175, 178, 182, 228
Perier, Madame, 'Vie de Pascal,' 102
Peter the Great at Sayes Court, 286, 287
Peterhouse, Cambridge, 15, 17, 45, 88, 153, 160
Petty, Dr., afterwards Sir William, 89, 124, 125
Phelp, Richard, bell-founder, 321, 323
Philosophical Society, the, 126
Philosophy Act, the, kept at Cambridge, 6; at Oxford, 93
Physicians, College of, built by Wren, 265
Pierce, Edward, sculptor under Wren, 207
Pigott, Mrs., only surviving descendant of Sir C. Wren, 231, 304, 317
Plague, the (in 1636), 25; (in 1665), 142, 143, 144, 154, 243
Plot, Dr., 142, 300
Pope, 'Moral Essays,' 208
— 'Dunciad,' 330
Popish Plot, the, 227
Portland, Earl of, 282, 303
Portland quarries, the, 221, 279
Prayer Book, the, 65, 69, 118
— of Edward VI., the first, 121
Prynne, William, 44, 45, 50, 70

'QUENCH COAL,' pamphlet by Prynne, 44
'Querela Cantabrigiensis,' 76

RAIKES, Captain, 'History of the Honourable Artillery Company,' 185
Randolph, Thomas, 90
Red Book of the Garter, the, 68

Renegado, form of penance and reconciliation for, 19, 20
Restoration, the, 79
Rooke, Laurence, Astronomy Professor at Gresham College, 125, 128
Rowe, Sir Thomas, 34, 35
Royal Exchange, the, rebuilt by C. Wren, 178
Royal Society, the, 95, 124, 129, 141, 145, 154, 159, 193, 194, 203, 208, 222, 223, 228, 230, 231, 239, 240, 246, 284, 299, 327, 333; 'History of,' by Sprat, 95
— 'History of,' by Weld, 124, 327
Ryswick, peace of (1697), 271
Ryves, Dr., Bruno, Dean of Chichester, and of Windsor, and Registrar of the Garter, 123

S. ALBAN'S, Lord, 146, 148, 241
— Alban's, Wood St., rebuilt by Wren, 248
— Andrew's, Holborn, rebuilt by Wren, 259, 297
— Andrew's-by-the-Wardrobe, rebuilt by Wren, 271
SS. Anne and Agnes' Church, rebuilt by Wren, 218
S. Anne's, Soho, 300
— Antholin's, Watling St., rebuilt by Wren, 233; destruction of, 234
— Augustine's Church, 234
— Bartholomew's, Bartholomew Lane, rebuilt by Wren, 218; destroyed to give site for the Sun Fire-office, 219
— Bartholomew's Day (1662), 122
— Bennet's, Gracechurch St., rebuilt by Wren, 250; destruction of, 250
— Bennet's, Paul's Wharf, rebuilt by Wren, 243
— Bennet Fink, rebuilt by Wren, 194; destruction of, 194

S. Bride's, Fleet St., rebuilt by Wren, 219, 220
— Christopher-le-Stocks, repaired by Wren, 185
— Clement Danes, rebuilt by Wren, 233
— — Eastcheap, rebuilt by Wren, 252
— Dionysius or S. Dionis, Back Church, rebuilt by Wren, 194; destruction of, 194
— Dunstan's in the East, repaired by Wren, 287, 288
— Edmund the King, rebuilt by Wren, 267
— Faith (crypt of S. Paul's), built by Wren, 262
— George's, Botolph Lane, rebuilt by Wren, 194
— George's Chapel, Windsor, 4, 5, 67, 68, 209
— Gregory's Church, 41, 99, 250
— James's, Garlickhithe, rebuilt by Wren, 243
— — Westminster, built by Wren, 241, 242, 310
— John's College, 31, 71
— Lawrence, Jewry, rebuilt by Wren, 206
— Magnus, London Bridge, 5; rebuilt by Wren, 204, 297
— Margaret's, Fish St., 5
— — Lothbury, rebuilt by Wren, 267
— — Pattens, rebuilt by Wren, 259
— Martin's-in-the-Fields, 191; rebuilt by Gibbs, 233
— Martin's, Ludgate Hill, rebuilt by Wren, 248
— Mary's, Abchurch, rebuilt by Wren, 252
— — Aldermanbury, rebuilt by Wren, 207
— — -at-Hill, 191
— — -le-Bow, rebuilt by Wren, 183

358 INDEX

SAI

S. Mary-le-Strand, built by Gibbs, 233, 305
—— Somerset, rebuilt by Wren, 273
—— Woolnoth, repaired by Wren, rebuilt by Hawksmore, 206
—— Magdalene, Fish St., rebuilt by Wren, 248
— Matthew's, Friday St., rebuilt by Wren, 250
— Michael's, Bassishaw, rebuilt by Wren, 219
—— Cornhill, rebuilt by Wren, 191
—— Crooked Lane, rebuilt by Wren, 262; destruction of (1830), 262
—— Queenhithe, repaired by Wren, 207
— Mary's, Royal College Hill, rebuilt by Strong, Wren's mastermason, 272
— Mildred's, Bread St., rebuilt by Wren, 240
—— Poultry, rebuilt by Wren, 205; destruction of, in 1872, 205
— Nicholas, Cole Abbey, rebuilt by Wren, 206
— Olave's, Jewry, rebuilt by Wren, 194
— Paul's Cathedral, old, repairs of, 41, 42; attacked by the Puritan mob (1640), 46–47; meeting of the Convocation of Canterbury at (1661), 119; Wren's proposed repairs of, 139, 140, 154; burning of, in the Great Fire (1666), 156, 158; removing the ruins of, 165; Sancroft's letters to Wren respecting, 166, 168; Wren's account of the effect of the fire upon, 169, 170, 171; sale of the ruins of, for the rebuilding of parochial churches, 186, 187; ruins of, blown up with gunpowder, 187, 188; New or present

SAN

building, different designs for, and Wren's model of, 196, 197; first stone of, laid by Wren, 200; Wren's care in laying the foundations of, 201; Bishop Compton's address to obtain contributions for, 220; quarries of Portland stone set apart for, 221; the crypt of, finished, 261, 262; part of the money for, taken by Parliament for the expenses of King William's wars, 273; placing of the organ in, 273, 274, 275; opening of the choir of, 279; Wren's order against swearing among the workmen in, 285; morning-prayer chapel of, opened, 288; burial of Jane Wren in, 300; thanksgiving for the victory of Blenheim at, 301; covering of the dome of, with lead, 303; last stone of, laid by Wren's son, 318, 319; the iron gates set up in, 324; Wren's design for east end of, 324, 325; iron fence round, 326; design of the commissioners to put up a balustrade, in, 328; late improvements in 334
S. Peter's, Cornhill, rebuilt by Wren, 233; charitable legacies belonging to, 233
— Sepulchre's Church, 182, 183
— Stephen's, Coleman St., rebuilt by Wren, 205
—— Walbrook, rebuilt by Wren, 192, 225, 226
— Swithin's, Cannon St., rebuilt by Wren, 219
— Vedast's, Foster Lane, steeple of, added by Wren, 273
Salisbury Cathedral, Wren's work at, 17
Sancroft, Dr., Dean of S. Paul's and Archbishop of Canterbury, appointed a S. Paul's commissioner, 154; sermon of, after

SAV

the Fire, 1 5 ; letters of, to Sir C. Wren, 166–168 ; contributions of, to the building of S. Paul's, 220 ; imprisonment of, in the Tower, 260, 261 ; refuses to take the oath of allegiance to William III., 264

Savoy conference, the, 120

Sayes Court occupied by Peter the Great, 286, 287

Scarborough, Sir Charles, 78, 224

Scudamore, Lord, 19

'Sessional Papers, R.I.B.A.,' 267, 268

Seven Bishops, the, trial of, 235, 260

Seward, 'Anecdotes of Distinguished Persons,' 222

Sheldon, Bishop of London and Archbishop of Canterbury, 140, 146

Sheldonian Theatre, the, built by Wren, 140, 331

Sherlock, Dean of S. Paul's, 281

Simpson, Dr. Sparrow, 'Documents illustrating the History of S. Paul's,' 27, 274, 280, 288, 323

Smith, Bernard, or Father, builder of organ at S. Paul's, 275, 288

South, Dr., 69, 141

Spain, expedition of the Prince of Wales to, 7, 9

'Spectator, the,' 179

Sprat, Dr., Dean of Westminster and Bishop of Rochester, his account of the meetings of the Royal Society, 95 ; 'History of Royal Society,' 95 ; letters of, to Christopher Wren, 105, 132, 133 ; his sermon before the Commons, 209 ; is succeeded by Atterbury, 289

Steele, Sir R., 'The Tatler,' 239

Strafford, Lord, 48, 49, 50

Strong, Edward, Wren's master-mason, 272, 284, 297, 303

— Thomas, brother of Edward, 200

WAL

TANGIERS, fortifications of, 132 ; Tenison, Thomas, Bishop of Lincoln and Archbishop of Canterbury, his secret ordination by Bishop Duppa, 123 ; founding of a library at S. Martin's by, 226 ; building of the Chapel of the Holy Trinity, Conduit St., by, 243

Temple Bar, built by Wren, 179

Tijou, M., worker in iron, maker of the gates in S. Paul's, 324, 326

Tilbury Fort, 216

Torricelli, his invention of the barometer, 100, 101

Tower of London, the, 44, 58, 59, 69, 71, 87, 114, 115, 187, 211, 212, 260, 261

Tradescant, John, collector of the objects of natural history in the Oxford Museum, 217

Trelawney, Bishop of Winchester, 235

Trinity College, Oxford, 144, 145, 146

Trinity College, Cambridge, 146

Turner, Bishop of Ely, 260

VANBRUGH, Sir John, 286, 305

Van Vianen, Christian, 37

Ven, Colonel, 68

Verrio, painter, his work at Whitehall and Windsor, 252

WADHAM COLLEGE, Oxford, 73, 77, 79, 93, 95, 105

Waller, Edmund, 9, 196

Waller, Sir William, sack of the city of Chichester by, 79, 123

Wallis, Dr., 77, 78, 112, 141, 222, 223

Walpole, 'Anecdotes of Painting,' 37, 268

WAL

Walworth, Sir William, his tomb, 262
Ward, 'Lives of the Gresham Professors,' 79, 89, 128, 226
Ward, Dr. Seth., Bishop of Exeter, of Salisbury, 90, 124, 125, 171, 206
'Warwickshire Worthies,' 3, 330
Weather-clock, the invention of, by Wren, 89
Weavers, the, at Norwich, 23
Weld, 'History of the Royal Society,' 124, 193, 327
Westminster Abbey, 57, 230, 289, 293, 320, 331
— School, 41, 57, 69, 90, 231
White, Bishop of Peterborough, 260, 281
Whitehall, 144, 149, 252, 299, 317
Whittington, Sir Richard, 272
Wilkins, Dr. John, Bishop of Chester, 74, 77, 93, 94, 95, 124, 206
William, Prince of Orange, 49
William III., 208, 263, 268, 299
Williams, Bishop of Lincoln, and Archbishop of York, 57, 59
Wilson, Bishop of Sodor and Man, 220
Winchester, Wren's scheme for palace at, 234, 235
— House, conference at, 10, 11
Windsor, 4, 16, 37, 40, 68, 263, 264, 265, 300
Wiseman, attack of the mob on Westminster Abbey, led by, 57
Wood, 'Athenæ Oxonienses,' 153
— 'Fasti,' 223
Wood, Philip, carvings of, 253-255
Woodward, Dr., 202, 203
Worcester, battle of (1651), 91, 93
'Workman, the British,' 253
Wren, Capt., 161, 162
— Charles, son of Bishop Wren, 161
Wren, Christopher, Dr., birth of, 5; education of, 31; given the

WRE

living of Fonthill Bishops, 31; of East Knoyle, 31; made Dean of Windsor and Registrar of the Garter, 34; made rector of Great Haseley, 38; building at Windsor for Charles I. designed by, 40; his care for the treasures of the Order of the Garter, 67; letter of, to the Knights of the Garter, 80, 81; death of, 96
Wren, Sir Christopher, birth of, 32; sent to school at Westminster, 41; his Latin letter to his father, 42, 43; goes to Oxford, 73, 74; his life there, 77, 78; his translation of the 'Clavis Aurea,' 78, 79; his early Inventions, 88, 89, 90; friendship of, with Evelyn, 93, 94; made Gresham professor of astronomy, 97; his first lecture, 97, 98; discovery of the barometer by, 101; origin of the Royal Society in meetings in his rooms, 124; is made Savilian professor, 125; and doctor of civil laws at Oxford and Cambridge, 126; his letter to Lord Brouncker on Experiments, 126, 127; writes the preamble to the Charter of the Royal Society, 129; declines the commission to direct the fortifications of Tangiers, 132; his designs for the chapel at Pembroke Hall, Cambridge, 134; his letter to Dr. Bathurst, 144; his journey abroad, 146; his journal, 149-152; his return to London and inspection of S. Paul's, 154; his plan for rebuilding the city after the fire, 157, 158, 172, 173; Sancroft's letters to him as to the patching of S. Paul's, 166-171; his work at Salisbury Cathedral, 171; letter of, to Faith Coghill, 177; his marriage, 178; rebuilding of the Exchange by, 178; building

WRE

of Temple Bar by, 178; petition of, to Charles II., 180–182; rebuilding of Bow Church by, 183–184; of S. Christopher-le-Stocks, 184; is made a member of the Honourable Artillery Company, 185; resigns the Savilian astronomy professorship, 186; appointed architect of S. Paul's, 187; clears away the ruins of old S. Paul's, 187; his experiment in blowing up the tower with gunpowder, 188; his use of a battering ram, 188; birth of his eldest son, 191; repair of S. Mary-at-Hill by, 191; building of S. Stephen's, Walbrook, by, 192, 225; knighted by Charles II., 194; rebuilding of Drury Lane by, 196; salary as architect of S. Paul's, 196; his model for S. Paul's, 196–198; lays the first stone of S. Paul's, 200; death of his wife, 203; his second marriage, 203; rebuilding of eight city churches by, 204–207; building of the Monument by, 207; his designs for a monument to Charles I., 209; building of the chapel at Emmanuel College by, 216; of the Observatory at Greenwich, 216; birth of his daughter Jane, 217; rebuilding of five more city churches by, 218, 219; the marking out of the dome of S. Paul's by, 222; death of his second wife, 226; elected President of the Royal Society, 228; Christ Church gateway built by, 232; All Hallows, Bread Street, rebuilt by, 232; S. Peter's, Cornhill, and S. Clement Danes rebuilt by, 233; his design for a palace at Winchester, 234, 235; Chelsea Hospital built by, 240; S. James's, Westminster, built by,

WRE

241; Chichester Cathedral repaired by, 245; Fawley Court built by, 245; made Controller of the Works, 246; elected member for Plympton, 247; eight more city churches built by, 248–252; death of his sister Susan, 261; buildings by, erected at Windsor, 264, 265; College of Physicians built by, 265; halls of city companies rebuilt by, 266; Hampton Court palace rebuilt by, 257, 268; scheme of, for Greenwich Palace, 269; his difficulties in placing the organ of S. Paul's, 273; invention by, of a pulpit on wheels, 280; letter of, to his son in Paris, 282, 283; chosen Grand Master of the Freemasons, 285; Marlborough House built by, 286; S. Dunstan's-in-the-East repaired by, 287, 288; statement of, as to repairs of Westminster Abbey, 289–293; elected member for Weymouth, 298; death of his daughter Jane, 300; second letter of, to his son, 302, 303; letter of, on church building, 305–313; private houses built by, 317; last stone of S. Paul's laid by his son, 318; attack on, by S. Paul's Commissioners, 320; his petition to Queen Anne, 320, 322; his unfulfilled design for east end of S. Paul's, 324, 325; dismissal of, by George I., from the post of surveyor-general, 329; purchase of Wroxhall Abbey by, 330; his studies and papers in cipher respecting the longitude at sea, 331, 332; his death 333; his burial and monument, 334

Wren, Christopher, son of Sir C. Wren, 200, 265, 269, 281, 282, 283, 302, 303, 304, 318, 330

B B

Wren, Francis, 5
— Geoffrey, 4, 5
— Jane, daughter of Sir C. Wren, 217, 269, 288, 300, 301
— Matthew, birth and education of, 6 ; sent with the Prince to Spain, 7, 8 ; return and statement of, to three Bishops respecting the Prince of Wales, 10–13 ; elected Master of Peterhouse, 15 ; made Dean of Windsor, 16 ; his marriage, 16 ; made Bishop of Hereford, 17 ; Clerk of the Closet, 17 ; service composed by, for the Reconciliation of Renegados, 19, 20 ; made Bishop of Norwich, 23 ; translated to Ely, 44 ; his care for his diocese, 45, 46 ; Sir Harbottle Grimston's and Hampden's attack upon him, 48, 49 ; officiates at the marriage of Princess Mary, 49 ; resigns the Deanery of the Chapels Royal, 51 ; articles of accusation drawn up against him in the Commons, 55 ; his imprisonment, 58 ; his defence, 61–66 ; death of his wife, 85 ; his life in the Tower, 86 ; refuses freedom on Cromwell's terms, 100 ; his conferences with Dr. Barwick, 110–113 ; released from prison, 115, 116 ; revision of the Prayer Book by, 120 ; consecration and dedication of Pembroke Chapel by, 152 ; second visitation, 153 ; death and funeral of, 159, 160, 161
Wren, Matthew, son of Bishop Wren, 60, 78, 85, 88, 92, 103, 112, 124, 160, 161, 194
— Stephen, grandson of Sir C. Wren, 224
— Susan, daughter of Dean Wren, 34, 41. *See* Holder.
— Thomas, son of Bishop Wren, 161, 162, 224
— William, 4, 5
— Sir William, son of Bishop Wren, 161, 162
Wrenne, ancient form of spelling Wren, 4
Wrenne, John, 4
Wroxhall Abbey, purchase of, by Sir C. Wren, 330

YORK, Duke of, 160, 185, 228, 234. *See* James II.

A LIST OF

C. KEGAN PAUL & CO.'S PUBLICATIONS.

7.81.

1 *Paternoster Square,*
London.

A LIST OF

C. KEGAN PAUL & CO.'S PUBLICATIONS.

ADAMS (F. O.) F.R.G.S.—THE HISTORY OF JAPAN. From the Earliest Period to the Present Time. New Edition, revised. 2 volumes. With Maps and Plans. Demy 8vo. price 21s. each.

ADAMSON (H. T.) B.D.—THE TRUTH AS IT IS IN JESUS. Crown 8vo. cloth, price 8s. 6d.

THE THREE SEVENS. Crown 8vo. cloth, price 5s. 6d.

A. K. H. B.—FROM A QUIET PLACE. A New Volume of Sermons. Crown 8vo. cloth, price 5s.

ALBERT (Mary)—HOLLAND AND HER HEROES TO THE YEAR 1585. An Adaptation from 'Motley's Rise of the Dutch Republic.' Small crown 8vo. price 4s. 6d.

ALLEN (Rev. R.) M.A.—ABRAHAM; HIS LIFE, TIMES, AND TRAVELS, 3,800 years ago. With Map. Second Edition. Post 8vo. price 6s.

ALLEN (Grant) B.A.—PHYSIOLOGICAL ÆSTHETICS. Large post 8vo. 9s.

ALLIES (T. W.) M.A.—PER CRUCEM AD LUCEM. The Result of a Life. 2 vols. Demy 8vo. cloth, price 25s.

A LIFE'S DECISION. Crown 8vo. cloth, price 7s. 6d.

ANDERSON (R. C.) C.E.—TABLES FOR FACILITATING THE CALCULATION OF EVERY DETAIL IN CONNECTION WITH EARTHEN AND MASONRY DAMS. Royal 8vo. price £2. 2s.

ARCHER (Thomas)—ABOUT MY FATHER'S BUSINESS. Work amidst the Sick, the Sad, and the Sorrowing. Cheaper Edition. Crown 8vo. price 2s. 6d.

ARMSTRONG (Richard A.) B.A.—LATTER-DAY TEACHERS. Six Lectures. Small crown 8vo. cloth, price 2s. 6d.

ARNOLD (Arthur)—SOCIAL POLITICS. Demy 8vo. cloth, price 14s.

FREE LAND. Crown 8vo. cloth, price 6s.

BADGER (George Percy) D.C.L.—AN ENGLISH-ARABIC LEXICON. In which the equivalent for English Words and Idiomatic Sentences are rendered into literary and colloquial Arabic. Royal 4to. cloth, price £9. 9s.

BAGEHOT (Walter)—THE ENGLISH CONSTITUTION. A New Edition, Revised and Corrected, with an Introductory Dissertation on Recent Changes and Events. Crown 8vo. price 7s. 6d.

LOMBARD STREET. A Description of the Money Market. Seventh Edition. Crown 8vo. price 7s. 6d.

SOME ARTICLES ON THE DEPRECIATION OF SILVER, AND TOPICS CONNECTED WITH IT. Demy 8vo. price 5s.

BAGOT (Alan)—ACCIDENTS IN MINES: Their Causes and Prevention. Crown 8vo. price 6s.

BAKER (*Sir Sherston, Bart.*)—HALLECK'S INTERNATIONAL LAW; or, Rules Regulating the Intercourse of States in Peace and War. A New Edition, revised, with Notes and Cases. 2 vols. Demy 8vo. price 38s.

THE LAWS RELATING TO QUARANTINE. Crown 8vo. cloth, price 12s. 6d.

BALDWIN (*Capt. J. H.*) *F.Z.S. Bengal Staff Corps.*—THE LARGE AND SMALL GAME OF BENGAL AND THE NORTH-WESTERN PROVINCES OF INDIA. 4to. With numerous Illustrations. Second Edition. Price 21s.

BARNES (*William*)—AN OUTLINE OF ENGLISH SPEECHCRAFT. Crown 8vo. price 4s.

OUTLINES OF REDECRAFT (LOGIC). With English Wording. Crown 8vo. cloth, price 3s.

BARTLEY (*G. C. T.*)—DOMESTIC ECONOMY: Thrift in Every-Day Life. Taught in Dialogues suitable for children of all ages. Small cr. 8vo. price 2s.

BAUR (*Ferdinand*) *Dr. Ph., Professor in Maulbronn.*—A PHILOLOGICAL INTRODUCTION TO GREEK AND LATIN FOR STUDENTS. Translated and adapted from the German. By C. KEGAN PAUL, M.A. Oxon., and the Rev. E. D. STONE, M.A., late Fellow of King's College, Cambridge, and Assistant Master at Eton. Crown 8vo. price 6s.

BAYNES (*Rev. Canon R. H.*)—AT THE COMMUNION TIME. A Manual for Holy Communion. With a preface by the Right Rev. the Lord Bishop of Derry and Raphoe. Cloth, price 1s. 6d.

BELLINGHAM (*Henry*) *M.P., Barrister-at-Law*—SOCIAL ASPECTS OF CATHOLICISM AND PROTESTANTISM IN THEIR CIVIL BEARING UPON NATIONS. Translated and adapted from the French of M. le Baron de Haulleville. With a preface by His Eminence Cardinal Manning. Second and Cheaper Edition. Crown 8vo. price 3s. 6d.

BENT (*J. Theodore*)—GENOA: How the Republic Rose and Fell. With 18 Illustrations. Demy 8vo. cloth, price 18s.

BONWICK (*J.*) *F.R.G.S.*—PYRAMID FACTS AND FANCIES. Crown 8vo. price 5s.

EGYPTIAN BELIEF AND MODERN THOUGHT. Large post 8vo. cloth, price 10s. 6d.

BOWEN (*H. C.*) *M.A., Head Master of the Grocers' Company's Middle Class School at Hackney.*

STUDIES IN ENGLISH, for the use of Modern Schools. Small crown 8vo. price 1s. 6d.

ENGLISH GRAMMAR FOR BEGINNERS. Fcp. 8vo. cloth, price 1s.

BOWRING (*Sir John*)—AUTOBIOGRAPHICAL RECOLLECTIONS OF SIR JOHN BOWRING. With Memoir by LEWIN B. BOWRING. Demy 8vo. price 14s.

BRIDGETT (*Rev. T. E.*)—HISTORY OF THE HOLY EUCHARIST IN GREAT BRITAIN. 2 vols. Demy 8vo. cloth, price 18s.

BRODRICK (*the Hon. G. C.*)—POLITICAL STUDIES. Demy 8vo. cloth, price 14s.

BROOKE (*Rev. S. A.*) *M.A., Chaplain in Ordinary to Her Majesty the Queen, and Minister of Bedford Chapel, Bloomsbury.*

LIFE AND LETTERS OF THE LATE REV. F. W. ROBERTSON, M.A., Edited by.
 I. Uniform with the Sermons. 2 vols. With Steel Portrait. Price 7s. 6d.
 II. Library Edition. 8vo. With Portrait. Price 12s.
 III. A Popular Edition. In 1 vol. 8vo. price 6s.

BROOKE (Rev. S. A.) M.A.—cont.

    THE SPIRIT OF THE CHRISTIAN LIFE. A New Volume of Sermons. Crown 8vo. cloth, price 7s. 6d.

    THE FIGHT OF FAITH. Sermons preached on various occasions. Fifth Edition. Crown 8vo. price 7s. 6d.

    THEOLOGY IN THE ENGLISH POETS.—Cowper, Coleridge, Wordsworth, and Burns. Fourth and Cheaper Edition. Post 8vo. price 5s.

    CHRIST IN MODERN LIFE. Fifteenth and Cheaper Edition. Crown 8vo. price 5s.

    SERMONS. First Series. Eleventh Edition. Crown 8vo. price 6s.

    SERMONS. Second Series. Fourth Edition. Crown 8vo. price 7s.

BROOKE (W. G.) M.A.—THE PUBLIC WORSHIP REGULATION ACT. With a Classified Statement of its Provisions, Notes, and Index. Third Edition, revised and corrected. Crown 8vo. price 3s. 6d.

    SIX PRIVY COUNCIL JUDGMENTS—1850–72. Annotated by. Third Edition. Crown 8vo. price 9s.

BROUN (J. A.)—MAGNETIC OBSERVATIONS AT TREVANDRUM AND AUGUSTIA MALLEY. Vol. I. 4to. price 63s.

    The Report from above, separately, sewed, price 21s.

BROWN (Rev. J. Baldwin) B.A.—THE HIGHER LIFE. Its Reality, Experience, and Destiny. Fifth Edition. Crown 8vo. price 5s.

    DOCTRINE OF ANNIHILATION IN THE LIGHT OF THE GOSPEL OF LOVE. Five Discourses. Third Edition. Crown 8vo. price 2s. 6d.

    THE CHRISTIAN POLICY OF LIFE. A Book for Young Men of Business. New and Cheaper Edition. Crown 8vo. cloth, price 3s. 6d.

BROWN (J. Croumbie) LL.D.—REBOISEMENT IN FRANCE; or, Records of the Replanting of the Alps, the Cevennes, and the Pyrenees with Trees, Herbage, and Bush. Demy 8vo. price 12s. 6d.

    THE HYDROLOGY OF SOUTHERN AFRICA. Demy 8vo. price 10s. 6d.

BROWNE (W. R.)—THE INSPIRATION OF THE NEW TESTAMENT. With a Preface by the Rev. J. P. NORRIS, D.D. Fcp. 8vo. cloth, price 2s. 6d.

BURCKHARDT (Jacob)—THE CIVILIZATION OF THE PERIOD OF THE RENAISSANCE IN ITALY. Authorised translation, by S. G. C. Middlemore. 2 vols. Demy 8vo. price 24s.

BURTON (Mrs. Richard)—THE INNER LIFE OF SYRIA, PALESTINE, AND THE HOLY LAND. With Maps, Photographs, and Coloured Plates. 2 vols. Second Edition. Demy 8vo. price 24s.

    ⁎⁎ Also a Cheaper Edition in one volume. Large post 8vo. cloth, price 10s. 6d.

BURTON (Capt. Richard F.)—THE GOLD MINES OF MIDIAN AND THE RUINED MIDIANITE CITIES. A Fortnight's Tour in North Western Arabia. With numerous Illustrations. Second Edition. Demy 8vo. price 18s.

    THE LAND OF MIDIAN REVISITED. With numerous Illustrations on Wood and by Chromolithography. 2 vols. Demy 8vo. cloth, price 32s.

BUSBECQ (Ogier Ghiselin de)—HIS LIFE AND LETTERS. By CHARLES THORNTON FORSTER, M.A., and F. H. BLACKBURNE DANIELL, M.A. 2 vols. With Frontispieces. Demy 8vo. cloth, price 24s.

CANDLER (H.)—The Groundwork of Belief. Crown 8vo. cloth, price 7s.

CARPENTER (Dr. Philip P.)—His Life and Work. Edited by his brother, Russell Lant Carpenter. With Portrait and Vignettes. Second Edition. Crown 8vo. cloth, price 7s. 6d.

CARPENTER (W. B.) LL.D., M.D., F.R.S., &c.—The Principles of Mental Physiology. With their Applications to the Training and Discipline of the Mind, and the Study of its Morbid Conditions. Illustrated. Fifth Edition. 8vo. price 12s.

CERVANTES—The Ingenious Knight Don Quixote de la Mancha. A New Translation from the Originals of 1605 and 1608. By A. J. Duffield. With Notes. 3 vols. Demy 8vo. price 42s.

CHEYNE (Rev. T. K.)—The Prophecies of Isaiah. Translated with Critical Notes and Dissertations. 2 vols. Demy 8vo. cloth, price 25s.

CLAIRAUT—Elements of Geometry. Translated by Dr. Kaines. With 145 Figures. Crown 8vo. cloth, price 4s. 6d.

CLAYDEN (P. W.)—England under Lord Beaconsfield. The Political History of the Last Six Years, from the end of 1873 to the beginning of 1880. Second Edition, with Index and continuation to March 1880. Demy 8vo. cloth, price 16s.

CLODD (Edward) F.R.A.S.—The Childhood of the World: a Simple Account of Man in Early Times. Sixth Edition. Crown 8vo. price 3s.
A Special Edition for Schools. Price 1s.

The Childhood of Religions. Including a Simple Account of the Birth and Growth of Myths and Legends. Third Thousand. Crown 8vo. price 5s.
A Special Edition for Schools. Price 1s. 6d.

Jesus of Nazareth. With a brief sketch of Jewish History to the Time of His Birth. Small crown 8vo. cloth, price 6s.

COGHLAN (J. Cole) D.D.—The Modern Pharisee and other Sermons. Edited by the Very Rev. H. H. Dickinson, D.D., Dean of Chapel Royal, Dublin. New and Cheaper Edition. Crown 8vo. cloth, 7s. 6d.

COLERIDGE (Sara)—Phantasmion. A Fairy Tale. With an Introductory Preface by the Right Hon. Lord Coleridge, of Ottery St. Mary. A New Edition. Illustrated. Crown 8vo. price 7s. 6d.

Memoir and Letters of Sara Coleridge. Edited by her Daughter. With Index. Cheap Edition. With one Portrait. Price 7s. 6d.

COLLINS (Mortimer)—The Secret of Long Life. Small crown 8vo. cloth, price 3s. 6d.

CONNELL (A. K.)—Discontent and Danger in India. Small crown 8vo. cloth, price 3s. 6d.

COOKE (Prof. J. P.) of the Harvard University.—Scientific Culture. Crown 8vo. price 1s.

COOPER (H. J.)—The Art of Furnishing on Rational and Æsthetic Principles. New and Cheaper Edition. Fcp. 8vo. cloth, price 1s. 6d.

CORFIELD (Professor) M.D.—Health. Crown 8vo. cloth, price 6s.

CORY (William)—A Guide to Modern English History. Part I.—MDCCCXV.–MDCCCXXX. Demy 8vo. cloth, price 9s.

COURTNEY. (W. L.)—THE METAPHYSICS OF JOHN STUART MILL.
Crown 8vo. cloth, price 5s. 6d.

COX (Rev. Sir George W.) M.A., Bart.—A HISTORY OF GREECE FROM THE EARLIEST PERIOD TO THE END OF THE PERSIAN WAR. New Edition. 2 vols. Demy 8vo. price 36s.

THE MYTHOLOGY OF THE ARYAN NATIONS. New Edition. 2 vols. Demy 8vo. price 28s.

A GENERAL HISTORY OF GREECE FROM THE EARLIEST PERIOD TO THE DEATH OF ALEXANDER THE GREAT, with a sketch of the subsequent History to the present time. New Edition. Crown 8vo. price 7s. 6d.

TALES OF ANCIENT GREECE. New Edition. Small crown 8vo. price 6s.

SCHOOL HISTORY OF GREECE. New Edition. With Maps. Fcp. 8vo. price 3s. 6d.

THE GREAT PERSIAN WAR FROM THE HISTORY OF HERODOTUS. New Edition. Fcp. 8vo. price 3s. 6d.

A MANUAL OF MYTHOLOGY IN THE FORM OF QUESTION AND ANSWER. New Edition. Fcp. 8vo. price 3s.

AN INTRODUCTION TO THE SCIENCE OF COMPARATIVE MYTHOLOGY AND FOLK-LORE. Crown 8vo. cloth, price 9s.

COX (Rev. Sir G. W.) M.A., Bart., and JONES (Eustace Hinton)—POPULAR ROMANCES OF THE MIDDLE AGES. Second Edition, in 1 vol. Crown 8vo. cloth, price 6s.

COX (Rev. Samuel)—SALVATOR MUNDI; or, Is Christ the Saviour of all Men? Sixth Edition. Crown 8vo. price 5s.

THE GENESIS OF EVIL, AND OTHER SERMONS, mainly expository. Second Edition. Crown 8vo. cloth, price 6s.

A COMMENTARY ON THE BOOK OF JOB. With a Translation. Demy 8vo. cloth, price 15s.

CRAUFURD (A. H.)—SEEKING FOR LIGHT: Sermons. Crown 8vo. cloth, price 5s.

CRAVEN (Mrs.)—A YEAR'S MEDITATIONS. Crown 8vo. cloth, price 6s.

CRAWFURD (Oswald)—PORTUGAL, OLD AND NEW. With Illustrations and Maps. Demy 8vo. cloth, price 16s.

CROZIER (John Beattie) M.B.—THE RELIGION OF THE FUTURE. Crown 8vo. cloth, price 6s.

DALTON (John Neale) M.A., R.N.—SERMONS TO NAVAL CADETS. Preached on board H.M.S. 'Britannia.' Second Edition. Small crown 8vo. cloth, price 3s. 6d.

DAVIDSON (Rev. Samuel) D.D., LL.D. — THE NEW TESTAMENT, TRANSLATED FROM THE LATEST GREEK TEXT OF TISCHENDORF. A New and thoroughly revised Edition. Post 8vo. price 10s. 6d.

CANON OF THE BIBLE: Its Formation, History, and Fluctuations. Third and revised Edition. Small crown 8vo. price 5s.

DAVIES (Rev. J. L.) M.A.—THEOLOGY AND MORALITY. Essays on Questions of Belief and Practice. Crown 8vo. price 7s. 6d.

DAWSON (Geo.) M.A.—Prayers, with a Discourse on Prayer. Edited by his Wife. Fifth Edition. Crown 8vo. price 6s.
— Sermons on Disputed Points and Special Occasions. Edited by his Wife. Third Edition. Crown 8vo. price 6s.
— Sermons on Daily Life and Duty. Edited by his Wife. Third Edition. Crown 8vo. price 6s.

DE REDCLIFFE (Viscount Stratford) P.C., K.G., G.C.B.—Why am I a Christian? Fifth Edition. Crown 8vo. price 3s.

DESPREZ (Philip S.) B.D.—Daniel and John; or, the Apocalypse of the Old and that of the New Testament. Demy 8vo. cloth, price 12s.

DE TOCQUEVILLE (A.)—Correspondence and Conversations of, with Nassau William Senior, from 1834 to 1859. Edited by M. C. M. Simpson. 2 vols. Post 8vo. price 21s.

DOWDEN (Edward) LL.D.—Shakspere: a Critical Study of his Mind and Art. Fifth Edition. Post 8vo. price 12s.
— Studies in Literature, 1789-1877. Large post 8vo. price 12s.

DREWRY (G. O.) M.D.—The Common-Sense Management of the Stomach. Fifth Edition. Fcp. 8vo. price 2s. 6d.

DREWRY (G. O.) M.D., and BARTLETT (H. C.) Ph.D., F.C.S.—Cup and Platter: or, Notes on Food and its Effects. New and Cheaper Edition. Small 8vo. price 1s. 6d.

DUFFIELD (A. J.)—Don Quixote: his Critics and Commentators. With a brief account of the minor works of Miguel de Cervantes Saavedra, and a statement of the aim and end of the greatest of them all. A handy book for general readers. Crown 8vo. cloth, price 3s. 6d.

DU MONCEL (Count)—The Telephone, the Microphone, and the Phonograph. With 74 Illustrations. Small crown 8vo. cloth, price 5s.

EDEN (Frederick)—The Nile without a Dragoman. Second Edition. Crown 8vo. price 7s. 6d.

EDGEWORTH (F. Y.)—Mathematical Psychics. An Essay on the Application of Mathematics to Social Science. Demy 8vo. cloth, 7s. 6d.

EDIS (Robert W.) F.S.A. &c.—Decoration and Furniture of Town Houses: a Series of Cantor Lectures, delivered before the Society of Arts, 1880. Amplified and Enlarged. With 29 Full-page Illustrations and numerous Sketches. Second Edition. Square 8vo. cloth, price 12s. 6d.

Educational Code of the Prussian Nation, in its Present Form. In accordance with the Decisions of the Common Provincial Law, and with those of Recent Legislation. Crown 8vo. cloth, price 2s. 6d.

ELSDALE (Henry)—Studies in Tennyson's Idylls. Crown 8vo. price 5s.

ELYOT (Sir Thomas)—The Boke named the Gouernour. Edited from the First Edition of 1531 by Henry Herbert Stephen Croft, M.A., Barrister-at-Law. With Portraits of Sir Thomas and Lady Elyot, copied by permission of her Majesty from Holbein's Original Drawings at Windsor Castle. 2 vols. Fcp. 4to. cloth, price 50s.

EVANS (Mark)—THE STORY OF OUR FATHER'S LOVE, told to Children. Fifth and Cheaper Edition. With Four Illustrations. Fcp. 8vo. price 1s. 6d.

    A BOOK OF COMMON PRAYER AND WORSHIP FOR HOUSEHOLD USE, compiled exclusively from the Holy Scriptures. Fcp. 8vo. price 1s.

    THE GOSPEL OF HOME LIFE. Crown 8vo. cloth, price 4s. 6d.

    THE KING'S STORY-BOOK. In Three Parts. Fcp. 8vo. cloth, price 1s. 6d. each.

    ** Parts I. and II. with Eight Illustrations and Two Picture Maps, now ready.

EX-CIVILIAN—LIFE IN THE MOFUSSIL: or Civilian Life in Lower Bengal. 2 vols. Large post 8vo. price 14s.

FELKIN (H. M.)—TECHNICAL EDUCATION IN A SAXON TOWN. Published for the City and Guilds of London Institute for the Advancement of Technical Education. Demy 8vo. cloth, price 2s.

FIELD (Horace) B.A. Lond.—THE ULTIMATE TRIUMPH OF CHRISTIANITY. Small crown 8vo. cloth, price 3s. 6d.

FINN (The late James) M.R.A.S.—STIRRING TIMES; or, Records from Jerusalem Consular Chronicles of 1853 to 1856. Edited and Compiled by his Widow; with a Preface by the Viscountess STRANGFORD. 2 vols. Demy 8vo. price 30s.

FLOREDICE (W. H.)—A MONTH AMONG THE MERE IRISH. Small crown 8vo. cloth, price 5s.

FOLKESTONE RITUAL CASE: the Arguments, Proceedings, Judgment, and Report. Demy 8vo. price 25s.

FORMBY (Rev. Henry)—ANCIENT ROME AND ITS CONNECTION WITH THE CHRISTIAN RELIGION: An Outline of the History of the City from its First Foundation down to the Erection of the Chair of St. Peter, A.D. 42-47. With numerous Illustrations of Ancient Monuments, Sculpture, and Coinage, and of the Antiquities of the Christian Catacombs. Royal 4to. cloth extra, £2. 10s; roxburgh half-morocco, £2. 12s. 6d.

FOWLE (Rev. T. W.) M.A.—THE RECONCILIATION OF RELIGION AND SCIENCE. Being Essays on Immortality, Inspiration, Miracles, and the Being of Christ. Demy 8vo. price 10s. 6d.

    THE DIVINE LEGATION OF CHRIST. Crown 8vo. cloth, price 7s.

FRASER (Donald)—EXCHANGE TABLES OF STERLING AND INDIAN RUPEE CURRENCY, upon a new and extended system, embracing Values from One Farthing to One Hundred Thousand Pounds, and at rates progressing, in Sixteenths of a Penny, from 1s. 9d. to 2s. 3d. per Rupee. Royal 8vo. price 10s. 6d.

FRISWELL (J. Hain)—THE BETTER SELF. Essays for Home Life. Crown 8vo. price 6s.

GARDINER (Samuel R.) and J. BASS MULLINGER, M.A.—INTRODUCTION TO THE STUDY OF ENGLISH HISTORY. Large crown 8vo. cloth, price 9s.

GARDNER (J.) M.D.—LONGEVITY: THE MEANS OF PROLONGING LIFE AFTER MIDDLE AGE. Fourth Edition, revised and enlarged. Small crown 8vo. price 4s.

***GEBLER** (Karl Von)*—Galileo Galilei and the Roman Curia, from Authentic Sources. Translated with the sanction of the Author, by Mrs. George Sturge. Demy 8vo. cloth, price 12s.

***GEDDES** (James)*—History of the Administration of John de Witt, Grand Pensionary of Holland. Vol. I. 1623—1654. With Portrait. Demy 8vo. cloth, price 15s.

***GEORGE** (Henry)*—Progress and Poverty: an Inquiry into the Causes of Industrial Depressions, and of Increase of Want with Increase of Wealth. The Remedy. Post 8vo. cloth, price 7s. 6d.

***GILBERT** (Mrs.)*—Autobiography and other Memorials. Edited by Josiah Gilbert. Third and Cheaper Edition. With Steel Portrait and several Wood Engravings. Crown 8vo. price 7s. 6d.

***GLOVER** (F.) M.A.*—Exempla Latina. A First Construing Book with Short Notes, Lexicon, and an Introduction to the Analysis of Sentences. Fcp. 8vo. cloth, price 2s.

***GODWIN** (William)*—William Godwin: His Friends and Contemporaries. With Portraits and Facsimiles of the Handwriting of Godwin and his Wife. By C. Kegan Paul. 2 vols. Large post 8vo. price 28s.

The Genius of Christianity Unveiled. Being Essays never before published. Edited, with a Preface, by C. Kegan Paul. Crown 8vo. price 7s. 6d.

***GOLDSMID** (Sir Francis Henry) Bart., Q.C., M.P.*—Memoir of. With Portrait. Crown 8vo. cloth, price 5s.

***GOODENOUGH** (Commodore J. G.) R.N., C.B., C.M.G.*—Memoir of, with Extracts from his Letters and Journals. Edited by his Widow. With Steel Engraved Portrait. Square 8vo. cloth, price 5s.

*** Also a Library Edition with Maps, Woodcuts, and Steel Engraved Portrait. Square post 8vo. price 14s.

***GOSSE** (Edmund W.)*—Studies in the Literature of Northern Europe. With a Frontispiece designed and etched by Alma Tadema. Large post 8vo. cloth, price 12s.

***GOULD** (Rev. S. Baring) M.A.*—The Vicar of Morwenstow: a Memoir of the Rev. R. S. Hawker. With Portrait. Third Edition, revised. Square post 8vo. price 10s. 6d.

Germany, Present and Past. 2 vols. Large crown 8vo. cloth, price 21s.

***GRAHAM** (William) M.A.*—The Creed of Science, Religious, Moral, and Social. Demy 8vo. cloth, price 12s.

***GRIFFITH** (Thomas) A.M.*—The Gospel of the Divine Life: a Study of the Fourth Evangelist. Demy 8vo. cloth, price 14s.

***GRIMLEY** (Rev. H. N.) M.A.*—Tremadoc Sermons, chiefly on the Spiritual Body, the Unseen World, and the Divine Humanity. Second Edition. Crown 8vo. price 6s.

***GRÜNER** (M. L.)*—Studies of Blast Furnace Phenomena. Translated by L. D. B. Gordon, F.R.S.E., F.G.S. Demy 8vo. price 7s. 6d.

***GURNEY** (Rev. Archer)*—Words of Faith and Cheer. A Mission of Instruction and Suggestion. Crown 8vo. price 6s.

HAECKEL (Prof. Ernst)—THE HISTORY OF CREATION. Translation revised by Professor E. RAY LANKESTER, M.A., F.R.S. With Coloured Plates and Genealogical Trees of the various groups of both plants and animals. 2 vols. Second Edition. Post 8vo. cloth, price 32s.

THE HISTORY OF THE EVOLUTION OF MAN. With numerous Illustrations. 2 vols. Post 8vo. price 32s.

FREEDOM IN SCIENCE AND TEACHING. With a Prefatory Note by T. H. HUXLEY, F.R.S. Crown 8vo. cloth, price 5s.

HALF-CROWN SERIES :—

SISTER DORA : a Biography. By MARGARET LONSDALE.

TRUE WORDS FOR BRAVE MEN : a Book for Soldiers and Sailors. By the late CHARLES KINGSLEY.

AN INLAND VOYAGE. By R. L. STEVENSON.

TRAVELS WITH A DONKEY. By R. L. STEVENSON.

A NOOK IN THE APENNINES. By LEADER SCOTT.

NOTES OF TRAVEL : being Extracts from the Journals of Count VON MOLTKE.

LETTERS FROM RUSSIA. By Count VON MOLTKE.

ENGLISH SONNETS. Collected and Arranged by J. DENNIS.

LYRICS OF LOVE. FROM SHAKESPEARE TO TENNYSON. Selected and Arranged by W. D. ADAMS.

LONDON LYRICS. By F. LOCKER.

HOME SONGS FOR QUIET HOURS. By the Rev. Canon R. H. BAYNES.

HALLECK'S INTERNATIONAL LAW ; or, Rules Regulating the Intercourse of States in Peace and War. A New Edition, revised, with Notes and Cases, by Sir SHERSTON BAKER, Bart. 2 vols. Demy 8vo. price 38s.

HARTINGTON (The Right Hon. the Marquis of) M.P.—ELECTION SPEECHES IN 1879 AND 1880. With Address to the Electors of North East Lancashire. Crown 8vo. cloth, price 3s. 6d.

HAWEIS (Rev. H. R.) M.A.—CURRENT COIN. Materialism—The Devil — Crime — Drunkenness — Pauperism — Emotion — Recreation — The Sabbath. Third Edition. Crown 8vo. price 6s.

SPEECH IN SEASON. Fourth Edition. Crown 8vo. price 9s.

THOUGHTS FOR THE TIMES. Eleventh Edition. Crown 8vo. price 7s. 6d.

UNSECTARIAN FAMILY PRAYERS, New and Cheaper Edition. Fcp. 8vo. price 1s. 6d.

ARROWS IN THE AIR. Second Edition. Crown 8vo. cloth, price 6s.

HAWKINS (Edwards Comerford)—SPIRIT AND FORM. Sermons preached in the Parish Church of Leatherhead. Crown 8vo. cloth, price 6s.

HAYES (A. H.), Junr.—NEW COLORADO AND THE SANTA FÉ TRAIL. With Map and 60 Illustrations. Crown 8vo. cloth, price 9s.

HEIDENHAIN (Rudolf) M.D.—ANIMAL MAGNETISM : PHYSIOLOGICAL OBSERVATIONS. Translated from the Fourth German Edition by L. C. WOOLDRIDGE, with a Preface by G. R. ROMANES, F.R.S. Crown 8vo. price 2s. 6d.

HELLWALD (Baron F. Von)—THE RUSSIANS IN CENTRAL ASIA. A Critical Examination, down to the Present Time, of the Geography and History of Central Asia. Translated by Lieut.-Col. THEODORE WIRGMAN, LL.B. With Map. Large post 8vo. price 12s.

HINTON (J.)—THE PLACE OF THE PHYSICIAN. To which is added ESSAYS ON THE LAW OF HUMAN LIFE, AND ON THE RELATIONS BETWEEN ORGANIC AND INORGANIC WORLDS. Second Edition. Crown 8vo. price 3s. 6d.

PHYSIOLOGY FOR PRACTICAL USE. By Various Writers. With 50 Illustrations. Third and Cheaper Edition. Crown 8vo. price 5s.

AN ATLAS OF DISEASES OF THE MEMBRANA TYMPANI. With Descriptive Text. Post 8vo. price £6. 6s.

THE QUESTIONS OF AURAL SURGERY. With Illustrations. 2 vols. Post 8vo. price 12s. 6d.

CHAPTERS ON THE ART OF THINKING, AND OTHER ESSAYS. With an Introduction by SHADWORTH HODGSON. Edited by C. H. HINTON. Crown 8vo. cloth, price 8s. 6d.

THE MYSTERY OF PAIN. New Edition. Fcp. 8vo. cloth limp, 1s.

LIFE AND LETTERS. Edited by ELLICE HOPKINS, with an Introduction by Sir W. W. GULL, Bart., and Portrait engraved on Steel by C. H. JEENS. Third Edition. Crown 8vo. price 8s. 6d.

HOOPER (Mary)—LITTLE DINNERS: HOW TO SERVE THEM WITH ELEGANCE AND ECONOMY. Thirteenth Edition. Crown 8vo. price 5s.

COOKERY FOR INVALIDS, PERSONS OF DELICATE DIGESTION, AND CHILDREN. Crown 8vo. price 3s. 6d.

EVERY-DAY MEALS. Being Economical and Wholesome Recipes for Breakfast, Luncheon, and Supper. Second Edition. Crown 8vo. cloth, price 5s.

HOPKINS (Ellice)—LIFE AND LETTERS OF JAMES HINTON, with an Introduction by Sir W. W. GULL, Bart., and Portrait engraved on Steel by C. H. JEENS. Third Edition. Crown 8vo. price 8s. 6d.

HORNER (The Misses)—WALKS IN FLORENCE. A New and thoroughly Revised Edition. 2 vols. Crown 8vo. Cloth limp. With Illustrations.

    VOL. I.—Churches, Streets, and Palaces. Price 10s. 6d.
    VOL. II.—Public Galleries and Museums. Price 5s.

HOUSEHOLD READINGS ON PROPHECY. By A LAYMAN. Small crown 8vo. cloth, price 3s. 6d.

HULL (Edmund C. P.)—THE EUROPEAN IN INDIA. With a Medical Guide for Anglo-Indians. By R. S. MAIR, M.D., F.R.C.S.E. Third Edition, Revised and Corrected. Post 8vo. price 6s.

HUTTON (Arthur) M.A.—THE ANGLICAN MINISTRY: its Nature and Value in relation to the Catholic Priesthood. With a Preface by His Eminence Cardinal Newman. Demy 8vo. cloth, price 14s.

JENKINS (E.) and RAYMOND (J.)—THE ARCHITECT'S LEGAL HANDBOOK. Third Edition, Revised. Crown 8vo. price 6s.

JENKINS (Rev. R. C.) M.A.—THE PRIVILEGE OF PETER and the Claims of the Roman Church confronted with the Scriptures, the Councils, and the Testimony of the Popes themselves. Fcp. 8vo. price 3s. 6d.

JENNINGS (Mrs. Vaughan)—RAHEL: HER LIFE AND LETTERS. With a Portrait from the Painting by Daffinger. Square post 8vo. price 7s. 6d.

JOEL (L.)—A CONSUL'S MANUAL AND SHIPOWNER'S AND SHIPMASTER'S PRACTICAL GUIDE IN THEIR TRANSACTIONS ABROAD. With Definitions of Nautical, Mercantile, and Legal Terms; a Glossary of Mercantile Terms in English, French, German, Italian, and Spanish; Tables of the Money, Weights, and Measures of the Principal Commercial Nations and their Equivalents in British Standards; and Forms of Consular and Notarial Acts. Demy 8vo. cloth, price 12s.

JOHNSTONE (C. F.) M.A.—HISTORICAL ABSTRACTS: being Outlines of the History of some of the less known States of Europe. Crown 8vo. cloth, price 7s. 6d.

JONES (Lucy)—PUDDINGS AND SWEETS; being Three Hundred and Sixty-five Receipts approved by experience. Crown 8vo. price 2s. 6d.

JOYCE (P. W.) LL.D. &c.—OLD CELTIC ROMANCES. Translated from the Gaelic. Crown 8vo. cloth, price 7s. 6d.

KAUFMANN (Rev. M.) B.A.—SOCIALISM: Its Nature, its Dangers, and its Remedies considered. Crown 8vo. price 7s. 6d.

UTOPIAS; or, Schemes of Social Improvement, from Sir Thomas More to Karl Marx. Crown 8vo. cloth, price 5s.

KAY (Joseph) M.A., Q.C.—FREE TRADE IN LAND. Edited by his Widow. With Preface by the Right Hon. JOHN BRIGHT, M.P. Sixth Edition. Crown 8vo. cloth, price 5s.

KENT (C.)—CORONA CATHOLICA AD PETRI SUCCESSORIS PEDES OBLATA. DE SUMMI PONTIFICIS LEONIS XIII. ASSUMPTIONE EPIGRAMMA. In Quinquaginta Linguis. Fcp. 4to. cloth, price 15s.

KERNER (Dr. A.) Professor of Botany in the University of Innsbruck.—FLOWERS AND THEIR UNBIDDEN GUESTS. Translation edited by W. OGLE, M.A., M.D. With Illustrations. Square 8vo. cloth, price 9s.

KIDD (Joseph) M.D.—THE LAWS OF THERAPEUTICS; or, the Science and Art of Medicine. Second Edition. Crown 8vo. price 6s.

KINAHAN (G. Henry) M.R.I.A., of H.M.'s Geological Survey.—THE GEOLOGY OF IRELAND, with numerous Illustrations and a Geological Map of Ireland. Square 8vo. cloth.

KINGSLEY (Charles) M.A.—LETTERS AND MEMORIES OF HIS LIFE. Edited by his WIFE. With Two Steel Engraved Portraits, and Illustrations on Wood, and a Facsimile of his Handwriting. Thirteenth Edition. 2 vols. Demy 8vo. price 36s.

*** Also the Ninth Cabinet Edition, in 2 vols. Crown 8vo. cloth, price 12s.

ALL SAINTS' DAY, and other Sermons. Edited by the Rev. W. HARRISON. Third Edition. Crown 8vo. price 7s. 6d.

TRUE WORDS FOR BRAVE MEN. A Book for Soldiers' and Sailors' Libraries. Eighth Edition. Crown 8vo. price 2s. 6d.

KNIGHT (Professor W.)—STUDIES IN PHILOSOPHY AND LITERATURE. Large post 8vo. cloth, price 7s. 6d.

KNOX (Alexander A.)—THE NEW PLAYGROUND; or, Wanderings in Algeria. Large crown 8vo. cloth, price 10s. 6d.

LACORDAIRE (Rev. Père)—LIFE : Conferences delivered at Toulouse. A New and Cheaper Edition. Crown 8vo. price 3s. 6d.

LEE (Rev. F. G.) D.C.L.—THE OTHER WORLD; or, Glimpses of the Supernatural. 2 vols. A New Edition. Crown 8vo. price 15s.

LEWIS (Edward Dillon)—A DRAFT CODE OF CRIMINAL LAW AND PROCEDURE. Demy 8vo. cloth, price 21s.

LIFE IN THE MOFUSSIL ; or, Civilian Life in Lower Bengal. By an Ex-Civilian. Large post 8vo. price 14s.

LINDSAY (W. Lauder) M.D., F.R.S.E., &c.—MIND IN THE LOWER ANIMALS IN HEALTH AND DISEASE. 2 vols. Demy 8vo. cloth, price 32s. Vol. I.—Mind in Health.   Vol. II.—Mind in Disease.

LLOYD (Francis), and TEBBITT (Charles)—EXTENSION OF EMPIRE, WEAKNESS? DEFICITS, RUIN? With a Practical Scheme for the Reconstruction of Asiatic Turkey. Small crown 8vo. cloth, price 3s. 6d.

LONSDALE (Margaret)—SISTER DORA: a Biography. With Portrait. Twenty-fourth Edition. Crown 8vo. cloth, price 2s. 6d.

LORIMER (Peter) D.D.—JOHN KNOX AND THE CHURCH OF ENGLAND. His Work in her Pulpit, and his Influence upon her Liturgy, Articles, and Parties. Demy 8vo. price 12s.

JOHN WICLIF AND HIS ENGLISH PRECURSORS. By GERHARD VICTOR LECHLER. Translated from the German, with additional Notes. 2 vols. Demy 8vo. price 21s.

MACLACHLAN (Mrs.)—NOTES AND EXTRACTS ON EVERLASTING PUNISHMENT AND ETERNAL LIFE, ACCORDING TO LITERAL INTERPRETATION. Small crown 8vo. cloth, price 3s. 6d.

MACNAUGHT (Rev. John)—CŒNA DOMINI : An Essay on the Lord's Supper, its Primitive Institution, Apostolic Uses, and Subsequent History. Demy 8vo. price 14s.

MAGNUS (Mrs.)—ABOUT THE JEWS SINCE BIBLE TIMES. From the Babylonian Exile till the English Exodus. Small crown 8vo. cloth, price 5s.

MAIR (R. S.) M.D., F.R.C.S.E.—THE MEDICAL GUIDE FOR ANGLO-INDIANS. Being a Compendium of Advice to Europeans in India, relating to the Preservation and Regulation of Health. With a Supplement on the Management of Children in India. Second Edition. Crown 8vo. limp cloth, price 3s. 6d.

MANNING (His Eminence Cardinal)—THE TRUE STORY OF THE VATICAN COUNCIL. Crown 8vo. price 5s.

MARKHAM (Capt. Albert Hastings) R.N.—THE GREAT FROZEN SEA : A Personal Narrative of the Voyage of the *Alert* during the Arctic Expedition of 1875-6. With Six Full-page Illustrations, Two Maps, and Twenty-seven Woodcuts. Fourth and Cheaper Edition. Crown 8vo. cloth, price 6s.

A POLAR RECONNAISSANCE: being the Voyage of the 'Isbjörn' to Novaya Zemlya in 1879. With 10 Illustrations. Demy 8vo. cloth, price 16s.

MARTINEAU (Gertrude)—OUTLINE LESSONS ON MORALS. Small crown 8vo. cloth, price 3s. 6d.

McGRATH (Terence)—PICTURES FROM IRELAND. New and Cheaper Edition. Crown 8vo. cloth, price 2s.

MERRITT (Henry)—ART-CRITICISM AND ROMANCE. With Recollections and Twenty-three Illustrations in *eau-forte*, by Anna Lea Merritt. 2 vols. Large post 8vo. cloth, price 25s.

MILLER (Edward)—THE HISTORY AND DOCTRINES OF IRVINGISM; or, the so-called Catholic and Apostolic Church. 2 vols. Large post 8vo. price 25s.

THE CHURCH IN RELATION TO THE STATE. Large crown 8vo. cloth, price 7s. 6d.

MILNE (James)—TABLES OF EXCHANGE for the Conversion of Sterling Money into Indian and Ceylon Currency, at Rates from 1s. 8d. to 2s. 3d. per Rupee. Second Edition. Demy 8vo. cloth, price £2. 2s.

MINCHIN (J. G.)—BULGARIA SINCE THE WAR: Notes of a Tour in the Autumn of 1879. Small crown 8vo. cloth, price 3s. 6d.

MOCKLER (E.)—A GRAMMAR OF THE BALOOCHEE LANGUAGE, as it is spoken in Makran (Ancient Gedrosia), in the Persia-Arabic and Roman characters. Fcp. 8vo. price 5s.

MOFFAT (R. S.)—ECONOMY OF CONSUMPTION: a Study in Political Economy. Demy 8vo. price 18s.

THE PRINCIPLES OF A TIME POLICY: being an Exposition of a Method of Settling Disputes between Employers and Employed in regard to Time and Wages, by a simple Process of Mercantile Barter, without recourse to Strikes or Locks-out. Reprinted from 'The Economy of Consumption,' with a Preface and Appendix containing Observations on some Reviews of that book, and a Re-criticism of the Theories of Ricardo and J. S. Mill on Rent, Value, and Cost of Production. Demy 8vo. price 3s. 6d.

MORELL (J. R.)—EUCLID SIMPLIFIED IN METHOD AND LANGUAGE. Being a Manual of Geometry. Compiled from the most important French Works, approved by the University of Paris and the Minister of Public Instruction. Fcp. 8vo. price 2s. 6d.

MORSE (E. S.) Ph.D.—FIRST BOOK OF ZOOLOGY. With numerous Illustrations. New and Cheaper Edition. Crown 8vo. price 2s. 6d.

MUNRO (Major-Gen. Sir Thomas) Bart. K.C.B., Governor of Madras. SELECTIONS FROM HIS MINUTES AND OTHER OFFICIAL WRITINGS. Edited, with an Introductory Memoir, by Sir ALEXANDER ARBUTHNOT, K.C.S.I., C.I.E. 2 vols. Demy 8vo. cloth, price 30s.

NELSON (J. H.) M.A.—A PROSPECTUS OF THE SCIENTIFIC STUDY OF THE HINDÛ LAW. Demy 8vo. cloth, price 9s.

NEWMAN (J. H.) D.D.—CHARACTERISTICS FROM THE WRITINGS OF. Being Selections from his various Works. Arranged with the Author's personal Approval. Third Edition. With Portrait. Crown 8vo. price 6s.

*** A Portrait of the Rev. Dr. J. H. Newman, mounted for framing, can be had, price 2s. 6d.

NEW WERTHER. By LOKI. Small crown 8vo. cloth, price 2s. 6d.

NICHOLAS (T.)—THE PEDIGREE OF THE ENGLISH PEOPLE. Fifth Edition. Demy 8vo. price 16s.

NICHOLSON (Edward Byron)—THE GOSPEL ACCORDING TO THE HEBREWS. Its Fragments Translated and Annotated with a Critical Analysis of the External and Internal Evidence relating to it. Demy 8vo. cloth, price 9s. 6d.

A NEW COMMENTARY ON THE GOSPEL ACCORDING TO MATTHEW. Demy 8vo. cloth, price 12s.

THE RIGHTS OF AN ANIMAL. Crown 8vo. cloth, price 3s. 6d.

NICOLS (Arthur) F.G.S., F.R.G.S.—CHAPTERS FROM THE PHYSICAL HISTORY OF THE EARTH: an Introduction to Geology and Palæontology. With numerous Illustrations. Crown 8vo. cloth, price 5s.

NORMAN PEOPLE (THE), and their Existing Descendants in the British Dominions and the United States of America. Demy 8vo. price 21s.

NUCES: EXERCISES ON THE SYNTAX OF THE PUBLIC SCHOOL LATIN PRIMER. New Edition in Three Parts. Crown 8vo. each 1s.
*** The Three Parts can also be had bound together in cloth, price 3s.

OATES (Frank) F.R.G.S.—MATABELE LAND AND THE VICTORIA FALLS. A Naturalist's Wanderings in the Interior of South Africa. Edited by C. G. OATES, B.A. With numerous Illustrations and 4 Maps. Demy 8vo. cloth.

OF THE IMITATION OF CHRIST. Four Books. Demy 32mo. cloth limp, 1s.
*** Also in various bindings.

O'MEARA (Kathleen)—FREDERIC OZANAM, Professor of the Sorbonne: His Life and Work. Second Edition. Crown 8vo. cloth, price 7s. 6d.

HENRI PERREYVE AND HIS COUNSELS TO THE SICK. Small crown 8vo. cloth, price 5s.

OUR PUBLIC SCHOOLS—ETON, HARROW, WINCHESTER, RUGBY, WESTMINSTER, MARLBOROUGH, THE CHARTERHOUSE. Crown 8vo. cloth, price 6s.

OWEN (F. M.)—JOHN KEATS: a Study. Crown 8vo. cloth, price 6s.

OWEN (Rev. Robert) B.D.—SANCTORALE CATHOLICUM; or, Book of Saints. With Notes, Critical, Exegetical, and Historical. Demy 8vo. cloth, price 18s.

AN ESSAY ON THE COMMUNION OF SAINTS. Including an Examination of the Cultus Sanctorum. Price 2s.

PARCHMENT LIBRARY. Choicely printed on hand-made paper, limp parchment antique, 6s. each; vellum, 7s. 6d. each.

SHAKSPERE'S SONNETS. Edited by EDWARD DOWDEN, Author of 'Shakspere: his Mind and Art,' &c. With a Frontispiece etched by Leopold Lowenstam, after the Death Mask.

ENGLISH ODES. Selected by EDMUND W. GOSSE, Author of 'Studies in the Literature of Northern Europe.' With Frontispiece on India paper by Hamo Thornycroft, A.R.A.

OF THE IMITATION OF CHRIST. By THOMAS À KEMPIS. A revised Translation. With Frontispiece on India paper, from a Design by W. B. Richmond.

TENNYSON'S THE PRINCESS: a Medley. With a Miniature Frontispiece by H. M. Paget, and a Tailpiece in Outline by Gordon Browne.

POEMS: Selected from PERCY BYSSHE SHELLEY. Dedicated to Lady Shelley. With Preface by RICHARD GARNET and a Miniature Frontispiece.

TENNYSON'S 'IN MEMORIAM.' With a Miniature Portrait in *eau-forte* by Le Rat, after a Photograph by the late Mrs. Cameron.

PARKER (Joseph) D.D.—THE PARACLETE: An Essay on the Personality and Ministry of the Holy Ghost, with some reference to current discussions. Second Edition. Demy 8vo. price 12s.

PARR (Capt. H. Hallam, C.M.G.)—A SKETCH OF THE KAFIR AND ZULU WARS: Guadana to Isandhlwana. With Maps. Small crown 8vo. cloth, price 5s.

PARSLOE (Joseph) — OUR RAILWAYS. Sketches, Historical and Descriptive. With Practical Information as to Fares and Rates, &c., and a Chapter on Railway Reform. Crown 8vo. price 6s.

PATTISON (Mrs. Mark) —THE RENAISSANCE OF ART IN FRANCE. With Nineteen Steel Engravings. 2 vols. Demy 8vo. cloth, price 32s.

PAUL (C. Kegan) —WILLIAM GODWIN: HIS FRIENDS AND CONTEMPORARIES. With Portraits and Facsimiles of the Handwriting of Godwin and his Wife. 2 vols. Square post 8vo. price 28s.

THE GENIUS OF CHRISTIANITY UNVEILED. Being Essays by William Godwin never before published. Edited, with a Preface, by C. Kegan Paul. Crown 8vo. price 7s. 6d.

MARY WOLLSTONECRAFT. Letters to Imlay. New Edition with Prefatory Memoir by. Two Portraits in *eau-forte* by ANNA LEA MERRITT. Crown 8vo. cloth, price 6s.

PAYNE (Prof. J. F.) —FRÖBEL AND THE KINDERGARTEN SYSTEM. Second Edition.

A VISIT TO GERMAN SCHOOLS: ELEMENTARY SCHOOLS IN GERMANY. Notes of a Professional Tour to inspect some of the Kindergartens, Primary Schools, Public Girls' Schools, and Schools for Technical Instruction in Hamburgh, Berlin, Dresden, Weimar, Gotha, Eisenach, in the autumn of 1874. With Critical Discussions of the General Principles and Practice of Kindergartens and other Schemes of Elementary Education. Crown 8vo. price 4s. 6d.

PENRICE (Maj. J.) B.A. —A DICTIONARY AND GLOSSARY OF THE KO-RAN. With Copious Grammatical References and Explanations of the Text. 4to. price 21s.

PESCHEL (Dr. Oscar) —THE RACES OF MAN AND THEIR GEOGRAPHICAL DISTRIBUTION. Large crown 8vo. price 9s.

PETERS (F. A.) —THE NICOMACHEAN ETHICS OF ARISTOTLE. Translated by. Crown 8vo. cloth, price 6s.

PINCHES (Thomas) M.A. —SAMUEL WILBERFORCE: FAITH—SERVICE—RECOMPENSE. Three Sermons. With a Portrait of Bishop Wilberforce (after a Portrait by Charles Watkins). Crown 8vo. cloth, price 4s. 6d.

PLAYFAIR (Lieut.-Col.) Her Britannic Majesty's Consul-General in Algiers.

TRAVELS IN THE FOOTSTEPS OF BRUCE IN ALGERIA AND TUNIS. Illustrated by facsimiles of Bruce's original Drawings, Photographs, Maps, &c. Royal 4to. cloth, bevelled boards, gilt leaves, price £3. 3s.

POLLOCK (Frederick) —SPINOZA, HIS LIFE AND PHILOSOPHY. Demy 8vo. cloth, price 16s.

POLLOCK (W. H.) —LECTURES ON FRENCH POETS. Delivered at the Royal Institution. Small crown 8vo. cloth, price 5s.

POOR (Laura E.) —SANSKRIT AND ITS KINDRED LITERATURES. Studies in Comparative Mythology. Small crown 8vo. cloth, price 5s.

POUSHKIN (A. S.) —RUSSIAN ROMANCE. Translated from the Tales of Belkin, &c. By Mrs. J. Buchan Telfer (*née* Mouravieff). New and Cheaper Edition. Crown 8vo. price 3s. 6d.

PRESBYTER—UNFOLDINGS OF CHRISTIAN HOPE. An Essay shewing that the Doctrine contained in the Damnatory Clauses of the Creed commonly called Athanasian is Unscriptural. Small crown 8vo. price 4s. 6d.

PRICE (Prof. Bonamy)—CURRENCY AND BANKING. Crown 8vo. Price 6s.

CHAPTERS ON PRACTICAL POLITICAL ECONOMY. Being the Substance of Lectures delivered before the University of Oxford. Large post 8vo. price 12s.

PROTEUS AND AMADEUS. A Correspondence. Edited by AUBREY DE VERE. Crown 8vo. price 5s.

PULPIT COMMENTARY (THE). Edited by the Rev. J. S. EXELL and the Rev. Canon H. D. M. SPENCE.

    GENESIS. By Rev. T. WHITELAW, M.A. ; with Homilies by the Very Rev. J. F. MONTGOMERY, D.D., Rev. Prof. R. A. REDFORD, M.A., LL.B., Rev. F. HASTINGS, Rev. W. ROBERTS, M.A. An Introduction to the Study of the Old Testament by the Rev. Canon FARRAR, D.D., F.R.S. ; and Introductions to the Pentateuch by the Right Rev. H. COTTERILL, D.D., and Rev. T. WHITELAW, M.A. Fourth Edition. One vol. price 15s.

    NUMBERS. By the Rev. R. WINTERBOTHAM, LL.B. ; with Homilies by the Rev. Professor W. BINNIE, D.D., Rev. E. S. PROUT, M.A., Rev. D. YOUNG, Rev. J. WAITE, B.A., and an Introduction by the Rev. THOMAS WHITELAW, M.A. Price 15s.

    JOSHUA. By Rev. J. J. LIAS, M.A. ; with Homilies by Rev. S. R. ALDRIDGE, LL.B., Rev. R. GLOVER, Rev. E. DE PRESSENSÉ, D.D., Rev. J. WAITE, B.A., Rev. F. W. ADENEY, M.A. ; and an Introduction by the Rev. A. PLUMMER, M.A. Second Edition. Price 12s. 6d.

    JUDGES AND RUTH. By the Right Rev. Lord A. C. HERVEY, D.D., and Rev. J. MORRISON, D.D. ; with Homilies by Rev. A. F. MUIR, M.A., Rev. W. F. ADENEY, M.A., Rev. W. M. STATHAM, and Rev. Professor J. THOMSON, M.A. Second Edition. Price 10s. 6d.

    1 SAMUEL. By the Very Rev. R. P. SMITH, D.D. ; with Homilies by Rev. DONALD FRASER, D.D., Rev. Prof. CHAPMAN, and Rev. B. DALE. Third Edition. Price 15s.

    EZRA, NEHEMIAH, AND ESTHER. By Rev. Canon G. RAWLINSON, M.A.; with Homilies by Rev. Prof. J. R. THOMSON, M.A., Rev. Prof. R. A. REDFORD, LL.B., M.A., Rev. W. S. LEWIS, M.A., Rev. J. A. MACDONALD, Rev. A. MACKENNAL, B.A., Rev. W. CLARKSON, B.A., Rev. F. HASTINGS, Rev. W. DINWIDDIE, LL.B., Rev. Prof. ROWLANDS, B.A., Rev. G. WOOD, B.A., Rev. Prof. P. C. BARKER, LL.B., M.A., and Rev. J. S. EXELL. Fourth Edition. One vol. price 12s. 6d.

PUNJAUB (THE) AND NORTH-WESTERN FRONTIER OF INDIA. By an Old Punjaubee. Crown 8vo. price 5s.

RABBI JESHUA. An Eastern Story. Crown 8vo. cloth, price 3s. 6d.

RAVENSHAW (John Henry) B.C.S.—GAUR : ITS RUINS AND INSCRIPTIONS. Edited by his Widow. With 44 Photographic Illustrations, and 25 facsimiles of Inscriptions. Royal 4to. cloth, price £3. 13s. 6d.

READ (Carveth)—ON THE THEORY OF LOGIC : An Essay. Crown 8vo. price 6s.

REALITIES OF THE FUTURE LIFE. Small crown 8vo. cloth, price 1s. 6d.

RENDELL (J. M.)—CONCISE HANDBOOK OF THE ISLAND OF MADEIRA. With Plan of Funchal and Map of the Island. Fcp. 8vo. cloth, 1s. 6d.

B

REYNOLDS (*Rev. J. W.*)—THE SUPERNATURAL IN NATURE. A Verification by Free Use of Science. Second Edition, revised and enlarged. Demy 8vo. cloth, price 14s.

THE MYSTERY OF MIRACLES. By the Author of 'The Supernatural in Nature.' Crown 8vo. cloth, price 6s.

RIBOT (*Prof. Th.*)—ENGLISH PSYCHOLOGY. Second Edition. A Revised and Corrected Translation from the latest French Edition. Large post 8vo. price 9s.

HEREDITY: A Psychological Study on its Phenomena, its Laws, its Causes, and its Consequences. Large crown 8vo. price 9s.

RINK (*Chevalier Dr. Henry*)—GREENLAND: ITS PEOPLE AND ITS PRODUCTS. By the Chevalier Dr. HENRY RINK, President of the Greenland Board of Trade. With sixteen Illustrations, drawn by the Eskimo, and a Map. Edited by Dr. Robert Brown. Crown 8vo. price 10s. 6d.

ROBERTSON (*The late Rev. F. W.*) *M.A., of Brighton.*—LIFE AND LETTERS OF. Edited by the Rev. Stopford Brooke, M.A., Chaplain in Ordinary to the Queen.
    I. Two vols., uniform with the Sermons. With Steel Portrait. Crown 8vo. price 7s. 6d.
    II. Library Edition, in demy 8vo. with Portrait. Price 12s.
    III. A Popular Edition, in 1 vol. Crown 8vo. price 6s.

SERMONS. Four Series. Small crown 8vo. price 3s. 6d. each.

THE HUMAN RACE, and other Sermons. Preached at Cheltenham, Oxford, and Brighton. Large post 8vo. cloth, price 7s. 6d.

NOTES ON GENESIS. New and Cheaper Edition. Crown 8vo. price 3s. 6d.

EXPOSITORY LECTURES ON ST. PAUL'S EPISTLES TO THE CORINTHIANS. A New Edition. Small crown 8vo. price 5s.

LECTURES AND ADDRESSES, with other Literary Remains. A New Edition. Crown 8vo. price 5s.

AN ANALYSIS OF MR. TENNYSON'S 'IN MEMORIAM.' (Dedicated by Permission to the Poet-Laureate.) Fcp. 8vo. price 2s.

THE EDUCATION OF THE HUMAN RACE. Translated from the German of Gotthold Ephraim Lessing. Fcp. 8vo. price 2s. 6d.
    The above Works can also be had, bound in half-morocco.
*** A Portrait of the late Rev. F. W. Robertson, mounted for framing, can be had, price 2s. 6d.

RODWELL (*G. F.*) *F.R.A.S., F.C.S.*—ETNA: A HISTORY OF THE MOUNTAIN AND ITS ERUPTIONS. With Maps and Illustrations. Square 8vo. cloth, price 9s.

ROSS (*Alexander*) *D.D.*—MEMOIR OF ALEXANDER EWING, Bishop of Argyll and the Isles. Second and Cheaper Edition. Demy 8vo. cloth, price 10s. 6d.

SALTS (*Rev. Alfred*) *LL.D.*—GODPARENTS AT CONFIRMATION. With a Preface by the Bishop of Manchester. Small crown 8vo. cloth limp, price 2s.

SALVATOR (*Archduke Ludwig*)—LEVKOSIA, THE CAPITAL OF CYPRUS. Crown 4to. cloth, price 10s. 6d.

SAMUEL (*Sydney M.*)—JEWISH LIFE IN THE EAST. Small crown 8vo. cloth, price 3s. 6d.

SAYCE (Rev. Archibald Henry)—INTRODUCTION TO THE SCIENCE OF LANGUAGE. 2 vols. Large post 8vo. cloth, price 25*s*.

SCIENTIFIC LAYMAN. The New Truth and the Old Faith: are they Incompatible? Demy 8vo. cloth, price 10*s*. 6*d*.

SCOONES (W. Baptiste)—FOUR CENTURIES OF ENGLISH LETTERS: A Selection of 350 Letters by 150 Writers, from the Period of the Paston Letters to the Present Time. Second Edition. Large crown 8vo. cloth, price 9*s*.

SCOTT (Robert H.)—WEATHER CHARTS AND STORM WARNINGS. Second Edition. Illustrated. Crown 8vo. price 3*s*. 6*d*.

SENIOR (N. W.)—ALEXIS DE TOCQUEVILLE. Correspondence and Conversations with Nassau W. Senior, from 1833 to 1859. Edited by M. C. M Simpson. 2 vols. Large post 8vo. price 21*s*.

SHAKSPEARE (Charles)—SAINT PAUL AT ATHENS. Spiritual Christianity in relation to some aspects of Modern Thought. Five Sermons preached at St. Stephen's Church, Westbourne Park. With a Preface by the Rev. Canon FARRAR.

SHELLEY (Lady)—SHELLEY MEMORIALS FROM AUTHENTIC SOURCES. With (now first printed) an Essay on Christianity by Percy Bysshe Shelley. With Portrait. Third Edition. Crown 8vo. price 5*s*.

SHILLITO (Rev. Joseph)—WOMANHOOD: its Duties, Temptations, and Privileges. A Book for Young Women. Third Edition. Crown 8vo. price 3*s*. 6*d*.

SHIPLEY (Rev. Orby) M.A.—CHURCH TRACTS: OR, STUDIES IN MODERN PROBLEMS. By various Writers. 2 vols. Crown 8vo. price 5*s*. each.

PRINCIPLES OF THE FAITH IN RELATION TO SIN. Topics for Thought in Times of Retreat. Eleven Addresses delivered during a Retreat of Three Days to Persons living in the World. Demy 8vo. cloth, price 12*s*.

SISTER AUGUSTINE, Superior of the Sisters of Charity at the St. Johannis Hospital at Bonn. Authorised Translation by HANS THARAU, from the German 'Memorials of AMALIE VON LASAULX.' Second Edition. Large crown 8vo. cloth, price 7*s*. 6*d*.

SMITH (Edward) M.D., LL.B., F.R.S.—HEALTH AND DISEASE, as Influenced by the Daily, Seasonal, and other Cyclical Changes in the Human System. A New Edition. Post 8vo. price 7*s*. 6*d*.

PRACTICAL DIETARY FOR FAMILIES, SCHOOLS, AND THE LABOURING CLASSES. A New Edition. Post 8vo. price 3*s*. 6*d*.

TUBERCULAR CONSUMPTION IN ITS EARLY AND REMEDIABLE STAGES. Second Edition. Crown 8vo. price 6*s*.

SPEDDING (James)—REVIEWS AND DISCUSSIONS, LITERARY, POLITICAL, AND HISTORICAL NOT RELATING TO BACON. Demy 8vo. cloth, price 12*s*. 6*d*.

STAPFER (Paul)—SHAKSPEARE AND CLASSICAL ANTIQUITY: Greek and Latin Antiquity as presented in Shakspeare's Plays. Translated by EMILY J. CAREY. Large post 8vo. cloth, price 12*s*.

ST. BERNARD. A Little Book on the Love of God. Translated by MARIANNE CAROLINE and COVENTRY PATMORE. Cloth extra, gilt top, 4*s*. 6*d*.

STEPHENS (Archibald John) LL.D.—THE FOLKESTONE RITUAL CASE. The Substance of the Argument delivered before the Judicial Committee of the Privy Council on behalf of the Respondents. Demy 8vo. cloth, price 6*s*.

B 2

STEVENSON (Rev. W. F.)—HYMNS FOR THE CHURCH AND HOME. Selected and Edited by the Rev. W. Fleming Stevenson. The most complete Hymn Book published. The Hymn Book consists of Three Parts :—I. For Public Worship.—II. For Family and Private Worship.—III. For Children.
*** Published in various forms and prices, the latter ranging from 8*d*. to 6*s*. Lists and full particulars will be furnished on application to the Publishers.

STEVENSON (Robert Louis)—VIRGINIBUS PUERISQUE, and other Papers. Crown 8vo. cloth, price 6*s*.

SULLY (James) M.A. — SENSATION AND INTUITION. Demy 8vo. price 10*s*. 6*d*.

PESSIMISM : a History and a Criticism. Second Edition. Demy 8vo. price 14*s*.

SYME (David)—OUTLINES OF AN INDUSTRIAL SCIENCE. Second Edition. Crown 8vo. price 6*s*.

TAYLOR (Algernon)—GUIENNE. Notes of an Autumn Tour. Crown 8vo. cloth, price 4*s*. 6*d*.

THOMSON (J. Turnbull)—SOCIAL PROBLEMS ; OR, AN INQUIRY INTO THE LAWS OF INFLUENCE. With Diagrams. Demy 8vo. cloth, price 10*s*. 6*d*.

TODHUNTER (Dr. J.)—A STUDY OF SHELLEY. Crown 8vo. cloth, price 7*s*.

TWINING (Louisa)—WORKHOUSE VISITING AND MANAGEMENT DURING TWENTY-FIVE YEARS. Small crown 8vo. cloth, price 3*s*. 6*d*.

UPTON (Major R. D.)—GLEANINGS FROM THE DESERT OF ARABIA. Large post 8vo. cloth, price 10*s*. 6*d*.

VAUGHAN (H. Halford)—NEW READINGS AND RENDERINGS OF SHAKESPEARE'S TRAGEDIES. 2 vols. demy 8vo. cloth, price 25*s*.

VILLARI (Professor)—NICCOLO MACHIAVELLI AND HIS TIMES. Translated by Linda Villari. 2 vols. Large post 8vo. price 24*s*.

VYNER (Lady Mary)—EVERY DAY A PORTION. Adapted from the Bible and the Prayer Book, for the Private Devotions of those living in Widowhood. Collected and Edited by Lady Mary Vyner. Square crown 8vo. extra, price 5*s*.

WALDSTEIN (Charles) Ph.D.—THE BALANCE OF EMOTION AND INTELLECT ; an Introductory Essay to the Study of Philosophy. Crown 8vo. cloth, price 6*s*.

WALLER (Rev. C. B.)—THE APOCALYPSE, reviewed under the Light of the Doctrine of the Unfolding Ages, and the Relation of All Things. Demy 8vo. price 12*s*.

WATSON (Sir Thomas) Bart., M.D.—THE ABOLITION OF ZYMOTIC DISEASES, and of other similar Enemies of Mankind. Small crown 8vo. cloth, price 3*s*. 6*d*.

WEDMORE (Frederick)—THE MASTERS OF GENRE PAINTING. With Sixteen Illustrations. Crown 8vo. cloth, price 7*s*. 6*d*.

WHEWELL (William) D.D.—HIS LIFE AND SELECTIONS FROM HIS CORRESPONDENCE. By Mrs. STAIR DOUGLAS. With a Portrait from a Painting by SAMUEL LAURENCE. Demy 8vo. cloth, price 21*s*.

WHITE (A. D.) LL.D.—WARFARE OF SCIENCE. With Prefatory Note by Professor Tyndall. Second Edition. Crown 8vo. price 3*s*. 6*d*.

C. Kegan Paul & Co.'s Publications. 21

WHITNEY (Prof. William Dwight)—ESSENTIALS OF ENGLISH GRAMMAR, for the Use of Schools. Crown 8vo. price 3s. 6d.

WICKSTEED (P. H.)—DANTE: Six Sermons. Crown 8vo. cloth, price 5s.

WILLIAMS (Rowland) D.D.—PSALMS, LITANIES, COUNSELS, AND COLLECTS FOR DEVOUT PERSONS. Edited by his Widow. New and Popular Edition. Crown 8vo. price 3s. 6d.

STRAY THOUGHTS COLLECTED FROM THE WRITINGS OF THE LATE ROWLAND WILLIAMS, D.D. Edited by his Widow. Crown 8vo. cloth, price 3s. 6d.

WILLIS (R.) M.D.—SERVETUS AND CALVIN: a Study of an Important Epoch in the Early History of the Reformation. 8vo. price 16s.

WILLIAM HARVEY. A History of the Discovery of the Circulation of the Blood: with a Portrait of Harvey after Faithorne. Demy 8vo. cloth, price 14s. Portrait separate.

WILSON (Erasmus)—EGYPT OF THE PAST. With Chromo-lithograph and numerous Illustrations in the text. Crown 8vo. cloth.

WILSON (H. Schütz)—THE TOWER AND SCAFFOLD. A Miniature Monograph. Large fcp. 8vo. price 1s.

WOLLSTONECRAFT (Mary)—LETTERS TO IMLAY. New Edition, with Prefatory Memoir by C. KEGAN PAUL, author of 'William Godwin: His Friends and Contemporaries,' &c. Two Portraits in *eau-forte* by Anna Lea Merritt. Crown 8vo. cloth, price 6s.

WOLTMANN (Dr. Alfred), and WOERMANN (Dr. Karl)— HISTORY OF PAINTING. Edited by Sidney Colvin. Vol. I. Painting in Antiquity and the Middle Ages. With numerous Illustrations. Medium 8vo. cloth, price 28s.; bevelled boards, gilt leaves, price 30s.

WOOD (Major-General J. Creighton)—DOUBLING THE CONSONANT. Small crown 8vo. cloth, price 1s. 6d.

WORD WAS MADE FLESH. Short Family Readings on the Epistles for each Sunday of the Christian Year. Demy 8vo. cloth, price 10s. 6d.

WRIGHT (Rev. David) M.A.—WAITING FOR THE LIGHT, AND OTHER SERMONS. Crown 8vo. price 6s.

YOUMANS (Eliza A.)—AN ESSAY ON THE CULTURE OF THE OBSERVING POWERS OF CHILDREN, especially in connection with the Study of Botany. Edited, with Notes and a Supplement, by Joseph Payne, F.C.P., Author of 'Lectures on the Science and Art of Education,' &c. Crown 8vo. price 2s. 6d.

FIRST BOOK OF BOTANY. Designed to Cultivate the Observing Powers of Children. With 300 Engravings. New and Cheaper Edition. Crown 8vo. price 2s. 6d.

YOUMANS (Edward L.) M.D.—A CLASS BOOK OF CHEMISTRY, on the Basis of the New System. With 200 Illustrations. Crown 8vo. price 5s.

THE INTERNATIONAL SCIENTIFIC SERIES.

I. FORMS OF WATER: a Familiar Exposition of the Origin and Phenomena of Glaciers. By J. Tyndall, LL.D., F.R.S. With 25 Illustrations. Seventh Edition. Crown 8vo. price 5s.

II. PHYSICS AND POLITICS; or, Thoughts on the Application of the Principles of 'Natural Selection' and 'Inheritance' to Political Society. By Walter Bagehot. Fifth Edition. Crown 8vo. price 4s.

III. FOODS. By Edward Smith, M.D., LL.B., F.R.S. With numerous Illustrations. Seventh Edition. Crown 8vo. price 5s.

IV. MIND AND BODY: the Theories of their Relation. By Alexander Bain, LL.D. With Four Illustrations. Tenth Edition. Crown 8vo. price 4s.

V. THE STUDY OF SOCIOLOGY. By Herbert Spencer. Tenth Edition. Crown 8vo. price 5s.

VI. ON THE CONSERVATION OF ENERGY. By Balfour Stewart, M.A., LL.D., F.R.S. With 14 Illustrations. Fifth Edition. Crown 8vo. price 5s.

VII. ANIMAL LOCOMOTION; or, Walking, Swimming, and Flying. By J. B. Pettigrew, M.D., F.R.S., &c. With 130 Illustrations. Second Edition. Crown 8vo. price 5s.

VIII. RESPONSIBILITY IN MENTAL DISEASE. By Henry Maudsley, M.D. Third Edition. Crown 8vo. price 5s.

IX. THE NEW CHEMISTRY. By Professor J. P. Cooke, of the Harvard University. With 31 Illustrations. Fifth Edition. Crown 8vo. price 5s.

X. THE SCIENCE OF LAW. By Professor Sheldon Amos. Fourth Edition. Crown 8vo. price 5s.

XI. ANIMAL MECHANISM: a Treatise on Terrestrial and Aerial Locomotion. By Professor E. J. Marey. With 117 Illustrations. Second Edition. Crown 8vo. price 5s.

XII. THE DOCTRINE OF DESCENT AND DARWINISM. By Professor Oscar Schmidt (Strasburg University). With 26 Illustrations. Fourth Edit. Crown 8vo. price 5s.

XIII. THE HISTORY OF THE CONFLICT BETWEEN RELIGION AND SCIENCE. By J. W. Draper, M.D., LL.D. Fifteenth Edition. Crown 8vo. price 5s.

XIV. FUNGI: their Nature, Influences, Uses, &c. By M. C. Cooke, M.D., LL.D. Edited by the Rev. M. J. Berkeley, M.A., F.L.S. With numerous Illustrations. Second Edition. Crown 8vo. price 5s.

XV. THE CHEMICAL EFFECTS OF LIGHT AND PHOTOGRAPHY. By Dr. Hermann Vogel (Polytechnic Academy of Berlin). Translation thoroughly revised. With 100 Illustrations. Third Edition. Crown 8vo. price 5s.

XVI. THE LIFE AND GROWTH OF LANGUAGE. By William Dwight Whitney, Professor of Sanscrit and Comparative Philology in Yale College, Newhaven. Third Edition. Crown 8vo. price 5s.

XVII. MONEY AND THE MECHANISM OF EXCHANGE. By W. Stanley Jevons, M.A., F.R.S. Fourth Edition. Crown 8vo. price 5s.

XVIII. THE NATURE OF LIGHT. With a General Account of Physical Optics. By Dr. Eugene Lommel, Professor of Physics in the University of Erlangen. With 188 Illustrations and a Table of Spectra in Chromo-lithography. Third Edition. Crown 8vo. price 5s.

XIX. ANIMAL PARASITES AND MESSMATES. By Monsieur Van Beneden, Professor of the University of Louvain, Correspondent of the Institute of France. With 83 Illustrations. Second Edition. Crown 8vo. price 5s.

XX. FERMENTATION. By Professor Schützenberger, Director of the Chemical Laboratory at the Sorbonne. With 28 Illustrations. Third Edition. Crown 8vo. price 5s.

XXI. THE FIVE SENSES OF MAN. By Professor Bernstein, of the University of Halle. With 91 Illustrations. Second Edition. Crown 8vo. price 5s.

XXII. THE THEORY OF SOUND IN ITS RELATION TO MUSIC. By Professor Pietro Blaserna, of the Royal University of Rome. With numerous Illustrations. Second Edition. Crown 8vo. price 5s.

XXIII. STUDIES IN SPECTRUM ANALYSIS. By J. Norman Lockyer, F.R.S. With six photographic Illustrations of Spectra, and numerous engravings on Wood. Crown 8vo. Second Edition. Price 6s. 6d.

XXIV. A HISTORY OF THE GROWTH OF THE STEAM ENGINE. By Professor R. H. Thurston. With numerous Illustrations. Second Edition. Crown 8vo. cloth, price 6s. 6d.

XXV. EDUCATION AS A SCIENCE. By Alexander Bain, LL.D. Third Edition. Crown 8vo. cloth, price 5s.

XXVI. THE HUMAN SPECIES. By Prof. A. de Quatrefages. Third Edition. Crown 8vo. cloth, price 5s.

XXVII. MODERN CHROMATICS. With Applications to Art and Industry. By Ogden N. Rood. With 130 original Illustrations. Second Edition. Crown 8vo. cloth, price 5s.

XXVIII. THE CRAYFISH: an Introduction to the Study of Zoology. By Professor T. H. Huxley. With 82 Illustrations. Third Edition. Crown 8vo. cloth, price 5s.

XXIX. THE BRAIN AS AN ORGAN OF MIND. By H. Charlton Bastian, M.D. With numerous Illustrations. Second Edition. Crown 8vo. cloth, price 5s.

XXX. THE ATOMIC THEORY. By Prof. Wurtz. Translated by G. Cleminshaw, F.C.S. Second Edition. Crown 8vo. cloth, price 5s.

XXXI. THE NATURAL CONDITIONS OF EXISTENCE AS THEY AFFECT ANIMAL LIFE. By Karl Semper. With 2 Maps and 106 Woodcuts. Second Edition. Crown 8vo. cloth, price 5s.

XXXII. GENERAL PHYSIOLOGY OF MUSCLES AND NERVES. By Prof. J. Rosenthal. Second Edition. With Illustrations. Crown 8vo. cloth, price 5s.

XXXIII. SIGHT: an Exposition of the Principles of Monocular and Binocular Vision. By Joseph le Conte, LL.D. With 132 Illustrations. Crown 8vo. cloth, price 5s.

XXXIV. ILLUSIONS: a Psychological Study. By James Sully. Crown 8vo. cloth, price 5s.

XXXV. VOLCANOES: WHAT THEY ARE AND WHAT THEY TEACH. By Professor J. W. Judd, F.R.S. With 92 Illustrations on Wood. Crown 8vo. cloth, price 5s.

MILITARY WORKS.

ANDERSON (Col. R. P.)—VICTORIES AND DEFEATS: an Attempt to explain the Causes which have led to them. An Officer's Manual. Demy 8vo. price 14s.

ARMY OF THE NORTH GERMAN CONFEDERATION: a Brief Description of its Organisation, of the Different Branches of the Service and their rôle in War, of its Mode of Fighting, &c. Translated from the Corrected Edition, by permission of the Author, by Colonel Edward Newdigate. Demy 8vo. price 5s.

BLUME (Maj. W.)—THE OPERATIONS OF THE GERMAN ARMIES IN FRANCE, from Sedan to the end of the War of 1870-71. With Map. From the Journals of the Head-quarters Staff. Translated by the late E. M. Jones, Maj. 20th Foot, Prof. of Mil. Hist., Sandhurst. Demy 8vo. price 9s.

BOGUSLAWSKI (Capt. A. von)—TACTICAL DEDUCTIONS FROM THE WAR OF 1870-1. Translated by Colonel Sir Lumley Graham, Bart., late 18th (Royal Irish) Regiment. Third Edition, Revised and Corrected. Demy 8vo. price 7s.

BRACKENBURY (Lieut.-Col.) C.B., R.A., A.A.G.—MILITARY HANDBOOKS FOR REGIMENTAL OFFICERS. I. Military Sketching and Reconnaissance, by Lieut.-Col. F. J. Hutchison, and Capt. H. G. MacGregor. Second Edition. With 15 Plates. Small 8vo. cloth, price 6s. II. The Elements of Modern Tactics Practically applied to English Formations, by Major Wilkinson Shaw. Second and Cheaper Edition. With 25 Plates and Maps. Small cr. 8vo. cloth, price 9s.

BRIALMONT (Col. A.)—HASTY INTRENCHMENTS. Translated by Lieut. Charles A. Empson, R.A. With Nine Plates. Demy 8vo. price 6s.

CLERY (C.) Lieut.-Col.—MINOR TACTICS. With 26 Maps and Plans. Fifth and revised Edition. Demy 8vo. cloth, price 16s.

DU VERNOIS (Col. von Verdy)—STUDIES IN LEADING TROOPS. An authorised and accurate Translation by Lieutenant H. J. T. Hildyard, 71st Foot. Parts I. and II. Demy 8vo. price 7s.

GOETZE (Capt. A. von)—OPERATIONS OF THE GERMAN ENGINEERS DURING THE WAR OF 1870–1. Published by Authority, and in accordance with Official Documents. Translated from the German by Colonel G. Graham, V.C., C.B., R.E. With 6 large Maps. Demy 8vo. price 21s.

HARRISON (Lieut.-Col. R.) — THE OFFICER'S MEMORANDUM BOOK FOR PEACE AND WAR. Third Edition. Oblong 32mo. roan, with pencil, price 3s. 6d.

HELVIG (Capt. H.)—THE OPERATIONS OF THE BAVARIAN ARMY CORPS. Translated by Captain G. S. Schwabe. With Five large Maps. In 2 vols. Demy 8vo. price 24s.

TACTICAL EXAMPLES: Vol. I. The Battalion, price 15s. Vol. II. The Regiment and Brigade, price 10s. 6d. Translated from the German by Col. Sir Lumley Graham. With nearly 300 Diagrams. Demy 8vo. cloth.

HOFFBAUER (Capt.)—THE GERMAN ARTILLERY IN THE BATTLES NEAR METZ. Based on the Official Reports of the German Artillery. Translated by Captain E. O. Hollist. With Map and Plans. Demy 8vo. price 21s.

LAYMANN (Capt.) — THE FRONTAL ATTACK OF INFANTRY. Translated by Colonel Edward Newdigate. Crown 8vo. price 2s. 6d.

NOTES ON CAVALRY TACTICS, ORGANISATION, &c. By a Cavalry Officer. With Diagrams. Demy 8vo. cloth, price 12s.

PARR (Capt H. Hallam) C.M.G.—THE DRESS, HORSES, AND EQUIPMENT OF INFANTRY AND STAFF OFFICERS. Crown 8vo. cloth, price 1s.

SCHELL (Maj. von)—THE OPERATIONS OF THE FIRST ARMY UNDER GEN. VON GOEBEN. Translated by Col. C. H. von Wright. Four Maps. demy 8vo. price 9s.

THE OPERATIONS OF THE FIRST ARMY UNDER GEN. VON STEINMETZ. Translated by Captain E. O. Hollist. Demy 8vo. price 10s. 6d.

SCHELLENDORF (Major-Gen. B. von) —THE DUTIES OF THE GENERAL STAFF. Translated from the German by Lieutenant Hare. Vol. I. Demy 8vo. cloth, price 10s. 6d.

SCHERFF (Maj. W. von)—STUDIES IN THE NEW INFANTRY TACTICS. Parts I. and II. Translated from the German by Colonel Lumley Graham. Demy 8vo. price 7s. 6d.

SHADWELL (Maj.-Gen.) C.B.—MOUNTAIN WARFARE. Illustrated by the Campaign of 1799 in Switzerland. Being a Translation of the Swiss Narrative compiled from the Works of the Archduke Charles, Jomini, and others. Also of Notes by General H. Dufour on the Campaign of the Valtelline in 1635. With Appendix, Maps, and Introductory Remarks. Demy 8vo. price 16s.

SHERMAN (Gen. W. T.)—MEMOIRS OF GENERAL W. T. SHERMAN, Commander of the Federal Forces in the American Civil War. By Himself. 2 vols. With Map. Demy 8vo. price 24s. *Copyright English Edition.*

STUBBS (Lieut.-Col. F. W.) — THE REGIMENT OF BENGAL ARTILLERY. The History of its Organisation, Equipment, and War Services. Compiled from Published Works, Official Records, and various Private Sources. With numerous Maps and Illustrations. 2 vols. Demy 8vo. price 32s.

STUMM (Lieut. Hugo), German Military Attaché to the Khivan Expedition.— RUSSIA'S ADVANCE EASTWARD Based on the Official Reports of. Translated by Capt. C. E. H. VINCENT, With Map. Crown 8vo. price 6s.

VINCENT (Capt. C. E. H.)—ELEMENTARY MILITARY GEOGRAPHY, RECONNOITRING, AND SKETCHING. Compiled for Non-commissioned Officers and Soldiers of all Arms. Square crown 8vo. price 2s. 6d.

VOLUNTEER, THE MILITIAMAN, AND THE REGULAR SOLDIER, by a Public Schoolboy. Crown 8vo. cloth, price 5s.

WARTENSLEBEN (Count H. von.)—
THE OPERATIONS OF THE SOUTH
ARMY IN JANUARY AND FEBRUARY,
1871. Compiled from the Official
War Documents of the Head-quarters of the Southern Army. Translated by Colonel C. H. von Wright.
With Maps. Demy 8vo. price 6s.

THE OPERATIONS OF THE FIRST ARMY
UNDER GEN. VON MANTEUFFEL.
Translated by Colonel C. H. von
Wright. Uniform with the above.
Demy 8vo. price 9s.

WICKHAM (Capt. E. H., R.A.)—
INFLUENCE OF FIREARMS UPON
TACTICS: Historical and Critical
Investigations. By an OFFICER OF
SUPERIOR RANK (in the German
Army). Translated by Captain E. H.
Wickham, R.A. Demy 8vo. price
7s. 6d.

WOINOVITS (Capt. I.) — AUSTRIAN
CAVALRY EXERCISE. Translated by
Captain W. S. Cooke. Crown 8vo.
price 7s.

POETRY.

ADAMS (W. D. — LYRICS OF LOVE,
from Shakespeare to Tennyson. Selected and arranged by. Fcp. 8vo.
cloth extra, gilt edges, price 3s. 6d.

ANTIOPE: a Tragedy. Large crown 8vo.
cloth, price 6s.

AUBERTIN (J. J.)—CAMOENS' LUSIADS.
Portuguese Text, with Translation by.
Map and Portraits. 2 vols. Demy
8vo. price 30s.

- SEVENTY SONNETS OF CAMOENS. Portuguese Text and Translation, with
some original Poems. Dedicated to
Capt. Richard F. Burton. Printed on
hand made paper, cloth, bevelled
boards, gilt top, price 7s. 6d.

AVIA—THE ODYSSEY OF HOMER. Done
into English Verse by. Fcp. 4to.
cloth, price 15s.

BANKS (Mrs. G. L.)—RIPPLES AND
BREAKERS: Poems. Square 8vo.
cloth, price 5s.

BARNES (William)—POEMS OF RURAL
LIFE, IN THE DORSET DIALECT.
New Edition, complete in one vol.
Crown 8vo. cloth, price 8s. 6d.

BENNETT (Dr. W. C.)—NARRATIVE
POEMS AND BALLADS. Fcp. 8vo.
sewed, in Coloured Wrapper, price 1s.

SONGS FOR SAILORS. Dedicated by
Special Request to H.R.H. the Duke
of Edinburgh. With Steel Portrait
and Illustrations. Crown 8vo. price
3s. 6d.

An Edition in Illustrated Paper
Covers, price 1s.

SONGS OF A SONG WRITER. Crown
8vo. price 6s.

BEVINGTON (L. S.)—KEY NOTES.
Small crown 8vo. cloth, price 5s.

BOWEN (H. C.) M.A.—SIMPLE ENGLISH POEMS. English Literature for
Junior Classes. In Four Parts. Parts
I. II. and III. price 6d. each,
and Part IV. price 1s.

BRYANT (W. C.)—POEMS. Red-line
Edition. With 24 Illustrations and
Portrait of the Author. Crown 8vo.
cloth extra, price 7s. 6d.

A Cheap Edition, with Frontispiece. Small crown 8vo. price 3s. 6d.

BUTLER (Alfred J.)—AMARANTH AND
ASPHODEL. Songs from the Greek
Anthology. Small crown 8vo. cloth,
price 2s.

BYRNNE (E. Fairfax)—MILICENT: a
Poem. Small crown 8vo. cloth,
price 6s.

CALDERON'S DRAMAS: the Wonder-Working Magician—Life is a Dream
—the Purgatory of St. Patrick. Translated by Denis Florence MacCarthy.
Post 8vo. price 10s.

CLARKE (Mary Cowden)—HONEY FROM
THE WEED. Verses. Crown 8vo.
cloth, 7s.

COLOMB (Colonel) — THE CARDINAL
ARCHBISHOP: a Spanish Legend.
In 29 Cancious. Small crown 8vo.
cloth, price 5s.

CONWAY (Hugh)—A LIFE'S IDYLLS.
Small crown 8vo. cloth, price 3s. 6d.

COPPÉE (Francois)—L'EXILÉE. Done
into English Verse, with the sanction
of the Author, by I. O. L. Crown
8vo. vellum, price 5s.

COWAN (Rev. William)—POEMS: chiefly Sacred, including Translations from some Ancient Latin Hymns. Fcp. 8vo. cloth, price 5s.

CRESSWELL (Mrs. G.)—THE KING'S BANNER: Drama in Four Acts. Five Illustrations. 4to. price 10s. 6d.

DAVIES (T. Hart)—CATULLUS. Translated into English Verse. Crown 8vo. cloth, price 6s.

DE VERE (Aubrey)—ALEXANDER THE GREAT: a Dramatic Poem. Small crown 8vo. price 5s.
THE INFANT BRIDAL, and other Poems. A New and Enlarged Edition. Fcp. 8vo. price 7s. 6d.
LEGENDS OF THE SAXON SAINTS. Small crown 8vo. cloth, price 6s.
THE LEGENDS OF ST. PATRICK, and other Poems. Small cr. 8vo. price 5s.
ST. THOMAS OF CANTERBURY: a Dramatic Poem. Large fcp. 8vo. price 5s.
ANTAR AND ZARA: an Eastern Romance. INISFAIL, and other Poems, Meditative and Lyrical. Fcp. 8vo. price 6s.
THE FALL OF RORA, THE SEARCH AFTER PROSERPINE, and other Poems, Meditative and Lyrical. Fcp. 8vo. 6s.

DOBELL (Mrs. Horace)—ETHELSTONE, EVELINE, and other Poems. Crown 8vo. cloth, 6s.

DOBSON (Austin) — VIGNETTES IN RHYME, and Vers de Société. Third Edition. Fcp. 8vo. price 5s.
PROVERBS IN PORCELAIN. By the Author of 'Vignettes in Rhyme.' Second Edition. Crown 8vo. price 6s.

DOROTHY: a Country Story in Elegiac Verse. With Preface. Demy 8vo. cloth, price 5s.

DOWDEN (Edward) LL.D.—POEMS. Second Edition. Fcp. 8vo. price 5s.

DOWNTON (Rev. H.) M.A.—HYMNS AND VERSES. Original and Translated. Small crown 8vo. cloth, price 3s. 6d.

DUTT (Toru)—A SHEAF GLEANED IN FRENCH FIELDS. New Edition, with Portrait. Demy 8vo. cloth, 10s. 6d.

EDWARDS (Rev. Basil) — MINOR CHORDS; or, Songs for the Suffering: a Volume of Verse. Fcp. 8vo. cloth, price 3s. 6d.; paper, price 2s. 6d.

ELLIOT (Lady Charlotte)—MEDUSA and other Poems. Crown 8vo. cloth, price 6s.

ELLIOTT (Ebenezer), The Corn Law Rhymer.—POEMS. Edited by his son, the Rev. Edwin Elliott, of St. John's, Antigua. 2 vols. crown 8vo. price 18s.

ENGLISH ODES. Selected, with a Critical Introduction by EDMUND W. GOSSE, and a miniature frontispiece by Hamo Thornycroft, A.R.A. Elzevir 8vo. limp parchment antique, price 6s.; vellum, 7s. 6d.

EPIC OF HADES (THE). By the Author of 'Songs of Two Worlds.' Twelfth Edition. Fcp. 8vo. price 7s. 6d.
*** Also an Illustrated Edition, with seventeen full-page designs in photomezzotint by George R. Chapman. 4to. cloth, extra gilt leaves, price 25s.; and a Large Paper Edition with Portrait, price 10s. 6d.

EVANS (Anne)—POEMS AND MUSIC. With Memorial Preface by ANN THACKERAY RITCHIE. Large crown 8vo. cloth, price 7s.

GOSSE (Edmund W.)—NEW POEMS. Crown 8vo. cloth, price 7s. 6d.

GREENOUGH (Mrs. Richard)—MARY MAGDALENE: a Poem. Large post 8vo. parchment antique, bevelled boards, price 6s.

GWEN: a Drama in Monologue. By the Author of the 'Epic of Hades.' Third Edition. Fcp. 8vo. cloth, price 5s.

HAWKER (Robt. Stephen)—THE POETICAL WORKS OF. Now first collected and arranged. With a Prefatory Notice by J. G. Godwin. With Portrait. Crown 8vo. cloth, price 12s.

HAWTREY (Edward M.)—CORYDALIS: a Story of the Sicilian Expedition. Small crown 8vo. cloth, price 3s. 6d.

HOLMES (E. G. A.)—POEMS. First and Second Series. Fcp. 8vo. price 5s. each.

INCHBOLD (J. W.)—ANNUS AMORIS: Sonnets. Fcp. 8vo. price 4s. 6d.

JENKINS (Rev. Canon)—THE GIRDLE LEGEND OF PRATO. Small crown 8vo. cloth, price 2s.

JEROVEAM'S WIFE, and other Poems. Fcp. 8vo. cloth, price 3s. 6d.

KING (Edward)—ECHOES FROM THE ORIENT. With Miscellaneous Poems. Small crown 8vo. cloth, price 3s. 6d.

KING (Mrs. Hamilton)—THE DISCIPLES. Fourth Edition, with Portrait and Notes. Crown 8vo. price 7s. 6d.

ASPROMONTE, and other Poems. Second Edition. Fcp. 8vo. price 4s. 6d.

LAIRD-CLOWES (W.)—LOVE'S REBELLION: a Poem. Fcp. 8vo. cloth, price 3s. 6d.

LANG (A.)—XXXII BALLADES IN BLUE CHINA. Elzevir 8vo. parchment. price 5s.

LEIGH (Arran and Isla)—BELLEROPHÔN. Small crown 8vo. cloth, price 5s.

LEIGHTON (Robert)—RECORDS, AND OTHER POEMS. With Portrait. Small crown 8vo. cloth, price 7s. 6d.

LOCKER (F.)—LONDON LYRICS. A New and Revised Edition, with Additions and a Portrait of the Author. Crown 8vo. cloth elegant, price 6s.

LOVE SONNETS OF PROTEUS. With Frontispiece by the Author. Elzevir 8vo. cloth, price 5s.

LOWNDES (Henry) — POEMS AND TRANSLATIONS. Crown 8vo. cloth, price 6s.

LUMSDEN (Lieut.-Col. H. W.)—BEOWULF: an Old English Poem. Translated into Modern Rhymes. Small crown 8vo. cloth, price 5s.

MACLEAN (Charles Donald)—LATIN AND GREEK VERSE TRANSLATIONS. Small crown 8vo. cloth, 2s.

MAGNUSSON (Eirikr) M.A., and PALMER (E. H.) M.A.—JOHAN LUDVIG RUNEBERG'S LYRICAL SONGS, IDYLLS, AND EPIGRAMS. Fcp. 8vo. cloth, price 5s.

MARIE ANTIONETTE: a Drama. Small crown 8vo. cloth, price 5s.

MIDDLETON (The Lady)—BALLADS. Square 16mo. cloth, price 3s. 6d.

MONMOUTH: a Drama, of which the outline is Historical. (Dedicated, by permission, to Mr. Henry Irving.) Small crown 8vo. cloth, price 5s.

MOORE (Mrs. Bloomfield)—GONDALINE'S LESSON: The Warden's Tale, Stories for Children, and other Poems. Crown 8vo. cloth, price 5s.

MORICE (Rev. F. D.) M.A.—THE OLYMPIAN AND PYTHIAN ODES OF PINDAR. A New Translation in English Verse. Crown 8vo. price 7s. 6d.

MORSHEAD (E. D. A.)—THE HOUSE ATREUS. Being the Agamemnon, Libation-Bearers, and Furies of Æschylus. Translated into English Verse. Crown 8vo. cloth, price 7s.

MORTERRA (Felix)—THE LEGEND OF ALLANDALE, and other Poems. Small crown 8vo. cloth, price 6s.

NADEN (Constance W.)—SONGS AND SONNETS OF SPRING TIME. Small crown 8vo. cloth, price 5s.

NICHOLSON (Edward B.) Librarian of the London Institution—THE CHRIST CHILD, and other Poems. Crown 8vo. cloth, price 4s. 6d.

NOAKE (Major R. Compton) — THE BIVOUAC; or, Martial Lyrist. With an Appendix: Advice to the Soldier. Fcp. 8vo. price 5s. 6d.

NOEL (The Hon Roden)—A LITTLE CHILD'S MONUMENT. Small crown 8vo. cloth, 3s. 6d.

NORRIS (Rev. Alfred)—THE INNER AND OUTER LIFE POEMS. Fcp. 8vo. cloth, price 6s.

ODE OF LIFE (THE). By the Author of 'The Epic of Hades' &c. Third Edition. Crown 8vo. cloth, price 5s.

O'HAGAN (John) — THE SONG OF ROLAND. Translated into English Verse. Large post 8vo. parchment antique, price 10s. 6d.

PALMER (Charles Walter)—THE WEED: a Poem. Small crown 8vo. cloth, price 3s.

PAUL (C. Kegan)—GOETHE'S FAUST. A New Translation in Rhyme. Crown 8vo. price 6s.

PAYNE (John)—SONGS OF LIFE AND DEATH. Crown 8vo. cloth, price 5s.

PENNELL (H. Cholmondeley)—PEGASUS RESADDLED. By the Author of 'Puck on Pegasus,' &c. &c. With Ten Full-page Illustrations by George Du Maurier. Second Edition. Fcp. 4to. cloth elegant, price 12s. 6d.

PFEIFFER (Emily)—GLAN ALARCH: His Silence and Song: a Poem. Second Edition. Crown 8vo. price 6s.

GERARD'S MONUMENT and other Poems. Second Edition. Crown 8vo. cloth, price 6s.

QUARTERMAN'S GRACE, and other Poems. Crown 8vo. cloth, price 5s.

POEMS. Second Edition. Crown 8vo. cloth, price 6s.

SONNETS AND SONGS. New Edition. 16mo. handsomely printed and bound in cloth, gilt edges, price 4s.

PIKE (Warburton)—THE INFERNO OF DANTE ALIGHIERI. Demy 8vo. cloth, price 5s.

RHOADES (James)—THE GEORGICS OF VIRGIL. Translated into English Verse. Small crown 8vo. cloth, price 5s.

ROBINSON (A. Mary F.)—A HANDFUL OF HONEYSUCKLE. Fcp. 8vo. cloth, price 3s. 6d.

THE CROWNED HIPPOLYTUS. Translated from Euripides. With New Poems. Small crown 8vo. cloth, price 5s.

SHELLEY (Percy Bysshe) — POEMS SELECTED FROM. Dedicated to Lady Shelley. With Preface by Richard Garnett. Printed on hand-made paper, with miniature frontispiece, Elzevir 8vo. limp parchment antique, price 6s.; vellum, price 7s. 6d.

SKINNER (James)—CŒLESTIA. The Manual of St. Augustine. The Latin Text side by side with an English Interpretation in Thirty-six Odes with Notes, *and a plea for the* study of Mystical Theology. Large crown 8vo. cloth, 6s.

SONGS OF TWO WORLDS. By the Author of 'The Epic of Hades.' Fifth Edition. Complete in one Volume, with Portrait. Fcp. 8vo. cloth, price 7s. 6d.

SONGS FOR MUSIC. By Four Friends. Containing Songs by Reginald A. Gatty, Stephen H. Gatty, Greville J. Chester, and Juliana Ewing. Square crown 8vo. price 5s.

STEDMAN (Edmund Clarence)—LYRICS AND IDYLLS, with other Poems. Crown 8vo. cloth, price 7s. 6d.

STEVENS (William)—THE TRUCE OF GOD, and other Poems. Small crown 8vo. cloth, price 3s. 6d.

SWEET SILVERY SAYINGS OF SHAKESPEARE. Crown 8vo. cloth gilt, price 7s. 6d.

TAYLOR (Sir H.)—Works Complete in Five Volumes. Crown 8vo. cloth, price 30s.

TENNYSON (Alfred) — Works Complete:—

THE IMPERIAL LIBRARY EDITION. Complete in 7 vols. Demy 8vo. price 10s. 6d. each; in Roxburgh binding, 12s. 6d.

AUTHOR'S EDITION. In Six Volumes. Post 8vo. cloth gilt; or half-morocco, Roxburgh style.

CABINET EDITION. 12 Volumes. Each with Frontispiece. Fcp. 8vo. price 2s. 6d. each.

CABINET EDITION. 12 vols. Complete in handsome Ornamental Case.

THE ROYAL EDITION. In 1 vol. With 25 Illustrations and Portrait. Cloth extra, bevelled boards, gilt leaves, price 21s.

THE GUINEA EDITION. Complete in 12 vols. neatly bound and enclosed in box. Cloth, price 21s.; French morocco or parchment, price 31s. 6d.

SHILLING EDITION. In 12 vols. pocket size, 1s. each, sewed.

THE CROWN EDITION. Complete in 1 vol. strongly bound in cloth, price 6s.; cloth, extra gilt leaves, price 7s. 6d.; Roxburgh, half-morocco, price 8s. 6d.

*** Can also be had in a variety of other bindings.

TENNYSON (Alfred)—cont.

TENNYSON'S SONGS SET TO MUSIC by various Composers. Edited by W. J. Cusins. Dedicated, by express permission, to Her Majesty the Queen. Royal 4to. cloth extra, gilt leaves, price 21s.; or in half-morocco, price 25s.

Original Editions:—

BALLADS, and other Poems. Fcp. 8vo. cloth, price 5s.

POEMS. Small 8vo. price 6s.

MAUD, and other Poems. Small 8vo. price 3s. 6d.

THE PRINCESS. Small 8vo. price 3s. 6d.

IDYLLS OF THE KING. Small 8vo. price 5s.

IDYLLS OF THE KING. Complete. Small 8vo. price 6s.

THE HOLY GRAIL, and other Poems. Small 8vo. price 4s. 6d.

GARETH AND LYNETTE. Small 8vo. price 3s.

ENOCH ARDEN, &c. Small 8vo. price 3s. 6d.

IN MEMORIAM. Small 8vo. price 4s.

HAROLD: a Drama. New Edition. Crown 8vo. price 6s.

QUEEN MARY: a Drama. New Edition. Crown 8vo. price 6s.

THE LOVER'S TALE. Fcp. 8vo. cloth, 3s. 6d.

SELECTIONS FROM THE ABOVE WORKS. Super royal 16mo. price 3s. 6d.; cloth gilt extra, price 4s.

SONGS FROM THE ABOVE WORKS. 16mo. cloth, price 2s. 6d.; cloth extra, 3s. 6d.

IDYLLS OF THE KING, and other Poems. Illustrated by Julia Margaret Cameron. 2 vols. folio, half-bound morocco, cloth sides, price £6. 6s. each.

TENNYSON FOR THE YOUNG AND FOR RECITATION. Specially arranged. Fcp. 8vo. 1s. 6d.

THE TENNYSON BIRTHDAY BOOK. Edited by Emily Shakespear. 32mo. cloth limp, 2s.; cloth extra, 3s.

⁎ A superior Edition, printed in red and black, on antique paper, specially prepared. Small crown 8vo. cloth, extra gilt leaves, price 5s.; and in various calf and morocco bindings.

An Index to IN MEMORIAM. Price 2s.

THOMPSON (Alice C.)—PRELUDES: a Volume of Poems. Illustrated by Elizabeth Thompson (Painter of 'The Roll Call'). 8vo. price 7s. 6d.

THRING (Rev. Godfrey), B.A.—HYMNS AND SACRED LYRICS. Fcp. 8vo. price 3s. 6d.

TODHUNTER (Dr. J.)—LAURELLA, and other Poems. Crown 8vo. 6s. 6d.

ALCESTIS: a Dramatic Poem. Extra fcp. 8vo. cloth, price 5s.

A STUDY OF SHELLEY. Crown 8vo. cloth, price 7s.

TOLINGSBY (Frere)—ELNORA: an Indian Mythological Poem. Fcp. 8vo. cloth, price 6s.

TRANSLATIONS FROM DANTE, PETRARCH, MICHAEL ANGELO, AND VITTORIA COLONNA. Fcp. 8vo. cloth, price 7s. 6d.

TURNER (Rev. C. Tennyson)—SONNETS, LYRICS, AND TRANSLATIONS. Crown 8vo. cloth, price 4s. 6d.

COLLECTED SONNETS, Old and New. With Prefatory Poem by ALFRED TENNYSON; also some Marginal Notes by S. T. COLERIDGE, and a Critical Essay by JAMES SPEDDING. Fcp. 8vo cloth, price 7s. 6d.

WALTERS (Sophia Lydia)—THE BROOK: a Poem. Small crown 8vo. cloth, price 3s. 6d.

A DREAMER'S SKETCH BOOK. With 21 Illustrations by Percival Skelton, R. P. Leitch, W. H. J. BOOT, and T. R. PRITCHETT. Engraved by J. D. Cooper. Fcp. 4to. cloth, price 12s. 6d.

WATERFIELD (W.)—HYMNS FOR HOLY DAYS AND SEASONS. 32mo. cloth, price 1s. 6d.

WATSON (William)—THE PRINCE'S QUEST, and other Poems. Crown 8vo. cloth, price 5s.

WAY (A.) M.A.—THE ODES OF HORACE LITERALLY TRANSLATED IN METRE. Fcp. 8vo. price 2s.

WEBSTER (Augusta)—DISGUISES: a Drama. Small crown 8vo. cloth, price 5s.

WET DAYS. By a Farmer. Small crown 8vo. cloth, price 6s.

WILKINS (William)—Songs of Study. Crown 8vo. cloth, price 6s.

WILLOUGHBY (*The Hon. Mrs.*)—On the North Wind—Thistledown: a Volume of Poems. Elegantly bound, small crown 8vo. price 7s. 6d.

WOODS (*James Chapman*)—A Child of the People, and other Poems. Small crown 8vo. cloth, price 5s.

YOUNG (*Wm.*)—Gottlob, etcetera. Small crown 8vo. cloth, price 3s. 6d.

WORKS OF FICTION IN ONE VOLUME.

BANKS (*Mrs. G. L.*)—God's Providence House. New Edition. Crown 8vo. cloth, price 3s. 6d.

BETHAM-EDWARDS (*Miss M.*)— Kitty. With a Frontispiece. Crown 8vo. price 6s.

Blue Roses; or, Helen Malinofska's Marriage. By the Author of 'Véra.' New and Cheaper Edition. With Frontispiece. Crown 8vo. cloth, price 6s.

FRISWELL (*J. Hain*)—One of Two; or, The Left-Handed Bride. Crown 8vo. cloth, price 3s. 6d.

GARRETT (*E.*)—By Still Waters: a Story for Quiet Hours. With Seven Illustrations. Crown 8vo. price 6s.

HARDY (*Thomas*)—A Pair of Blue Eyes. Author of 'Far from the Madding Crowd.' New Edition. Crown 8vo. price 6s.

The Return of the Native. New Edition. With Frontispiece. Crown 8vo. cloth, price 6s.

HOOPER (*Mrs. G.*)—The House of Raby. Crown 8vo. cloth, price 3s. 6d.

INGELOW (*Jean*)—Off the Skelligs: a Novel. With Frontispiece. Second Edition. Crown 8vo. cloth, price 6s.

MACDONALD (*G.*)—Malcolm. With Portrait of the Author engraved on Steel. Fourth Edition. Crown 8vo. price 6s.

The Marquis of Lossie. Second Edition. With Frontispiece. Crown 8vo. cloth, price 6s.

St. George and St. Michael. Second Edition. With Frontispiece. Crown 8vo. cloth, 6s.

MASTERMAN (*J.*)—Half-a-Dozen Daughters. Crown 8vo. cloth, price 3s. 6d.

MEREDITH (*George*) — Ordeal of Richard Feverel. New Edition. Crown 8vo. cloth, price 6s.

MEREDITH (*George*)—cont.
The Egoist: A Comedy in Narrative. New and Cheaper Edition, with Frontispiece. Crown 8vo. cloth, price 6s.

PALGRAVE (*W. Gifford*)—Hermann Agha: an Eastern Narrative. Third Edition. Crown 8vo. cloth, price 6s.

Pandurang Hari; or, Memoirs of a Hindoo. With an Introductory Preface by Sir H. Bartle E. Frere, G.C.S.I., C.B. Crown 8vo. price 6s.

PAUL (*Margaret Agnes*)—Gentle and Simple: A Story. New and Cheaper Edition, with Frontispiece. Crown 8vo. price 6s.

SAUNDERS (*John*) — Israel Mort, Overman: a Story of the Mine. Crown 8vo. price 6s.

Abel Drake's Wife. Crown 8vo. cloth, price 3s. 6d.

Hirell. Crown 8vo. cloth, price 3s. 6d.

SHAW (*Flora L.*)—Castle Blair; a Story of Youthful Lives. New and Cheaper Edition, with Frontispiece. Crown 8vo. price 6s.

STRETTON (*Hesba*) — Through a Needle's Eye: a Story. New and Cheaper Edition, with Frontispiece. Crown 8vo. cloth, price 6s.

TAYLOR (*Col. Meadows*) *C.S.I., M.R.I.A.*
Seeta: a Novel. New and Cheaper Edition. With Frontispiece. Crown 8vo. cloth, price 6s.

Tippoo Sultaun: a Tale of the Mysore War. New Edition, with Frontispiece. Crown 8vo. cloth, price 6s.

Ralph Darnell. New and Cheaper Edition. With Frontispiece. Crown 8vo. cloth, price 6s.

A Noble Queen. New and Cheaper Edition. With Frontispiece. Crown 8vo. cloth, price 6s.

TAYLOR (*Col. Meadows*)—cont.
THE CONFESSIONS OF A THUG. Crown 8vo. price 6s.

TARA: a Mahratta Tale. Crown 8vo. price 6s.

THOMAS (*Moy*)—A FIGHT FOR LIFE. Crown 8vo. cloth, price 3s. 6d.

WITHIN SOUND OF THE SEA. New and Cheaper Edition, with Frontispiece. Crown 8vo. cloth, price 6s.

BOOKS FOR THE YOUNG.

AUNT MARY'S BRAN PIE. By the Author of 'St. Olave's.' Illustrated. Price 3s. 6d.

BARLEE (*Ellen*)—LOCKED OUT: a Tale of the Strike. With a Frontispiece. Royal 16mo. price 1s. 6d.

BONWICK (*J.*) *F.R.G.S.*—THE TASMANIAN LILY. With Frontispiece. Crown 8vo. price 5s.

MIKE HOWE, the Bushranger of Van Diemen's Land. New and Cheaper Edition. With Frontispiece. Crown 8vo. price 3s. 6d.

BRAVE MEN'S FOOTSTEPS. By the Editor of 'Men who have Risen.' A Book of Example and Anecdote for Young People. With Four Illustrations by C. Doyle. Sixth Edition. Crown 8vo. price 3s. 6d.

CHILDREN'S TOYS, and some Elementary Lessons in General Knowledge which they teach. Illustrated. Crown 8vo. cloth, price 5s.

COLERIDGE (*Sara*)—PRETTY LESSONS IN VERSE FOR GOOD CHILDREN, with some Lessons in Latin, in Easy Rhyme. A New Edition. Illustrated. Fcp. 8vo. cloth, price 3s. 6d.

D'ANVERS (*N. R.*)—LITTLE MINNIE'S TROUBLES: an Every-day Chronicle. With 4 Illustrations by W. H. Hughes. Fcp. cloth, price 3s. 6d.

PARTED: a Tale of Clouds and Sunshine. With 4 Illustrations. Extra fcp. 8vo. cloth, price 3s. 6d.

PIXIE'S ADVENTURES; or, the Tale of a Terrier. With 21 Illustrations. 16mo. cloth, price 4s. 6d.

NANNY'S ADVENTURES: or, the Tale of a Goat. With 12 Illustrations. 16mo. cloth, price 4s. 6d.

DAVIES (*G. Christopher*) — RAMBLES AND ADVENTURES OF OUR SCHOOL FIELD CLUB. With Four Illustrations. Crown 8vo. price 5s.

DRUMMOND (*Miss*)—TRIPP'S BUILDINGS. A Study from Life, with Frontispiece. Small crown 8vo. price 3s. 6d.

EDMONDS (*Herbert*) — WELL SPENT LIVES: a Series of Modern Biographies. Crown 8vo. price 5s.

EVANS (*Mark*)—THE STORY OF OUR FATHER'S LOVE, told to Children; Fourth and Cheaper Edition of Theology for Children. With Four Illustrations. Fcp. 8vo. price 1s. 6d.

FARQUHARSON (*M.*)
 I. ELSIE DINSMORE. Crown 8vo. price 3s. 6d.
 II. ELSIE'S GIRLHOOD. Crown 8vo. price 3s. 6d.
 III. ELSIE'S HOLIDAYS AT ROSELANDS. Crown 8vo. price 3s. 6d.

HERFORD (*Brooke*)—THE STORY OF RELIGION IN ENGLAND: a Book for Young Folk. Cr. 8vo. cloth, price 5s.

INGELOW (*Jean*) — THE LITTLE WONDER-HORN. With Fifteen Illustrations. Small 8vo. price 2s. 6d.

JOHNSON (*Virginia W.*)—THE CATSKILL FAIRIES. Illustrated by ALFRED FREDERICKS. Cloth, price 5s.

KER (*David*)—THE BOY SLAVE IN BOKHARA: a Tale of Central Asia. With Illustrations. New and Cheaper Edition. Crown 8vo. price 3s. 6d.

THE WILD HORSEMAN OF THE PAMPAS. Illustrated. New and Cheaper Edition. Crown 8vo. price 3s. 6d.

LAMONT (*Martha MacDonald*)—THE GLADIATOR: a Life under the Roman Empire in the beginning of the Third Century. With 4 Illustrations by H. M. Paget. Extra fcp. 8vo. cloth, price 3s. 6d.

LEANDER (*Richard*) — FANTASTIC STORIES. Translated from the German by Paulina B. Granville. With Eight Full-page Illustrations by M. E. Fraser-Tytler. Crown 8vo. price 5s.

LEE (*Holme*)—HER TITLE OF HONOUR. A Book for Girls. New Edition. With a Frontispiece. Crown 8vo. price 5s.

LEWIS (*Mary A.*)—A RAT WITH THREE TALES. New and Cheaper Edition. With Four Illustrations by Catherine F. Frere. Price 3s. 6d.

MC CLINTOCK (*L.*)—SIR SPANGLE AND THE DINGY HEN. Illustrated. Square crown 8vo. price 2s. 6d.

MAC KENNA (*S. J.*)—PLUCKY FELLOWS. A Book for Boys. With Six Illustrations. Fourth Edition. Crown 8vo. price 3s. 6d.

AT SCHOOL WITH AN OLD DRAGOON. With Six Illustrations. Third Edition. Crown 8vo. price 5s.

MALDEN (*H. E.*)—PRINCES AND PRINCESSES: Two Fairy Tales. Illustrated. Small crown 8vo. price 2s. 6d.

MASTER BOBBY. By the Author of 'Christina North.' With Six Illustrations. Fcp. 8vo. cloth, price 3s. 6d.

NAAKE (*J. T.*)—SLAVONIC FAIRY TALES. From Russian, Servian, Polish, and Bohemian Sources. With Four Illustrations. Crown 8vo. price 5s.

PELLETAN (*E.*)—THE DESERT PASTOR. JEAN JAROUSSEAU. Translated from the French. By Colonel E. P. De L'Hoste. With a Frontispiece. New Edition. Fcp. 8vo. price 3s. 6d.

REANEY (*Mrs. G. S.*)—WAKING AND WORKING; or, From Girlhood to Womanhood. New and Cheaper Edition. With a Frontispiece. Cr. 8vo. price 3s. 6d.

BLESSING AND BLESSED: a Sketch of Girl Life. New and Cheaper Edition. Crown 8vo. cloth, price 3s. 6d.

ROSE GURNEY'S DISCOVERY. A Book for Girls. Dedicated to their Mothers. Crown 8vo. cloth, price 3s. 6d.

ENGLISH GIRLS: Their Place and Power. With Preface by the Rev. R. W. Dale. Third Edition. Fcp. 8vo. cloth, price 2s. 6d.

REANEY (*Mrs. G. S.*)—cont.

JUST ANYONE, and other Stories. Three Illustrations. Royal 16mo. cloth, price 1s. 6d.

SUNBEAM WILLIE, and other Stories. Three Illustrations. Royal 16mo. price 1s. 6d.

SUNSHINE JENNY and other Stories. 3 Illustrations. Royal 16mo. cloth, price 1s. 6d.

ROSS (*Mrs. E.*), ('Nelsie Brook')— DADDY'S PET. A Sketch from Humble Life. With Six Illustrations. Royal 16mo. price 1s.

SADLER (*S. W.*) *R.N.*—THE AFRICAN CRUISER: a Midshipman's Adventures on the West Coast. With Three Illustrations. New and Cheaper Edition. Crown 8vo. price 2s. 6d.

SEEKING HIS FORTUNE, and other Stories. With Four Illustrations. New and Cheaper Edition. Crown 8vo. 2s. 6d.

SEVEN AUTUMN LEAVES FROM FAIRY LAND. Illustrated with Nine Etchings. Square crown 8vo. price 3s. 6d.

STOCKTON (*Frank R.*)—A JOLLY FELLOWSHIP. With 20 Illustrations. Crown 8vo. cloth, price 5s.

STORR (*Francis*) *and TURNER* (*Hawes*). —CANTERBURY CHIMES; or, Chaucer Tales retold to Children. With Six Illustrations from the Ellesmere MS. Fcp. 8vo. cloth, price 3s. 6d.

STRETTON (*Hesba*)—DAVID LLOYD'S LAST WILL. With Four Illustrations. Royal 16 mo. price 2s. 6d.

THE WONDERFUL LIFE. Thirteenth Thousand. Fcp. 8vo. cloth, price 2s. 6d.

SUNNYLAND STORIES. By the Author of 'Aunt Mary's Bran Pie.' Illustrated. Small 8vo. price 3s. 6d.

TALES FROM ARIOSTO RE-TOLD FOR CHILDREN. By a Lady. With 3 Illustrations. Crown 8vo. cloth, price 4s. 6d.

WHITAKER (*Florence*)—CHRISTY'S INHERITANCE. A London Story. Illustrated. Royal 16mo. price 1s. 6d.

ZIMMERN (*H.*)—STORIES IN PRECIOUS STONES. With Six Illustrations. Third Edition. Crown 8vo. price 5s.

www.ingramcontent.com/pod-product-compliance
Lightning Source LLC
Chambersburg PA
CBHW022115290426
44112CB00008B/685